WHY ARE MOST BUILDINGS RECTANGULAR?

This book brings together a dozen of Philip Steadman's essays and papers on the geometry of architectural and urban form, written over the last 12 years. New introductions link the papers and set them in context. There are two large themes: a morphological approach to the history of architecture, and studies of possibility in built form. Within this framework the papers cover the geometrical character of the building stock as a whole; histories of selected building types; analyses of density and energy in relation to urban form; and systematic methods for enumerating building plans and built forms. They touch on a range of key topics of debate in architectural theory and building science. Illustrated with over 200 black and white images, this collection provides an accessible and coherent guide to this important work.

Philip Steadman is Emeritus Professor of Urban and Built Form Studies at the Bartlett School (Faculty of the Built Environment), University College London. He studied Architecture at Cambridge University from 1960 to 1965, and after graduating joined the newly formed Centre for Land Use and Built Form Studies at Cambridge (later the Martin Centre). In 1972 he was a visiting research fellow at Princeton University. In 1977 he went to the Open University to join the Centre for Configurational Studies, of which he was Director until 1998. He joined the Bartlett in 1999. Much of his research has been on the forms of buildings and cities, and their relationship to the use of energy.

He has published three previous books on geometry and architecture: *The Geometry of Environment* (with Lionel March, 1971), *Architectural Morphology* (1983) and *Building Types and Built Forms* (2014). His study of *The Evolution of Designs: Biological Analogy in Architecture and the Applied Arts* came out in 1979 and was republished in an updated edition in 2008. He has also written books on energy and the built environment, American cities, the effects of nuclear attack on Britain, and the painting technique of Johannes Vermeer (*Vermeer's Camera*, 2001).

Reviews of *The Evolution of Designs*, revised edition (Routledge):

"The most coherent British contribution to architectural theory since Lethaby" – *Andrew Saint, University College London, UK*

"A superb historical account… He has the rare ability of giving quite dense material a sense of lightness and narrative drive" – *Karl Kropf, Oxford Brookes University, UK*

Reviews of *Why are Most Buildings Rectangular?*:

"Steadman's book is a 'must read' for anyone with even a passing interest in why buildings are the way they are. I was completely absorbed by the analytical representations which expose buildings' underlying spatial characteristics. Steadman's explanations of buildings' evolution through time and across space in response to human psychology and societal change as well as the physics of materials, light and air, display his polymathic knowledge." – *Kevin Lomas, Professor, Building Simulation, Loughborough University, UK*

"Philip Steadman has taken the next step in the tradition of typological research that lies at the heart of the modern discipline of architecture. He approaches rigorously focused questions with a seemingly inexhaustible array of sources, throwing open conventional boundaries between building science, history, and architectural theory. Indeed, he shows that these belong together. Beyond offering a wealth of knowledge, Steadman has done a great service to architects and scholars by suggesting so many paths for further research in one place." – *Matthew Allen, Harvard University, USA*

"This collection of 12 articles by Philip Steadman and his colleagues reflect 35 years of highly original, creative architectural research. The rich insights from the study of evolutionary building geometries, the morphologies of building types, the urban built forms constitute a unique example of architectural research situated within the organization of complexity and the science of design. Philip Steadman presents a brilliant scientific record that continues to have profound influence." – *Niklaus Kohler, Prof.em. Karlsruhe Institute of Technology (KIT), Germany*

"It is a pleasure to follow the delicacy and precision with which Philip Steadman applies the science of building morphology to historical questions about why buildings have taken the shapes that they have over the course of time. Steadman's erudition and subtle wit make this a most enjoyable book for anyone with an interest in the history of building forms." – *Adrian Forty, Professor Emeritus of Architectural History, The Bartlett School of Architecture, University College London, UK*

"Continuing to demonstrate the fruitfulness of *possible form*, Philip Steadman asks deceptively simple questions and answers them with his enviable ability of combining academic rigour, lightness of touch and a deep sense of humanity. The articles in this volume are some of the pieces I would most want to spend time tracking down. They are all the more compelling when taken together." – *Karl Kropf, Oxford Brookes University, UK*

"*Why are Most Buildings Rectangular?* is a seminal read for ambitious students and professionals in architecture, planning and design sciences. The book collates a series of Steadman's ground-breaking papers on spatial theory for building typologies and spatial configuration that paved the way for generations of research in academia and developments in practice. His unique theoretical foundations proved decisive for fields as diverse as architectural theory, computational design and urban data sciences. A rare giant of scientific and theoretical rigour in the discipline of architecture and planning." – *Dr Christian Derix, SUPERSPACE, UK*

"Philip Steadman's new book is a clear ode to the work of Martin and March, forgotten or maybe never known by many architects today. It is powerful in showing that an analytic understanding of form helps designers to see, but certainly also to challenge, the *ranges of choices* that are available. The book focuses on geometry and building types and makes one long for a complementary book about systems and city types." – *Meta Berghauser Pont, Associate Professor, Department of Architecture and Civil Engineering, University of Technology Chalmers, Sweden*

WHY ARE MOST BUILDINGS RECTANGULAR?

And Other Essays on Geometry and Architecture

Philip Steadman

LONDON AND NEW YORK

First published 2018
by Routledge
2 Park Square, Milton Park, Abingdon, Oxon OX14 4RN

and by Routledge
711 Third Avenue, New York, NY 10017

Routledge is an imprint of the Taylor & Francis Group, an informa business

© 2018 Philip Steadman

The right of Philip Steadman to be identified as author of this work
has been asserted by him in accordance with sections 77 and 78 of the
Copyright, Designs and Patents Act 1988.

All rights reserved. No part of this book may be reprinted or reproduced
or utilised in any form or by any electronic, mechanical, or other means,
now known or hereafter invented, including photocopying and recording,
or in any information storage or retrieval system, without permission in
writing from the publishers.

Trademark notice: Product or corporate names may be trademarks or
registered trademarks, and are used only for identification and explanation
without intent to infringe.

British Library Cataloguing-in-Publication Data
A catalogue record for this book is available from the British Library

Library of Congress Cataloging-in-Publication Data
Names: Steadman, Philip, 1942– author.
Title: Why are most buildings rectangular? : and other essays on geometry
and architecture / Philip Steadman.
Description: New York : Routledge, 2017. | Includes bibliographical
references and index.
Identifiers: LCCN 2017006822| ISBN 9781138226548 (hb : alk. paper) |
ISBN 9781138226555 (pb : alk. paper)
Subjects: LCSH: Architecture—Composition, proportion, etc. |
Geometry in architecture.
Classification: LCC NA2760 .S758 2017 | DDC 720.2—dc23
LC record available at https://lccn.loc.gov/2017006822

ISBN: 978-1-138-22654-8 (hbk)
ISBN: 978-1-138-22655-5 (pbk)

Typeset in Bembo and Stone Sans
by Florence Production Ltd, Stoodleigh, Devon, UK

CONTENTS

Preface	*vii*
Acknowledgements	*xi*

PART I
Plan geometry, rectangular and circular   **1**

1 Why are most buildings rectangular?   3

2 Architectural doughnuts: circular plan buildings, with and without courtyards   21

PART II
The history and 'evolution' of building types   **41**

3 The contradictions of Jeremy Bentham's Panopticon penitentiary   43

4 Samuel Bentham's Panopticon   67

5 The changing department store building, 1850 to 1940   81

6 Evolution of a building type: the case of the multi-storey garage   103

PART III
Built form and urban form: geometry, energy and density   **129**

7 Wall area, volume and plan depth in the building stock   131
with Stephen Evans and Michael Batty

vi Contents

8 Energy and urban built form: an empirical and statistical approach   149
with Ian Hamilton and Stephen Evans

9 Density and built form: integrating 'Spacemate' with the work   167
of Martin and March

PART IV
Theoretical approaches to possibility in built form   **187**

10 The analysis and interpretation of small house plans: some
contemporary examples   189
Frank Brown with Philip Steadman

11 Generative design methods, and the exploration of worlds of
formal possibility   226

12 Architectural morphospace: mapping worlds of built forms   237
with Linda Mitchell

Index   *265*

PREFACE

The papers collected here range widely in subject matter, but they are linked by a small number of themes, and by a particular philosophical approach to the study of architecture. All of them are devoted in one way or another to the geometry of the plans and forms of buildings.

The first two papers have to do with the geometry of the entire population of buildings old and new. The title essay raises the question 'Why do the majority of actual buildings have a geometry that is largely rectangular?' This is a question that practitioners and students have perhaps been asking themselves recently, at a time when curvilinear structures like those of Frank Gehry and Zaha Hadid have attracted so much attention. The second paper looks at that small minority of buildings that have simple circular plans ('architectural doughnuts'), and examines how circularity affects their performance and usability.

Four more papers (Nos **3–6**) follow the 'morphological histories' of some selected building types, using that term to mean types distinguished by activity: Panopticon and radial prisons; department stores; and multi-storey garages. Each type is tracked over a period of decades, to see the effects on typical built forms of a range of influences or forces: wider processes of social and technological change, trends in building construction and services, competition between the institutions or companies that occupy the buildings, and responses to the functional failure of designs. In the studies of prisons, emphasis is put, for obvious reasons, on the patterns of visibility that different layouts allow. These analyses employ Michael Benedikt's *isovist*, a graphical device with which all that a person can see from a specific point is mapped.

All these histories are broadly 'evolutionary' in the old pre-Darwinian sense. In some cases the morphological changes are indeed gradual and incremental. In other cases they are abrupt, when forms are invented *de novo* like Jeremy Bentham's Panopticon, or some of the newly devised layouts for high-rise garages of the 1920s. Of all these types it is nevertheless the garages that undergo something closest to a Darwinian evolution – although the analogy is a dangerous one and needs to be carefully watched.

The focus moves, in a group of three further papers (**7–9**), to the urban scale, where in Michael Batty's phrase "geometry meets geography". Here the forms of large numbers of buildings are studied statistically – observed from a distance, so to say – to try to understand

viii Preface

overall properties that arise from the activities of many builders and architects, and the universal constraints under which they work. One of these papers (**7**) looks at *allometric* effects comparable with those found in the forms of animal species – allometry being the study of change in shape in the animal body with increase in size. Buildings show allometric effects when considered *en masse*, as a result of the constraints put on the depth of their plans by the provision of natural light and natural ventilation. Ranko Bon was the first to study the allometry of architectural form in the 1970s. This paper applies Bon's method of analysis to the whole of London.

A sequel paper (**8**) examines the consequences for the use of energy of these limits placed by lighting and ventilation on plans and built forms. Correlations are demonstrated between energy use, plan depth and surface area. The use of air conditioning breaks the constraint of natural ventilation: the paper goes on to examine how the resulting move to deeper-plan buildings affects the consumption of electricity. A third paper in this group (**9**) has to do with the relationship of urban density to built form. It revives the pioneering work on density of Lionel March and Leslie Martin at Cambridge in the 1970s, and links this to recent empirical studies of the densities and morphologies of housing developments in Holland, made by two Dutch researchers Meta Berghauser Pont and Per Haupt.

The book concludes with a sequence of three papers (**10–12**) concerned with methods for laying out all possibilities, exhaustively, for certain classes of plans or built forms, suitably defined. The first paper in this group looks at plans consisting of rectangular rooms within rectangular boundaries, of which small houses provide examples. The following two papers develop a methodology for generating and cataloguing rectangular plans represented not as room layouts, but in terms of larger zones, either day-lit or artificially lit. The resulting arrangements are set out across a *morphospace* of possible forms.

The concept of the morphospace is again borrowed from biology, where it means a graphical plot in 2D or 3D of the space of forms of actual plant or animal species, within some larger world of theoretically conceivable forms. In a similar spirit, the final papers show where the plans of a variety of real nineteenth- and twentieth-century buildings are to be found, within the worlds of theoretical possibility mapped in the architectural morphospace.

Some of these papers were first published in specialised and non-architectural journals: the purpose here is to offer them to a potentially wider audience. Others overlap considerably with the contents of my recent *Building Types and Built Forms*, but provide extra material or go into greater depth.[1]

A science of architecture as a 'science of the artificial'

Taken together, the papers in the second half of the book are offered as contributions to an architectural science that goes beyond the concerns of traditional building science with heat, light and sound, to address issues relating to built form and spatial arrangement. I see this work as part of a collective effort to include architectural research among Herbert Simon's "sciences of the artificial" – sciences devoted to studying the products of man, as against the phenomena of nature.[2]

This architectural science involves, as I see it, two complementary kinds of activity. A central premise of the 'sciences of the artificial' is that artefacts – despite their being made by humans – can embody knowledge of which their makers and others are unaware. Large artefacts like cities for example are built by the collective action of many participants; they may come as a result to acquire characteristics and regularities that are unknown and unanticipated. The allometric effects demonstrated by Bon provide an example. It follows that, in order to retrieve this hidden knowledge, artefacts – in our case buildings and cities – must be subjected to analysis and experiment. Papers **7**, **8** and **9** are studies of this kind. The advent of very large digital data sets describing many buildings – in the case of Papers **7** and **8**, a 3D computer model of all buildings in London out to the M25 motorway – has made this possible on an unprecedented scale.

Martin and March in their work on density at the Centre for Land Use and Built Form Studies uncovered another kind of 'hidden knowledge'. They compared the densities achieved by three elementary type-forms – towers, streets and courts – and found that, all other things being equal, the courts achieved the highest densities. Building in tall towers did not necessarily raise densities. This ran directly counter to much conventional architectural thinking.

Sciences in general, and a science of architecture in particular, do not just deal with existing objects: by finding general rules or laws they aim to define the limits on *possibility* for those classes of object. This is the second kind of activity in an architectural science. Papers **10** to **12** here fall into this category of work. Leslie Martin characterised his research with Lionel March in this way. Through the use of mathematical models of built forms, Martin says, "We become aware of another way of looking at a design problem through which we can consider more effectively and rigorously *the ranges of choice* that are open to us."[3]

The research reported here is conceived in this spirit. I worked with Martin and March in the 1960s and '70s and began my academic career in research devising methods for enumerating possible room layouts, one late product of which was Paper **10** here, written with Frank Brown. It will be clear I hope from the studies of historical house types in this paper that our purpose was not to try to automate design or to make the design process 'scientific' in any way – a meaningless idea, but something that certain critics have suggested. It was instead to show how knowledge of plan possibility can allow one to understand better the ranges of choice – in Martin's phrase – that are available to architects at different dates and in varying circumstances. Strict limits on possible plan arrangement certainly exist, imposed by geometry and topology. In my view it is better for designers to be aware of these, than to hit their heads against them blindly.

How then, in an architectural science, is one to set bounds on the classes of geometrical objects that might be considered as theoretically possible plans or built forms? As a first move in this research, one could limit consideration just to rectangular plans and forms, on the strength of the arguments in this volume's first paper. (Non-rectangular forms might be addressed later.) The small houses that Brown and I examined all had plans that could be reasonably approximated as packings of rectangles.

Beyond that one might think about how attention could be limited to forms that are 'building-like' in some very general senses. Up until 1940 almost all buildings were lit and ventilated naturally, bringing about the limits on plan depth identified by Bon. Electric lighting was introduced from the end of the nineteenth century, but natural ventilation maintained the depth constraint until the advent of air conditioning. As a result larger buildings consisted, very many of them, of elongated ranges of limited depth connected together into branching plans with wings and courts. The plans tended to have shapes resembling letters of the alphabet. They had day-lit zones along the window walls, and perhaps thin artificially lit strips in the interior. Many such buildings continue to be constructed today.

x Preface

The method of enumerating plans and forms explained here in Papers **11** and **12** makes use of the device of an 'archetypal building', embodying constraints that serve to produce arrangements of this general character. 'Architectural possibility' that is to say, is being bounded by introducing generic functional constraints, of kinds to which a large majority of real buildings are subject.

This is where scientific work on possible forms, and a morphological history of building types, come together. The subjects of the two halves of this book are connected. The descriptive historical morphology can allow the researcher to infer and formalise the constraints that have acted generally on built form at different dates. These can then be introduced to the enumerations of possibilities. Once a world of theoretically possible forms is generated, the researcher can plot the positions of many actual buildings in this theoretical world, and follow the morphological trajectories these types take over time – as in Paper **12**. The two fields of work interact and complement each other.

Nearly forty years ago I wrote an editorial for a journal, urging morphologists and architectural historians to get together.[4] I imagined a systematic programme of data collection on the geometry and construction of large samples of buildings, out of which "an evolutionary history of building and an architectural morphology" could be developed. It is chastening to find myself still saying much the same thing today. But art is long and life is short, and maybe some progress has been made in the meantime.

Notes

1   Philip Steadman, *Building Types and Built Forms*, Troubador, Leicestershire 2014.
2   Herbert Simon, *The Sciences of the Artificial*, MIT Press, Cambridge MA 1969.
3   Foreword by Leslie Martin to Lionel March and Philip Steadman, *The Geometry of Environment*, Royal Institute of British Architects, London 1971 p. 6. My emphasis.
4   Editorial, *Transactions of the Martin Centre for Architectural and Urban Studies*, Vol. 4, 1980 pp. 1–2.

ACKNOWLEDGEMENTS

I am very grateful to my co-authors, Mike Batty, Steve Evans, Ian Hamilton and Linda Mitchell (née Waddoups) for kindly allowing me to republish our joint work. I owe a special debt to Frank Brown who was the first author of Paper 10 on small house plans. Frank sadly did not live to see his paper reprinted: he died while the book was in press. Perhaps this republication can serve as a small memorial to our long and congenial collaboration. The publishers of the journals in which the papers first appeared have graciously allowed them to be reprinted; and the owners of copyright in the pictures have also given their permission. Individual credits are given in figure captions. The papers have been reproduced as originally printed, but with some editing to remove repetition [*signalled in italic in the text*] and with new introductions.

PART I

Plan geometry, rectangular and circular

1

WHY ARE MOST BUILDINGS RECTANGULAR?

(*Architectural Research Quarterly*, Volume 10, 2006, pp. 119–130)

The title of this paper points to an empirical fact about buildings: that the majority have geometrical forms that are predominantly rectangular. Why should this be? One approach to the question is to look at the minority of buildings that are not rectangular. These include buildings with circular or polygonal plans that consist of just one room. There are other buildings that have rectangular plans with many rooms, but depart from rectangularity around the edges, as for example in pitched roofs or curved bay windows. The angular or curved parts occur on the outer surfaces, not in the interior. All this suggests that the answer to the question has to do with the close packing of rooms and elements of construction. A rectangular geometry allows for greater flexibility in the ways that spaces and components of different sizes can be packed together.

When the paper was first published a few readers got the impression that the title implied a belief on my part that 'All buildings should be rectangular'. This is certainly not my position. Others imagined that the paper was an intervention in the critical and aesthetic debates that have surrounded the use by Frank Gehry, Zaha Hadid and followers of complex doubly curved forms in architecture – made possible from the 1990s by new 'parametric' software. Naively perhaps, I had not anticipated this. There is however some suggestion at the end of the paper as to why such curvacious forms might tend to appear more in high-profile projects by prominent designers, less in the general mass of everyday construction.

Introduction: is it the case?

Why are most buildings rectangular? This is a fundamental question that is rarely asked. Perhaps visiting Martians – assuming their interests tended to the geometrical – might want to raise the issue. Certainly from the evidence of science fiction films the dwellings of aliens seem to be non-rectangular – presumably to signal their exoticism and unEarthliness. The question is worth pursuing all the same, I believe, because of its implications for a theory of built form. By 'buildings' I do not just mean considered and prestigious works of architecture, which possibly tend more often than others to the non-orthogonal and curvilinear, for reasons that may become clear. I mean the totality of buildings of all types, the whole of the stock, both architect-designed and 'without architects', present and past. And to be slightly more specific about the question itself: I mean to ask 'Why is the geometry of the majority of buildings

4 Plan geometry, rectangular and circular

predominantly rectangular?' There will, certainly, be many small departures from rectangularity in otherwise rectangular buildings, and it would be rare indeed to find a building in which every single space and component was perfectly rectangular. We are talking about general tendencies here.

Is it actually true? Everyday experience would indicate that it is: but we do not have to rely just on subjective impressions. At least two surveys have been made, to my knowledge, of the extent of rectangularity in the building stock. The first was a survey of houses carried out in the 1930s by the American architect Albert Farwell Bemis, reported in his book *The Evolving House*.[1] Bemis was interested in the potential for prefabrication in housebuilding. Taking for granted that components making up any prefabricated system would have to be rectangular, he measured a sample of 217 conventionally constructed houses and apartments in Boston, to determine what percentage of their total volume – conceiving the building as a 'solid block' in each case – was organised according to a rectangular geometry. He found that proportion to be 83 per cent, the remaining 17 per cent being largely attributed to pitched roofs.[2] This measurement gave Bemis an indication of the extent to which current house designs could be replicated with standardised rectangular components.

The second survey was made by M J T Krüger in the 1970s, in the course of a study of urban morphology and the connectivities between streets, plots and buildings.[3] Krüger took as his sample the entire city of Reading (Berkshire), and included buildings of all types. He inspected just the outlines of their perimeters in plan, working from Ordnance Survey maps. (Of course these outlines would have been somewhat simplified in the maps.) He distinguished plan shapes that were completely rectangular in their geometry (all external walls were straight line segments, and the angles between them right angles) from plan with curved walls, or with straight walls but set at acute or obtuse angles. He found that 98 per cent of the plan shapes were rectangular on this definition. On the evidence of these two studies then – and acknowledging their limited historical and geographical scope – it *does* seem fair to say that the majority of buildings are predominantly rectangular.

Hypotheses

At least part of the answer to our question in relation to the vertical direction is no great mystery: rectangularity in buildings has much to do with the force of gravity. Floors are flat so that we, and pieces of furniture, can stand easily on them. Walls and piers and columns are made vertical so that they are structurally stable and the loads they carry are transferred directly to the ground – although there are obviously many exceptions. Larger buildings as a consequence tend to be made up, as geometrical objects, from the horizontal layers of successive floors. In trying to understand general rules or tendencies it is often informative to look at exceptions, at 'pathological cases'. When are floors *not* flat? The most obvious examples are vehicle and trolley ramps – but we humans seem to prefer to rise or descend, ourselves, on the flat treads of stairs or escalators. Theatres and lecture rooms have raked floors; but these, like staircases, are not locally sloped, and consist of the shallow steps on which the rows of seats are placed. Truly sloping floors on which the occupants of buildings are expected to walk are rare; and where they do occur – as in the helical galleries of Frank Lloyd Wright's Guggenheim Museum in New York – can be a little disturbing and uncomfortable.

The rectangularity of buildings in the horizontal plane is more mysterious. I have solicited explanations from a number of colleagues who combine an interest in architecture with a mathematical turn of mind, and they have offered different ideas.

1 The cause, they suggest, lies in the use by architects of instruments – specifically drawing boards with T-squares and set-squares – that make it easier to draw rectangles than other shapes. (Techniques for surveying and laying out plans on the ground might also favour rightangles.) We know that drawing apparatus of this general kind is very ancient. The earliest known examples are from Babylonia and are dated to around 2130 BC (Figure 1). However we also know that very many, in fact almost certainly the majority of buildings in history were built without drawings of any kind; and that many of these were nevertheless rectangular. So this explanation is clearly inadequate.

FIGURE 1 Carved representation of a drawing board with scribing instrument and scale, from a statue of Gudea of Ur, c.2130 BC

2 The cause is to be found deeper in our culture and intellectual makeup, and has to do with western mathematical conceptions of three-dimensional space – with the geometry of Euclid, and with the superimposition onto mental space of the orthogonal coordinate systems of Descartes. (Architects' drawing equipment would then be just one symptom of this wider conceptualisation.) However this argument is subject to the same objections as the first. What about all those rectangular buildings produced in non-western cultures, or in the west but before Greek geometry, or erected by builders who had absolutely no knowledge of western geometrical theory?

3 The cause is to be found yet deeper still in our psychology, and has to do with the way in which we conceptualise space in relation to the layout, mental image and functioning of our own bodies. Our awareness of gravity and the earth's surface creates the basic distinction between 'up' and 'down'. The design of the body for locomotion, and the placing of the eyes relative to the direction of this movement, creates the distinction – in this argument – between 'forward' and 'backward'. We now have two axes at rightangles. A third orthogonal axis, distinguishing 'left' from 'right', reflects the bilateral symmetry, in this direction, of arms, legs, eyes and ears. When we walk, we steer and turn by reference to this sense of left and right. We organise our buildings accordingly.[4]

6 Plan geometry, rectangular and circular

This third argument for a general rectangularity in buildings is subtler if even more speculative than the previous two. If true, it would clearly apply to humans and their buildings in all times and places. Such a mental and bodily disposition to see and move in the world relative to an orthogonal system of 'body coordinates' might conceivably – although this is *very* hypothetical – account for the extent to which we humans are comfortable in buildings whose geometry is itself rectangular. But this is *not* in my view the explanation – or at least not the sole explanation – for the occurrence of that rectangularity in the first place.

Where do departures from rectangularity occur in plans?

Once again it is instructive to examine some counter-examples. In what circumstances do we tend to find buildings, or parts of buildings, which are *not* rectangular in plan? Many buildings that comprise just one room – or one large room plus a few much smaller attached spaces, such as porches or lobbies – have plan perimeters whose shapes are circles, ellipses, hexagons or octagons. Primitive and vernacular houses provide many familiar examples of circular one-room plans: igloos, Mongolian yurts, tepees, Dogon and Tallensi huts (Figure 2). Temples, chapels and other small places of worship are often single spaces, and again their plan shapes are frequently non-rectangular. Circular temple plans could be cited from many cultures and periods. Figure 3 reproduces a detail of a plate from J-B Séroux d'Agincourt's *Histoire de l'Art, Architecture* showing circular religious buildings dating from the fourth to the sixteenth century. The space of the auditorium is dominant in the forms of some theatres, and here too we find that where the plan of the auditorium is a semi-circle, a horseshoe, or a trapezium, then it can give this shape to the perimeter of the building (Figure 4).

These are buildings whose plans consist of, or are dominated by, one single space. A second type of situation in which curvilinear or other non-orthogonal elements are often found – in the plans of buildings that may consist of many rooms – is around the building's outer edges. Many of the otherwise rectangular churches in Figure 3 have semi-circular apses. In simple rectangular modern houses we find semi-circular or angled bay windows. These provided one of the more frequent departures from rectangularity in Bemis's survey. (The most obvious non-orthogonality in many buildings in the vertical direction – as confirmed by Bemis – is in their pitched roofs; again on the outer surfaces of the built forms, by definition.)

Figure 5 illustrates the plans of an apartment building at Sausset-les-Pins in France, designed by André Bruyère and completed in 1964. From the exterior the block gives the impression of being designed according to an entirely 'free-form' curvilinear geometry. Closer inspection of the interior however shows the majority of the rooms in the flats to be simple rectangles, or near approximations to rectangles. The curved profile of the exterior is created by curving some of the exterior-facing walls of the living rooms, and by adding balconies with curved outlines. Many late twentieth-century office buildings that have bulging facades are similarly curved only on these exterior surfaces, with conventional rectangular layouts concealed behind.

Naval architecture offers some interesting parallels here. The hulls of ships are doubly curved, for obvious hydrodynamic reasons. In smaller boats with undivided interiors the plan shape of the single cabin follows directly the internal lines of the hull. But in ocean liners with many spaces, the interior layout tends to consist mostly of rectangular rooms, with only the curved walls of those cabins that lie on the two outer sides of the ship taking up the curvature of the hull (Figure 6).

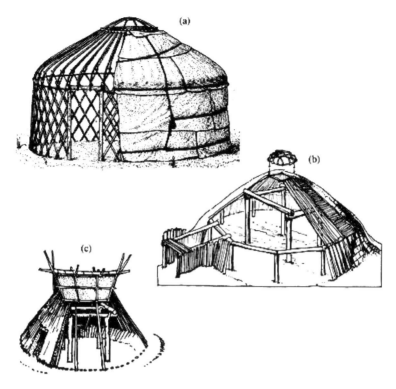

FIGURE 2 Traditional and vernacular houses with circular plans: (a) Mongolian yurt, (b) Mandan earth lodge, (c) Neolithic northern Japanese shelter; reprinted with permission from *Shelter*, Shelter Publications, Bolinas, California 1973. Drawings (b) and (c) are by Bob Easton

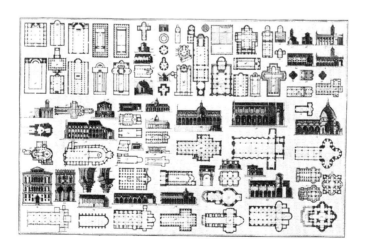

FIGURE 3 Detail of plate 'Summary and General Catalogue of the Buildings That Constitute the History of the Decadence of Architecture' from J-B Séroux d'Agincourt, *Histoire de l'Art par les Monuments Depuis sa Décadence au IVe Siècle jusqu'à son Renouvellement au XVIe* Paris, 1811–23, showing some religious buildings from the fourth to the sixteenth century with circular plans, as well as many rectangular buildings with semi-circular apses

8 Plan geometry, rectangular and circular

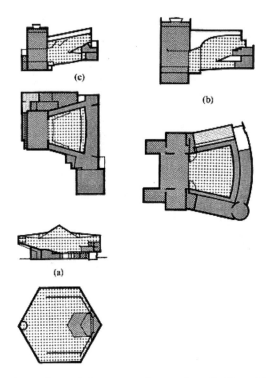

FIGURE 4 Plans and sections of twentieth-century theatres from R Ham, *Theatre Planning*, Architectural Press, London 1972, reproduced with permission from Taylor and Francis: (a) Festival Theatre, Chichester, (b) Shakespeare Memorial Theatre, Stratford-on-Avon, (c) Belgrade Theatre, Coventry

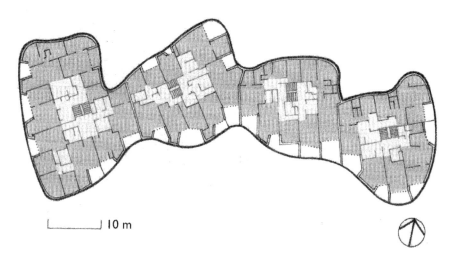

FIGURE 5 Plan of apartment building by André Bruyère, Sausset-les-Pins, France, 1964: redrawn from Bruyère's original. The balconies are shown in white

Why are most buildings rectangular? **9**

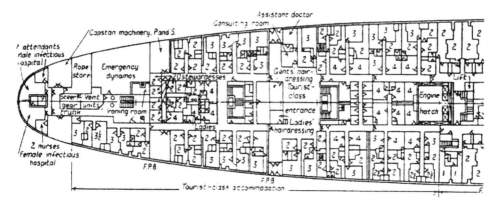

FIGURE 6 Part plan of B Deck of the 'Queen Mary' (from www.sterling.rmplc.co.uk/visions/decks.html, accessed May 2007)

If one were to ask the general public to name one contemporary building, above all others, whose form is definitively 'free' and non-rectangular, the most frequent answer might well be Frank Gehry's Guggenheim Museum in Bilbao. Without question the external titanium shell is geometrically complex. But if one looks deeper into the building one finds that in some places this shell is used to enclose large 'free-form' galleries, practically detached from the remainder of the structure and thus very nearly 'single-room buildings' in themselves (Figure 7). Meanwhile in those parts of the Museum where many rooms of comparable dimensions are located together, such as the multiple smaller galleries, and the administrative offices, the planning reverts to an orthogonal geometry.

It is true that in certain classically planned buildings with many rectangular rooms, as for example villas or country houses, there can be spaces deep in the interior, such as central halls, whose plans are circular, polygonal or elliptical (Figure 8). However these are produced by filling out the corners of rectangular spaces – in Beaux Arts terms the *poché* – with solid masonry, cupboards, lobbies or spiral stairs; and the overall planning discipline remains rectangular.

What all this evidence indicates, I would suggest, is that rectangularity in buildings in the horizontal plane has to do, crucially, with *the packing together of rooms in plan*. When many rooms of similar or varying sizes are fitted together so as to pack without interstices, it is *there* that rectangularity is found. Non-rectangular shapes occur on the edges of plans, or in single-room buildings, since in both cases the exigencies of close packing do not apply.

Packings of squares, triangles and hexagons

One reasonable objection to this line of argument would seem to be that it is possible to pack other two-dimensional shapes besides rectangles to fill the plane. Among regular figures (equal length sides, equal angles) there are just three shapes that tessellate in this way: squares, equilateral triangles and hexagons. Some architects have laid out plans very successfully on regular grids of triangles or hexagons. Figure 9 shows Frank Lloyd Wright's Sundt House project of 1941, and Figure 10 shows Bruce Goff's house for Joe Price of 1956. Use of a triangular organising grid does not force the designer into making all rooms simple triangles.

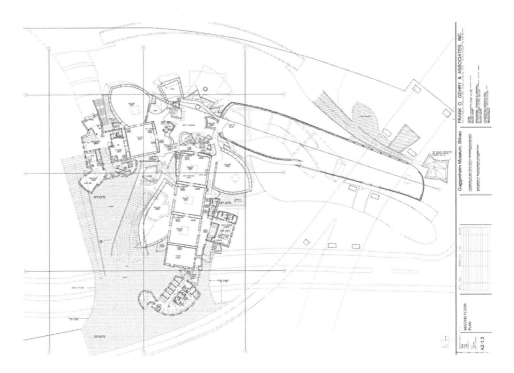

FIGURE 7 Third floor plan of the Guggenheim Museum, Bilbao by Frank Gehry, 1997, with kind permission of Gehry Partners LLP. Notice the rectangular planning of the smaller galleries and the office wing

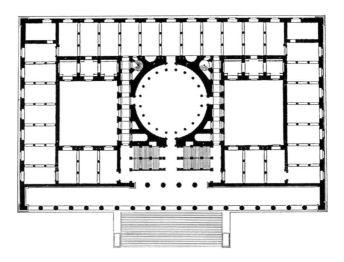

FIGURE 8 Plan of Altes Museum, Berlin by K F Schinkel, 1823–30, to show the central circular hall created within an otherwise rectangular plan

Why are most buildings rectangular? **11**

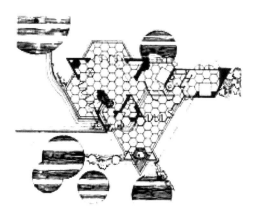 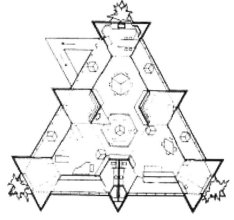

FIGURE 9 Plan of Sundt house project by Frank Lloyd Wright, 1941, laid out on a triangular grid

FIGURE 10 Plan of house for Joe Price by Bruce Goff, Bartlesville, Oklahoma, 1956–, also laid out on a triangular grid

The triangular units can be aggregated into parallelograms, trapezia and other shapes (including hexagons), as evidenced in the Wright and Goff plans. The triangular grid, that is, offers a certain *flexibility of room shape* to the architect. Similarly, unit hexagons in a hexagonal grid can be joined together to make other more complex shapes.

When I started to think about this particular issue of flexibility in planning, I imagined that a regular square grid perhaps offered *more* possibilities for room shapes, and *more* possibilities for arranging those shapes, than did a triangular or a hexagonal grid – and that here might lie part of an explanation for the prevalence of rectangularity in buildings. The following demonstration, though very far from providing any kind of mathematical proof, serves however to indicate that my intuition was wrong.

Consider three fragmentary square, triangular and hexagonal grids, each comprising nine grid cells, as in Figure 11. We can imagine that the plans of simple buildings – perhaps small houses – are to be laid out on the grids with their walls following selected grid lines. How many distinct shapes for rooms can be made by joining adjacent grid cells together, in each case? Let us confine our attention, since we are thinking about rooms in buildings, to *convex* shapes, convexity being a characteristic of most small architectural spaces. Let us also count shapes that are geometrically similar, but are of different sizes (they are made up of different numbers of grid cells) as being distinct. Thus on the square grid we can make three different square shapes, with one cell, four cells or nine cells. Our criterion of convexity means that there is only *one* shape that can be made on the hexagonal grid: the unit hexagonal cell itself. All shapes made by aggregations of hexagonal cells are non-convex. On the square grid by contrast it is possible to make six distinct shapes (Figure 12); but on the triangular grid it is possible to make ten distinct shapes (Figure 13). The triangular grid, contrary to what I had expected, offers a *greater* range of shapes for rooms than does the square grid.

Perhaps these shapes made by aggregating triangular units, although more numerous, cannot be packed together without gaps in as many distinct *arrangements* as can the shapes made from unit squares? For square grids, this question of possible arrangements was intensively studied,

12 Plan geometry, rectangular and circular

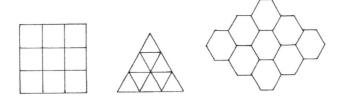

FIGURE 11 Fragments of grids, each comprised of nine cells whose shapes are squares, equilateral triangles, and regular hexagons

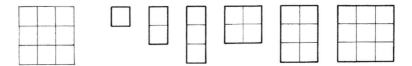

FIGURE 12 The six possible convex shapes made by aggregating unit cells in the square grid of Figure 11

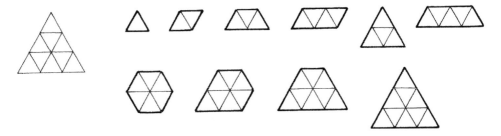

FIGURE 13 The ten possible convex shapes made by aggregating unit cells in the triangular grid of Figure 11

in effect, by several authors, during the 1970s and '80s. The purpose of that work was more general, as I shall explain. But one incidental result was to show for a 3 × 3 square grid, how many different arrangements are possible, of rectangular and square shapes made up from different numbers of grid cells, packed to fill the grid completely. These possibilities, of which there are 53, are all illustrated in Figure 14. (The enumeration is derived, with modifications and additions, from Bloch.[5]) No account is taken, in arriving at this total, of the particular orientation in which an arrangement is set on the page. That is to say, the same arrangement, simply rotated through 90° or 180° or 270°, is not regarded as 'different'. Certain arrangements can exist in distinct left-handed and right-handed versions. Just one representative is taken in each case. The count includes the two extreme cases in which the packing consists of nine unit squares, and of one single 3 × 3 square.

The enumeration of these square grid packings was made by computer. Essentially the same results were achieved by Mitchell, Steadman, Bloch, Krishnamurti, Earl and Flemming using several different algorithms.[6] I have carried out a similar exercise by hand for the grid

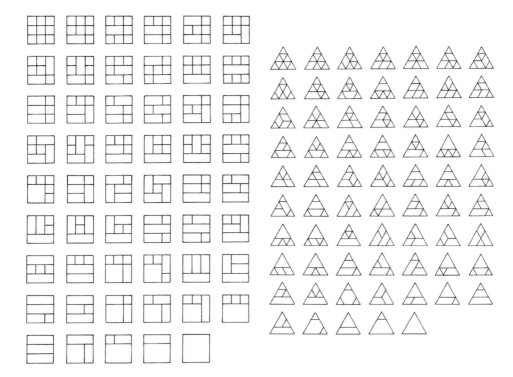

FIGURE 14 All 53 possible arrangements in which combinations of the rectangular shapes shown in Figure 12 can be packed, without interstices, into the square grid of Figure 11. Differences solely by rotation and reflection are ignored

FIGURE 15 All 68 possible arrangements in which combinations of the shapes shown in Figure 13 can be packed, without interstices, into the triangular grid of Figure 11. Differences solely by rotation and reflection are ignored

of nine triangular cells, to count the numbers of arrangements in which combinations of the shapes illustrated in Figure 13 can be packed to fill this grid. Once again, differences by rotation and reflection are ignored. Figure 15 shows my results. The number of possibilities is 68. Here once again, and contrary to my expectation, the triangular grid offers rather *more* possible arrangements of shapes than does the square grid.

The flexibility of dimensioning offered by rectangular packings

This demonstration however ignores one very important aspect of flexibility in the possible packings of shapes to fill the plane. The wider aim of the computer work mentioned above was to enumerate possibilities for packing rectangles of *any dimensions whatsoever* – not just rectangular shapes made by aggregating square cells of some given unit size.

Consider the packing of shapes on the square grid in Figure 16a. Here the arrangement is set on a system of x, y coordinates, as shown. The spacing of the grid lines in x and y is given by a series of dimensions x_1, x_2, x_3, y_1, y_2, y_3. In the packing of unit squares as shown in the figure these dimensions are of course all equal. Suppose however that the x and y values are changed. If they are all multiplied, or divided, in the same ratio, then the packing

14 Plan geometry, rectangular and circular

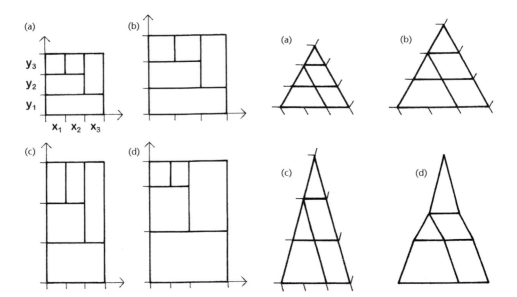

FIGURE 16 (a) A packing of rectangles within the square grid of Figure 11, set on an x, y coordinate system. The spacing of the grid lines is given by the dimensions x_1, x_2, x_3, y_1, y_2, y_3. (b) The same packing enlarged, by a similarity transformation. (c) The same packing stretched, by a shear transformation. (d) The same packing transformed by changing the spacing of the grid lines in different ratios

FIGURE 17 (a) A packing of shapes (compare Figure 13) within the triangular grid of Figure 11. (b) The same packing enlarged, by a similarity transformation. (c) The same packing stretched, by a shear transformation. (d) The same packing transformed by changing the spacing of the grid lines in different ratios

as a whole will simply be enlarged or shrunk in size, but will remain otherwise unchanged (Figure 16b). (In mathematical terms this is a *similarity transformation*.) If the x values are all multiplied in the same ratio, while the y values are all multiplied in a different ratio, the arrangement will be stretched or shrunk in one direction or the other (Figure 16c). (This is a *shear transformation*.) Finally, individual x and y values can be altered in different ratios, so as to cause local shrinking or stretching of different component rectangles (Figure 16d). All the shapes in the packing nevertheless remain rectangular throughout.

In this way any *dimensioned* version whatever of the basic arrangement of Figure 16a can in principle be generated. These versions are infinitely numerous, since any of the x and y grid dimensions can be altered by increments that can be as small as we wish. The same process of assigning dimensions can be carried out for all the different arrangements on 3 × 3 square grids in Figure 14; and indeed for all arrangements on 1 × 3, or 2 × 2, or 2 × 3, or 3 × 4 grids and so on. Such an approach makes it possible to generate absolutely any packing of rectangles, of whatever dimensions, within a simple rectangular boundary. This was the goal of the computer research referred to earlier (see note 6).

Now imagine a similar process of dimensioning being applied to the grid of nine equilateral triangles (Figure 17a) (or to the grid of nine unit hexagons). The entire pattern can be subjected

Why are most buildings rectangular? **15**

to a similarity transformation, enlarging or reducing it in size, without difficulty (Figure 17b). But any overall shear transformation results in changes in the internal angles of all the triangles (Figure 17c). And any change in the spacing of some of the grid lines results in changes in the internal angles of the triangles between those lines (Figure 17d) – indeed some 'grid lines' now become bent, and the very idea of a grid ceases to apply. In giving different dimensions to the grid spacing in square grids, we generate shapes that are always rectangles. In giving different dimensions to the spacings of lines in grids of equilateral triangles, by contrast, we generate shapes that are always triangles, certainly, but they are no longer equilateral triangles. A similar argument applies to the hexagonal grid.

Here, I would propose, we are approaching the heart of the issue, the key reason for the superior flexibility of rectangular packing over other shapes that fill the plane. That flexibility lies in part in the variety of possibilities for *configurations* of rectangles, irrespective of their sizes; but much more, in the flexibility of assigning different *dimensions* to those configurations, *while preserving their rectangularity*. *Any* rectangular packing can be dimensioned as desired in the general way illustrated in Figure 16 – in principle in an infinity of ways – and the component shapes will all still be rectangles.

Looking at this flexibility from another point of view: it is always possible to divide any rectangle within a packing into two rectangles, and to divide each of these rectangles into two further rectangles, and so on. In the context of plan layout, the designer can decide to turn one proposed rectangular room into two. More generally, he or she can squeeze groups of rectangular spaces together, or can pull them apart and slide others in between. In buildings once constructed, a new partition wall can divide any rectangular room into two rectangular parts. (It is equally possible to divide any triangle into two triangles – but those component triangles will have different internal angles from the first.)

I have confined discussion so far to packings of regular figures – squares, equilateral triangles, hexagons – and how these may be dimensioned. Beyond these, there are packings of other shapes, notably the semi-regular or Archimedean tessellations, which are made up of combinations of different regular figures. Some of these have served on occasion as the basis

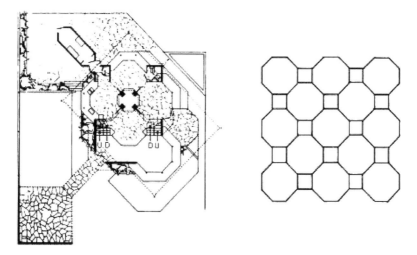

FIGURE 18 Plan of the Jones House by Bruce Goff, Bartlesville, Oklahoma 1958, laid out as a semi-regular tessellation of octagons and squares

16 Plan geometry, rectangular and circular

for architectural plans, as for example Bruce Goff's Jones House of 1958, whose rooms are alternate squares and octagons (Figure 18). And there is an infinite variety of irregular shapes that can fill the plane, examples of which form the basis of many of M C Escher's irritating puzzle pictures. But the argument about inflexibility of dimensioning applies, I would suggest, with even greater force in all these cases. Goff's planning of the Jones House is ingenious. But he picked a geometrical straitjacket for himself, and it is not surprising that few others have followed his lead.

Close packing of components in buildings and other artefacts

Up to this point we have looked only at the problems of arranging rooms in architectural plans. But the solid structure of any building – unless it is wholly of mud or concrete – itself consists of packings of three-dimensional components at a smaller scale: bricks, beams, door and window frames, floorboards, floor tiles. Here too, rectangularity generally prevails, for the same geometrical reasons, I would suggest, as already outlined. (And even concrete needs formwork, often assembled from rectangular members.) Rectangular rooms can readily be formed out of rectangular components of construction. This rectangularity of building components was Bemis's concern: to what extent would it be possible to construct houses from rectangular pre-made parts that would be larger than standard bricks or timbers, but could still be fitted together in many ways? In traditional brickwork, it is where walls meet at angles other than 90° that there is a need for differently shaped, hence more expensive 'specials'. Otherwise, so long as brick-based modular dimensions are generally adhered to, the standard brick will serve throughout. Pieces of timber in the form of parallelepipeds can always be cut into smaller paralellepipeds, and rectangular sheets of board into smaller rectangles. Building components must pack vertically as well as horizontally, so here is another reason besides gravity for the appearance of rectangularity in the vertical direction.

We find rectangularity in other types of artefact, for essentially the same reasons, I believe, of flexibility in the assembly or subdivision of parts. Woven cloth, with its weft and warp, is produced in rectangles because of the basic technology of the loom. Many types of traditional garment – shirts, ponchos, trousers, coats, kimonos – are then sewn from square or rectangular pieces cut from these larger sheets, so as not to waste any of the valuable and laboriously made cloth.[7] Such garments, when old, are picked apart and the pieces reused for other purposes. Figure 19 shows a nineteenth-century agricultural labourer's smock from Sussex, with the pattern of rectangular pieces from which it is assembled.

Paper too is manufactured in rectangles that can be cut in many ways without waste to create smaller sheets of different sizes. The rectangularity of the paper fits with the rectangularity of pages of printed type. In traditional printing methods each letter and space was represented by a separate rectangular slug of metal, the whole assemblage of letters – possibly of many different sizes – clamped together in a rectangular frame or 'chase' (Figure 20). The art of newspaper and magazine layout lies in the fitting together of differently sized pictures, headlines and blocks of type, to fill each page. Much furniture is built of course from essentially rectangular wooden components, and the furniture's rectangularity allows it to fit in the corners of rectangular rooms. In the denser parts of cities, complete rectangular buildings are packed close together on sites that are themselves rectangular; and these sites pack to fill the complete area of city blocks. This was part of the reason for Krüger's interest in plan shapes.

Why are most buildings rectangular? **17**

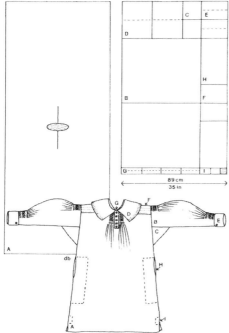

FIGURE 20 Rectangular metal slugs carrying letters or acting as spacers, clamped together into a rectangular frame or 'chase', as used in traditional printing methods. From P Gaskell, *A New Introduction to Bibliography*, Clarendon Press, Oxford 1974; reproduced by kind permission of Oxford University Press

FIGURE 19 Man's smock, probably from Sussex, 1860–80, and the pattern from which it was made. One rectangular piece of cloth serves for the body of the garment. All other pieces are also rectangular and are cut from a second rectangle of cloth without waste. From D K Burnham, *Cut My Cote*, Textile Department, Royal Ontario Museum, Toronto 1973, with the Museum's kind permission

A transition from round to rectangular in vernacular houses?

We have noticed how circularity in plan is often a characteristic of freestanding, widely spaced, single-room houses in pre-industrial societies. (The circular plan may derive in part from a system of construction where the roof is supported on a central pole, or forms a self-supporting cone or dome.) One might imagine that with increasing wealth there would be a change, at some point in time, from single-room to multi-room houses. Another possibility is that in circumstances where land was in short supply – as for example where it was necessary to confine many houses within a defensive perimeter – then those houses might have needed to be packed tightly together. In both cases the theory of rectangular packing proposed here might lead one to expect a transition in traditional houses from circular to rectangular plan shapes. Can one find actual evidence of such changes?

The American archaeologist Kent Flannery made a comparative analysis of the forms of villages and village houses in the period when permanent settlements first appeared after the end of the Pleistocene.[8] He looked at examples in the Near East, Africa, the Andes and

18 Plan geometry, rectangular and circular

Mesoamerica. He found two broad types of settlement: compounds consisting of small circular huts, and 'true villages' with larger rectangular houses. The round hut was characteristic of nomadic or semi-nomadic communities, and consisted of a single space, housing one or at most two people. The rectangular house typically had several rooms, accommodated an entire family, tended to be extended over time, and was found in fully sedentary communities. In some cases these rectangular houses were indeed concentrated together for the purposes of defence. In Flannery's own words:

> Rectangular structures replace circular ones through time in many archaeological areas around the world (although reversals of this trend occur).[9]

Figure 21 shows this process in action. The photograph is reproduced from Bernard Rudofsky's *Architecture Without Architects*, and shows an aerial view of Logone-Birni in the Cameroun.[10] There are freestanding circular huts with roofs both inside and outside the walled compounds. But the contiguous roofed structures within these compounds — together with some roofless enclosures that are packed closely with those buildings — are for the most part rectangular.

FIGURE 21 Aerial view of Logone-Birni in the Cameroun. Notice the freestanding circular huts, and the rectangular huts and rectangular unroofed enclosures packed within the compounds. From Bernard Rudofsky, *Architecture Without Architects*, Museum of Modern Art, New York 1964; photo by Marcel Griaule

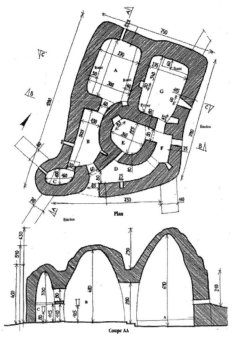

FIGURE 22 Plan of a stone *borie* in the Vaucluse region of France, with seven spaces; from Parc Naturel Régional du Luberon et Edisud, *Bories* 1994. The plan appears to represent a transitional stage between the circular single-room *borie*, and a packing of several rectangular spaces

Other examples can be seen in the vernacular architecture of Europe. The typical hut or *borie* of the Vaucluse region of France is a stone-built cylindrical one-room structure with a corbelled domical stone roof.[11] There are a few existing multi-room rectangular *bories*. In the example of Figure 22 the room layout seems to be in some sort of transitional stage between a squashing together of circles, and an emerging rectangularity. The *trullo* of Apulia has a stone structure similar to the *borie*. According to Fauzia Farneti the *trullo* was originally a temporary dwelling with a circular plan found in rural areas, and later evolved to have a rectangular exterior and a circular interior.[12] These rectangular *trulli*, in their final form, became the repeated structural units of multi-room houses.

A parting shot

Finally, why might we expect to find more departures from rectangularity in the work of 'high architects' than in the general run of more everyday buildings? Many contemporary architects, it seems to me, find the rectangular discipline imposed by the necessary constraints of the close packing of rooms – paradoxically, and despite its flexibility – to be an irksome prison; and they try to escape from it. They gravitate towards building types such as art museums and theatres, not just because these are prestigious and well-funded cultural projects with imaginative clients, but also because they can provide opportunities for spaces that are close to being 'single-room structures', which can be treated sculpturally. It is possible that architects might choose to adopt a non-orthogonal geometry in order, precisely, to set their work apart from the majority of the building stock. Rectangularity can be avoided on the external surfaces of buildings as we have seen: so there is much free play here for architectural articulation and elaboration of a non-orthogonal character. But this treatment comes at a cost, and in more utilitarian buildings it may be dispensed with.

Acknowledgements

Hypothesis 3 is due to Joe Rooney. Bill Hillier took me to see the *borie* of Figure 22, and told me about the paper by Kent Flannery. Jini Williams checked my enumerations in Figures 14 and 15 and found many mistakes, now corrected. Mary Harris and Penelope Woolfitt sent me information about the rectangular geometry of ethnic clothing, including xeroxed pages from Dorothy Burnham, *Cut My Cote* (Royal Ontario Museum, 1973). Philip Tabor, Adrian Forty, Sonit Bafna and an anonymous reviewer contributed ideas, information and suggestions. I am grateful to them all.

Notes

1 Albert Farwell Bemis and John Burchard, *The Evolving House* (Massachusetts Institute of Technology, Cambridge MA: Technology Press, 3 vols 1933–1936).
2 Ibid., Vol. 3 Appendix A pp. 303–316. Bemis extrapolated these data to the entire housing stock of the United States, based on the frequency of different house types, to give a figure of 88.5 per cent rectangularity. He also measured the rectangularity of the structural components of a sample detached house with hipped roof, bow windows and dormers. He found that 97 per cent of those components by number were rectangular.
3 Mario J T Krüger, 'An approach to built-form connectivity at an urban scale: system description and its representation' in *Environment and Planning B* Vol. 6 (1979) pp. 67–88.

20 Plan geometry, rectangular and circular

4 This proposal is due to Joe Rooney (personal communication).

5 Cecil J Bloch, *A Formal Catalogue of Small Rectangular Plans: Generation, Enumeration and Classification* (PhD thesis, Cambridge, England: University of Cambridge School of Architecture, 1979). Bloch enumerated packings of rectangles on 'minimal gratings' – that is to say where all grid lines coincide with the edges of rectangles. The number of distinct packings on 3 × 3 minimal gratings given by Bloch is 33. To these we must add – for the present enumeration – packings that correspond to 2 × 2 and 2 × 3 minimal gratings, suitably dimensioned to fill the 3 × 3 grid. Bloch did not count packings in which the number of rectangles equals the number of cells in the grating. These (on 1 × 1, 1 × 2, 1 × 3, 2 × 3 and 3 × 3 gratings) are also included here, appropriately dimensioned to the 3 × 3 grid in each case.

6 William J Mitchell, Philip Steadman and Robin S Liggett, 'Synthesis and optimisation of small rectangular floor plans', in *Environment and Planning B* Vol. 3 (1976) 37–70; Christopher F Earl, 'A note on the generation of rectangular dissections' in *Environment and Planning B* Vol. 4 (1977) 241–246; Ramesh Krishnamurti and Peter H O'N Roe, 'Algorithmic aspects of plan generation and enumeration' in *Environment and Planning B* Vol. 5 (1978) 157–177; Cecil J Bloch and Ramesh Krishnamurti, 'The counting of rectangular dissections' in *Environment and Planning B* Vol. 5 (1978) 207–214; Ulrich Flemming, 'Wall representations of rectangular dissections and their use in automated space allocation', in *Environment and Planning B* Vol. 5 (1978) 215–232; Cecil J Bloch, 'An algorithm for the exhaustive enumeration of rectangular dissections' in *Transactions of the Martin Centre for Architectural and Urban Studies* Vol. 3 (1978) 5–34. See also the general discussion in Philip Steadman, *Architectural Morphology* (London: Pion, 1979).

7 Dorothy K Burnham, *Cut My Cote* (Toronto, Canada: Textile Department, Royal Ontario Museum, 1973).

8 Kent V Flannery, 'The origins of the village as a settlement type in Mesoamerica and the Near East: a comparative study' in *Man, Settlement and Urbanism*, eds P J Ucko, R Tringham and G W Dimbleby (London: Duckworth, 1972) pp. 23–53.

9 Ibid., pp. 29–30.

10 Bernard Rudofsky, *Architecture Without Architects* (New York: Museum of Modern Art, 1964. Reprinted, London: Academy Editions, 1973).

11 Pierre Desaulle, *Les Bories de Vaucluse: Région de Bonnieux* (Paris: A. et J. Picard, 1965).

12 Paul Oliver, ed. *Encyclopedia of Vernacular Architecture of the World* (Cambridge: Cambridge University Press, 3 vols, 1997) p. 1568.

2

ARCHITECTURAL DOUGHNUTS

Circular plan buildings, with and without courtyards

(*Nexus Network Journal: Architecture and Mathematics*, Volume 17, 2015, pp. 759–783)

Not all buildings are rectangular. This paper concentrates on a particular class of non-rectangular buildings: those with plans defined by two concentric circles. I have christened these 'architectural doughnuts'. The inner circle might be a courtyard, creating a 'ring doughnut'; or it might be an important central space, creating a 'jam doughnut'. The ratio of the diameters of the circles in a jam doughnut can be important for the building's functioning and economic efficiency, depending on the activity housed. Geometrical data on a series of examples are presented in a 'morphospace' or world of possible doughnut plans.

The paper was published in a special issue of the Nexus Network Journal *in honour of Lionel March, with whom I published* The Geometry of Environment *in 1971. The topic relates obliquely to March's research at Cambridge University in the 1960s on 'land use and built form studies' [see Paper 9].*

Two kinds of architectural doughnut

By an 'architectural doughnut' I mean a building with a circular plan shape. There are two types of architectural doughnut. The first type is the 'ring doughnut' (geometrically a torus) with a courtyard at the centre. Figure 1 shows an example: the Narrenturm, an eighteenth-century hospital for the confinement of the mentally ill in Vienna. Offices for the Apple computer company, under construction in 2015 at Cupertino, California, provide another more recent case. The second type is the 'jam doughnut' (geometrically a cylinder) in which there is no central court. Instead the plan consists of some central space or function – the 'jam' – surrounded by subsidiary spaces – the 'dough'. An intermediate type has a central circular atrium rising the entire height of the building. The Italian architect Vittorio Bonadè Bottino built four hotels and hostels on this plan in the 1930s, with internal helical ramps giving access to the rooms.[1]

One functional difference between the 'ring doughnut' and 'jam doughnut' types has to do with the available patterns of visibility in each case. If a circular building without a courtyard has a completely open plan, then all points in the interior are visible from all other points. This is a general property of convex shapes. Circular plans have appealed to some architects

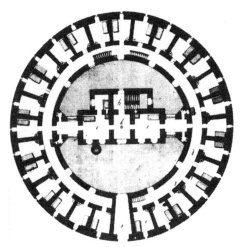 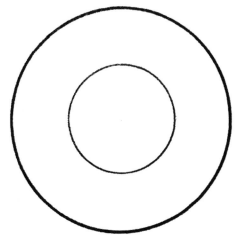

FIGURE 1 A 'ring doughnut' building: the Narrenturm, Vienna 1784, a hospital for the confinement of the mentally ill; from Dieter Jetter, 'Die psychiatrischen krankhaüser als Anstalten besonderer Art', *Confinia Psychiatrica* Volume 9, 1966, by kind permission of S Karger AG, Basel

FIGURE 2 Diagrammatic plan of a 'jam doughnut' building, as two concentric circles

who have wanted many peripheral spaces or positions to be observable from a central vantage point, as we shall see. Annular buildings with open plans by contrast have the property that there is no position from which the whole of the interior is visible at once – assuming that one cannot see across the courtyard and through windows on the far side, which in practice one usually cannot. Ring-shaped corridors – as in the Narrenturm – can be disorienting since they present much the same view at every point in the circuit.

I propose to concentrate on the 'jam doughnut' type.[2] We can represent the generic plan schematically as two concentric circles, the central circle representing the 'jam', and the outer ring representing the 'dough' (Figure 2). On any given floor, the ratio of the areas of the 'jam' and the 'dough' depend, obviously, on the diameters of the two circles. This ratio, and the absolute diameter values, can be important for the functioning of different building types having this type of plan, and can indeed decide whether a 'doughnut' plan is suitable or feasible in the first place. I discuss a series of examples below, for which diagrammatic plans are given to a standard scale in Table 3 on page 37.

The present paper pays distant homage to some work done by Lionel March with Leslie Martin at Cambridge in the 1970s, in which they investigated the geometrical effects and relative merits of placing buildings around the peripheries of sites, compared with concentrating development at the centres of sites.[3] They made reference in this work to the configuration of the Fresnel lens in optics, which is made up of many concentric ring-shaped elements. Martin and March drew a Fresnel pattern as a set of concentric squares, not circles, each ring having the same area as the central square (Figure 3). The pattern was used in the logo of the Centre for Land Use and Built Form Studies, set up in 1967 at the Cambridge University Department of Architecture, of which March was the first director. Here the

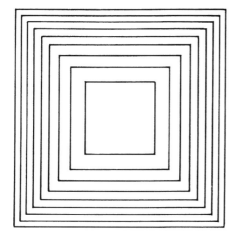
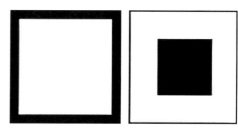

FIGURE 3 Fresnel pattern of concentric squares. The area of each ring is the same as the area of the central square. From Leslie Martin 'The grid as generator' in Martin and March eds, *Urban Space and Structures*, Cambridge University Press, 1972 p. 19, reproduced by permission of Lionel March

FIGURE 4 The logo of the Centre for Land Use and Built Form Studies, set up in 1967 at the Cambridge University School of Architecture. The design is by Philip Steadman. The areas of the black ring and the black square are the same

area of the black ring on the left is equal to the area of the central black square on the right (Figure 4). The research using the Fresnel principle was focused on the urban design scale. This present paper transfers similar considerations to the scale of the single building. Martin and March's theoretical patterns were rectangular. My doughnuts are (mostly) circular – although I will make brief mention of a few rectangular doughnut buildings.

Buildings with circular plans are relatively rare in the building stock. I have argued elsewhere [*Paper 1 above*] that the majority of buildings show a predominantly rectangular geometry in plan, because of the great flexibility that this allows for packing together many spaces of different dimensions and proportions.[4] Certain buildings escape these constraints of two-dimensional packing however, because they consist of just one large open space, or one large central space with some smaller spaces attached around the periphery. The examples of 'jam doughnuts' described here fall into those categories.

Circular plan buildings without courts are found in a wide range of sizes. At the lower end of the scale are vernacular huts like the *bories* of the Vaucluse region of France, or the Italian *trulli* of Apulia, both of them typically 2 or 3 m in diameter. Towards the upper end of the size range are the roundhouses that were built as railway engine sheds and maintenance depots in the nineteenth and twentieth centuries. The Camden Town roundhouse in London – now converted to an entertainment venue – has a diameter of 50 m.

The interiors of the small houses tend to be open and undivided. The plans of larger circular buildings can also be completely open – like the railway roundhouses. Where there are smaller spaces wrapped around in a ring, these are typically wedge-shaped, approximating to rectangles if their number is large. Even where peripheral spaces are not walled off, there may still be positions around the outer wall occupied by furniture, machines or equipment. In circular prisons there are positions for cells, in hospital wards for beds, in multi-storey garages for cars. In the railway roundhouses there are positions for locomotives.

Railway roundhouses

The roundhouse provided parking spaces for railway engines under cover, where they could be maintained and prepared. There was a central turntable, which was used for moving the engines onto short lengths of track radiating out from the centre. The Camden Town roundhouse had a turntable with a diameter of 11 m, and 19.5 m lengths of track for parking the locomotives (Figure 5). One engine was moved at a time, and the radial sections of track could be packed tightly around the edge of the turntable. Each had the standard British railway gauge of 1.435 m (4 ft 8½ in), allowing for twenty-four positions in the full circle, one of them the access track. (In other roundhouses there were separate tracks for entrance and exit.)

The length of a standard locomotive fixed the diameter of the turntable. This same dimension – with some extra allowance for track immediately adjoining the turntable – fixed the width of the outer ring. The space for each parked locomotive was wedge-shaped; but because locomotives are long and thin, not too much space was wasted. The diameter of the turntable determined the number of tracks – hence number of engines – that could be fitted in the ring. The length and width of the typical railway engine thus determined the dimensions of the entire plan.

In the twentieth century, roundhouses were largely abandoned in favour of rectangular engine sheds. I have not seen the reasons discussed in the somewhat sparse and specialised

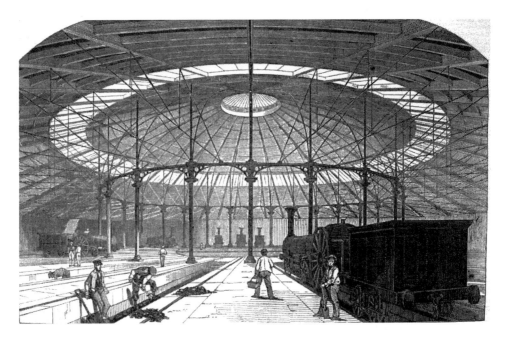

FIGURE 5 Interior view of the Camden Roundhouse, built as a locomotive shed and now an entertainment venue: *Illustrated London News*, 4 December 1847

history of the type.[5] The Camden roundhouse fell out of use because locomotives were made longer. One might speculate about other causes. The number of engines accommodated around the ring could not be increased. Perhaps the single-track entry and exit slowed down operations, and rectangular sheds with many parallel tracks allowed for speedier and more flexible deployment of the engines.

The railway roundhouse thus provides a historical example of a 'jam doughnut' where the dimensions of both 'jam' and 'dough' were more or less fixed by the function. In other building types, these dimensions could be varied.

Panopticon prisons

At the end of the eighteenth century the political philosopher and penal law reformer Jeremy Bentham and his brother Samuel conceived of a new kind of prison with a circular plan, the Panopticon ('everything seen').[6] The Benthams wanted the governor and staff of the Panopticon to be able to watch the prisoners continuously, day and night. This implied a ring of cells whose fronts were barred (the 'dough'), observed from the 'inspector's lodge' at the centre (the 'jam').

It is just possible that the Benthams drew some inspiration for the Panopticon from another contemporary type of cylindrical building whose purpose was to display large 360° panoramic paintings of landscapes, cityscapes or battle scenes.[7] Panoramas of this kind were patented by Robert Barker in the same year, 1787, in which Jeremy Bentham published his first Panopticon design. In both cases the cylindrical geometry was determined by the basic desire to have observers completely surrounded by what was observed – prisoners in the one case, paintings in the other. Panoramas became a popular form of entertainment in the nineteenth century. It has to be said however that, although mocking commentators in the press referred to the Panopticon as a 'penal panorama', there is no mention of Barker's invention anywhere in Jeremy Bentham's writings on prisons.

[*The Panopticon and its failings are discussed at length in the following Paper 3: some duplication here has been cut. One serious weakness of Jeremy Bentham's scheme was that the large hall at the middle of the plan had to be left empty in order that the cells could all be seen from the central observation point. The focus here is on that issue.*]

The Bentham brothers' second Panopticon scheme of 1791 was for a six-storey building with a ring of twenty-four cell positions, each measuring 4 m wide by 4.7 m deep [*see Paper 3 Figure 6*]. Jeremy never got this scheme built, despite twenty years of lobbying and much personal expense.[8] A few other Panoptical prisons were however constructed later, following the general lines of the Benthams's designs, where the central halls were again left almost completely empty. The largest and best-known of these is Stateville Penitentiary (today Stateville Correctional Center) near Joliet, Illinois, designed by the architectural firm of William Carbys Zimmermann and built between 1916 and 1924 [*see Paper 3 Figure 15*]. Eight four-storey rotundas were planned, of which four were completed. The single-person cells were just 2 m wide, and there were sixty-four cells in the complete circle.

The Panopticon was largely a failure as a model for prison design. By contrast the type that succeeded it in the nineteenth century and came to be reproduced in large numbers around the world was the 'radial prison', of which the Eastern State Penitentiary in Philadelphia and Pentonville in London [*see Paper 3 Figure 19*] were the first examples. These buildings consisted of long straight cell blocks radiating out from central observatories to create

26 Plan geometry, rectangular and circular

starfish-shaped plans. The huge circular hall of the Panopticon could be collapsed into a series of elongated rectangular halls. The whole of each hall could be watched from the observation point at the focus. Should the patrolling guards run into trouble, this could be seen from the centre, and reinforcements could be sent.

The Panopticon, in its various built and un-built versions, was thus an example of a 'jam doughnut' in which the width of the ring of cells (the 'dough') was variable only within narrow limits. Depending on the number of cells in the ring and their dimensions, this resulted in different areas for the 'jam' of the inspector's lodge and the open space around it. I have made a series of theoretical designs of increasing size and number of cells, where the cell sizes are standardised throughout at 4 m wide by 4.7 m deep, as in the Benthams' 1791 scheme. Table 1 gives dimensional statistics: the external radius of each building, the floor area of the central hall and observatory, the total floor area of the cells, and these areas as percentages of total floor area. The scheme with twenty-four cells approximates to the 1791 Panopticon. See how the cells make up 52 per cent of total area. With more cells this proportion reduces further.

Stateville had sixty-four cells in the ring, but these were only 2 m wide, so its plan is roughly comparable with the thirty-two-cell example in Table 1. However the cells were also shallow, with the result that collectively they represented just 26 per cent of total floor area. By comparison, at Pentonville the equivalent figure is 62 per cent. This was presumably a major consideration for the authorities at Stateville, when they replaced the demolished Panoptical rotundas with a rectangular cell block on the Pentonville model.

TABLE 1 Measurements of four theoretical designs for circular plan prisons of the Panopticon type, with increasing numbers of cells. The scheme with 24 cells approximates to Bentham's 1791 scheme

Number of cells	External radius (m)	Area of hall (m²)	Hall as % of total area	Area of cells (m²)	Cells as % of total area
24	15.3	353	48	400	52
32	20.4	774	59	533	41
40	25.5	1359	67	684	33
48	30.6	2107	72	835	28

Circular hospital wards

Jeremy Bentham never mentions this issue of wasted space anywhere in his copious writings on the Panopticon. A similar question was however debated at length at conferences and in print in connection with hospital wards, and with the idea put forward by the surgeon John Marshall in the 1870s that circular plans might have several advantages over the elongated rectangular design of ward that was then standard. The 'pavilion' hospital of the second half of the nineteenth century was made up of rectangular 'Nightingale wards', whose measurements in plan were typically 9 by 40 m (Figure 6). This allowed room for thirty-two beds. (The length was not absolutely fixed, and varied considerably in practice.) These wards were then spaced widely apart in order to provide the best possible natural ventilation, since the causes of many diseases were thought to lie in 'miasma' or polluted 'hospital air', which needed to be blown away.[9]

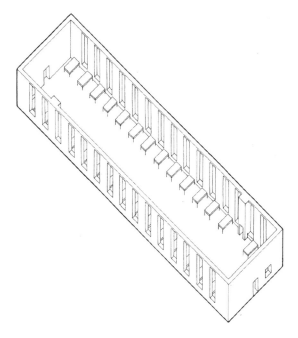

FIGURE 6 A typical thirty-bed Nightingale ward in a nineteenth-century pavilion hospital, in axonometric view: author's drawing

Marshall gave a paper to the Social Science Association 'On a circular system of hospital wards'.[10] The fact that the pavilion ward block was set so far away from its neighbours meant that it did not strictly have to be rectangular to fit with other parts of the hospital, and for that reason was free to take different shapes. Marshall argued that a circular plan would free up the ward's 'frontage'. It would have no 'blank ends', and "... would receive light, air and wind from every direction". It would also avoid angles and corners where dirt and stale air might be trapped.

Marshall provided a worked example, comparing a circular ward against a rectangular ward with the same number of beds and the same bed spacing. His calculation showed – as we might expect – that the circular design required much more floor area than the rectangular. Marshall however ignored the cost implication and saw the extra space as a benefit, offering among other things a greater volume of air per patient. He thought that nurses would find supervision easy; indeed one might have expected him to station them at the centre of the ward. Marshall however envisaged that the central point would be the place for the open fires and the (thermal) ventilation extract. Jeremy Taylor, who has written a history of these buildings, points out that strangely there is no mention of Panoptical surveillance in the entire published literature on circular wards.[11]

The circular plan was taken up enthusiastically in the early 1880s by a number of English hospital architects, who saw other merits besides those that attracted Marshall. Figure 7 shows a scheme for a thirty-two-bed ward for an infirmary by Henry Saxon Snell. The advantages included a supposed simplicity of construction, and the possibility that a flat roof could serve as a terrace for convalescents. Several designers were drawn by the aesthetic potential of the form, and published schemes with conical roofs suggestive of French chateaux, or with circular

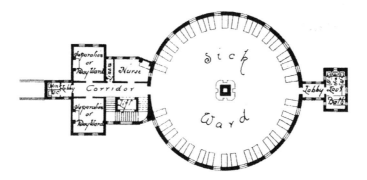

FIGURE 7 Scheme for a thirty-two-bed circular ward by Henry Saxon Snell, 1881. Nurses' rooms are at the left, and a bathroom at the right. From H S Snell, *Charitable and Parochial Establishments*, Batsford London 1881

classical arcades. A number of built examples exploited the fact that a small round tower could be fitted into the corner of a tight site where an existing hospital was being extended.

However Saxon Snell, who was previously a supporter, changed his views and launched a counter-attack on Marshall in a paper to the Congress of the Sanitary Institute of Great Britain.[12] His main reasons were to do with the capital and running costs of the unused space at the centres of large circular wards. I have made some schematic designs to illustrate Snell's general argument. I have laid out four circular wards with 8, 12, 16, 24 and 32 beds (Figure 8). The length of wall against which one bed is set is 2.4 m throughout, as in the standard Nightingale ward. The beds are 2 m long. Two extra 'bed spaces' are allowed for doors. Dimensional statistics for these alternatives are given in Table 2.

The expense of space in the twenty-four- and thirty-two-bed designs is very obvious. If we take the standard rectangular thirty-two-bed Nightingale ward and compute the floor area per bed, we obtain a value of 11 m². The figure for my thirty-two-bed circular ward is 16.6 m². The eight- and twelve-bed designs are more economical, but their plans illustrate different issues, to which Snell and other critics pointed. The feet of the beds are now very close together – nearly touching in the eight-bed case – and there is little room for manoeuvre between and around them. In most of the smaller circular wards that were actually constructed the beds were set further apart than this.

There were further potential problems with bigger circular ward plans, arising from their great depth in plan. Compared with the shallow 9 m depth of the standard rectangular ward, my twenty-four- and thirty-two-bed circular designs have diameters of 20 m and 26 m. It would have been very difficult to achieve through-ventilation in a building of this depth, and the centre would have received little daylight. Conditions on the south side of the plan could have become uncomfortably hot in summer, something that the rectangular Nightingale ward generally avoided by orienting the window walls east and west. In any event the fashion for circular wards lasted barely two decades, and just nine small schemes were built. Here is another example, like the Panopticon, where the intrinsic waste of space in the centre of the plan – together with other defects – led to the type's abandonment.

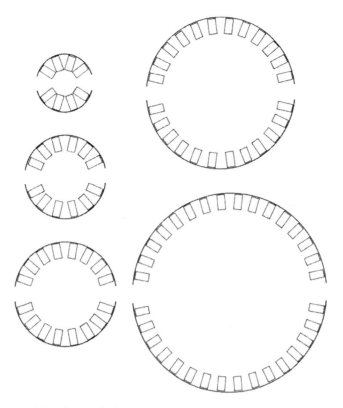

FIGURE 8 Theoretical circular ward plans with 8, 12, 16, 24 and 32 beds. The length of wall against which each bed is set is 2.4 m. The beds are 2 m long. Two extra 'bed spaces' are allowed for doors

TABLE 2 Measurements of five theoretical designs for circular hospital wards, with increasing numbers of beds (compare Figure 8)

Number of beds	External radius (m)	Area of circulation (m²)	Circulation as % of total area	Area for beds (m²)	Beds as % of total area
8	3.8	10.2	23	35.2	77
12	5.4	36.3	40	55.3	60
16	6.9	75.4	50	74.2	50
24	9.9	196.1	64	111.8	36
32	13.0	380.1	72	150.8	28

High-rise car parks

From the early 1920s a quite unprecedented new type of building began to appear in the major cities of the United States: the multi-storey parking garage [*see Paper 6*]. Here too architects and engineers imagined, at least initially, that circular or regular polygonal plans might be appropriate – the repeated spatial units now being the parking bays. Georg Müller, the German author of the first book on high-rise parking structures, reproduces drawings of

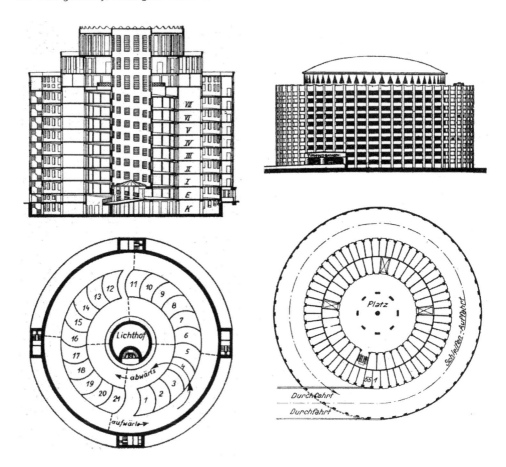

FIGURE 9 Two German schemes for circular plan multi-storey garages of the mid-1920s. From G Müller, *Grosstadt-Garagen*, Deutsche Bauzeitung, Berlin 1925

two un-built schemes of the mid-1920s.[13] These are illustrated in Figure 9. In both cases cars are to be driven up helical ramps and parked in bays alongside the ramps. Separate up and down ramps are needed. There is a minimum allowable curvature for the ramps, because of the turning circles of automobiles, which means that in these designs the ramps have to be wrapped around some central element. In the first design the two ramps are wound round a light well, with the parking spaces between the ramps. This is a 'ring doughnut' garage. In the second 'jam doughnut' plan there are again two ramps, around the outer perimeter. A *platz* [atrium] occupies the centre of the plan.

It is clear that, like the railway roundhouse, the dimensions of these buildings are determined by the size of the vehicles (or, more precisely, by the dimensions of the largest cars to be parked) and the sharpest allowable turning circle on the ramps. This latter constraint means that ramps cannot occupy the very centre of the plan – hence the central light well in the first plan, and the atrium in the second.

Parking garages are utilitarian structures in which two overriding goals in design are to minimise the cost of construction and to maximise the number of parking spaces on the given

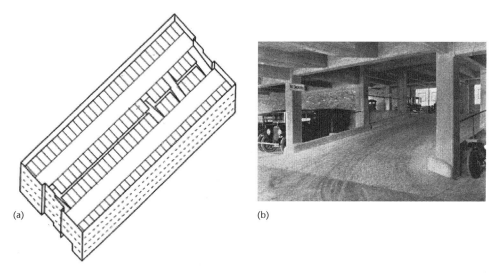

FIGURE 10 a) Theoretical design for a multi-storey garage with split-level floors and half-length 'D'Humy' ramps, axonometric view. Author's drawing. b) An interior view of a garage of this type built by the Ramp Buildings Corporation in the early 1920s. From G Müller, *Grosstadt-Garagen*, Deutsche Bauzeitung, Berlin 1925

site area. The more cars that can be parked for a given area of access ramp and/or access aisle, the lower the capital costs, and (in commercially-run garages) the greater the profits – so long as a smooth flow of cars in and out can be maintained. Experience with several different types of ramp garage in the 1920s and 1930s proved to their designers, relatively quickly it appears, that one particular design was most efficient on these criteria: a layout with split-level floors and half-length straight ramps, creating helical entry and exit routes (Figure 10). Dietrich Klose, in his encyclopaedic study of *Multi-Storey Car Parks and Garages*, quotes figures of between 25 m^2 and 31 m^2 gross area per car for such rectangular garages of the 1950s and early 1960s.[14]

By comparison the first of the circular German garage schemes has a gross floor area per car of 108 m^2 – in part because the parking bays are excessively large. For the second scheme, if we consider just the outer zone with the ramps and their car spaces, the figure is 115 m^2. The main reason that these figures are so big is because in both cases ramps are positioned on the outside of the parking bays. The width of a ramp is fixed, and the greater the diameter, the greater the ramp's area. It would have been more sensible to put the ramps inside the ring of car spaces.

Indeed this was what was done in one of the very few cylindrical car parks ever built: Marina City in Chicago, completed in 1962, and designed by Bertrand Goldberg Associates (Figure 11). Marina City has two 65-storey circular plan towers, of which 15 storeys provide parking on a continuously sloped helical floor. The whole of this part of the structure is a ramp, and the cars are parked on the outer edge of the sloping floor. There are thirty-two car spaces around the periphery in each turn; up and down ramps in a middle ring; and at the centre a service core with elevators and stairs. Above these are forty storeys of apartments.

32 Plan geometry, rectangular and circular

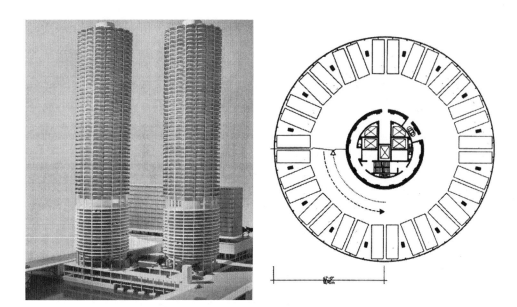

FIGURE 11 Marina City, Chicago, architects Bertrand Goldberg Associates, 1962; general view, and plan of one parking floor. Photo by Hedrich Blessing, Chicago History Museum. Plan by kind permission of the Bertrand Goldberg Archive, Art Institute of Chicago, and Geoffrey Goldberg

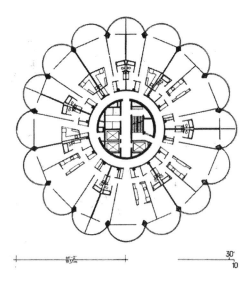

FIGURE 12 Marina City, Chicago, plan of an apartment floor. By kind permission of the Bertrand Goldberg Archive, Art Institute of Chicago, and Geoffrey Goldberg

The overall diameter of the plan (32.5 m) is thus a compromise between the constraints on the dimensions of both the parking floors and the apartment floors, meaning that the apartment plans are rather deep (11.4 m not counting the balconies) and have internal kitchens and bathrooms (Figure 12).[15] On the parking floors the gross area per car is 30.4 m². (This counts the service core, which would be necessary even if there were no apartments.) Marina City thus comes close to the figures for gross area per car achieved by rectangular garages around this same period. Construction costs for the helical floor were on the other hand probably higher than for the flat floors and short straight ramps of standard split-level commercial garages.

'Park at your desk' offices

This is a paper about circular buildings. But it is worth noting that similar issues about wrapping strips of accommodation around central cores can arise with square or near-square buildings. Staying with the car parking theme: in 1950 the architect Leroy L Warner took high-rise garage design into new territory in the Cafritz office block in Washington DC, with the slogan 'Park at Your Desk'.[16] At the centre of this building is a multi-storey car park with helical ramps and parking places off the ramps, like a squared-up version of the German circular plan garages (Figure 13). Set around the car parking is a ring of relatively shallow day-lit offices. Workers can drive into the building, drive up to their floor, park, and walk the last few metres to their desks. (One wonders about air quality in the offices.)

Warner built another block of similar design, also in Washington, the Universal South Building of 1959. Both this and the Cafritz Building survive. Their example has not however been generally followed. I suspect two causes, both intrinsic to the basic geometrical strategy of wrapping the car parking around the ramps, and wrapping the offices round the parking. First, the small square plan of the garage produces a relatively high figure for the gross area per car (including ramps) of 34 m². Second it is unlikely that there were enough parking

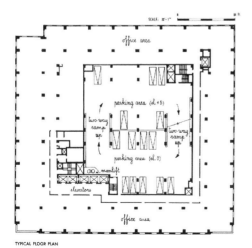
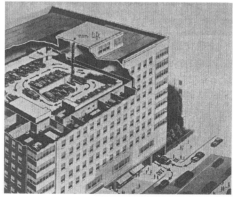

FIGURE 13 The Cafritz office building, Washington DC, architect Leroy L Warner, 1950: plan and cutaway perspective. The building was marketed with the slogan 'Park at Your Desk'. From G Baker and B Funaro, *Parking*, Reinhold, New York 1958

34 Plan geometry, rectangular and circular

spaces, even at the outset, to meet the building's needs. The total gross area of office space on each floor is 2200 m². Just for the sake of illustration let us assume a rough allocation of 15 m² per occupant, a figure typical for middle management in the 1950s. This would imply some 150 people per floor, for just 29 car places. Office area and parking area were seriously mismatched.

The Cafritz and Universal South Buildings are constrained by their downtown positions, but other contemporary American office buildings on larger sites which also combined parking with offices in the one structure tended to put the cars in a series of deep-plan podium floors (or perhaps below ground) with the offices in a shallow-plan block above.

Offices, naturally lit and ventilated, or air-conditioned

The tower housing the headquarters of Capitol Records in Los Angeles, completed in 1956, is claimed as the world's first office building with a circular plan. The architects were Welton Becket and Associates, who based the design on sketches by a graduate student, Lou Naidorf, who had just joined the practice. The word 'iconic' is used lazily and indiscriminately today in connection with high-rise offices, but the Capitol Records building is truly iconic, its form resembling a stack of vinyl discs on the spindle of a 1950s record player. The tower comprises 13 storeys and has an external diameter of 29.5 m.[17]

We can contrast Capitol Records with Australia's first true skyscraper at Australia Square in Sydney, completed in 1967, which also has a circular plan (and which its owners inevitably describe as 'iconic') (Figure 14). This building comprises fifty storeys and has an overall diameter

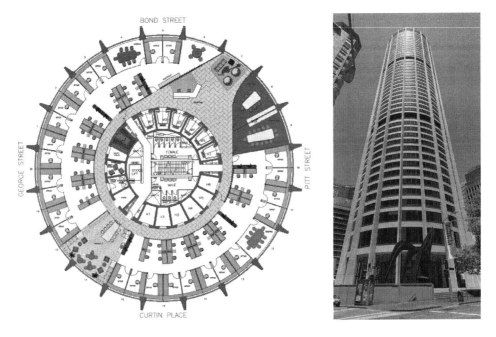

FIGURE 14 The office tower of Australia Square, Sydney, architects Harry Seidler and Associates, 1967; general view and plan of an office floor. Photo and drawing by kind permission of Australia Square

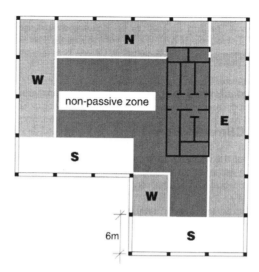

FIGURE 15 The 'passive zone' around the perimeter of a commercial building defined for the purposes of the LT environmental and energy calculation method. The width of the zone is typically twice the storey height. From N Baker, D Hoch and K Steemers, *The LT Method: Energy Design Tool for Non Domestic Buildings*, Commission of the European Communities, n.d. By kind permission of Nick Baker

of 44.5 m. The architects were Harry Seidler and Associates. Both these office towers, and others like them, are 'doughnuts' in which the 'dough' is a ring (or two rings) of offices, either cellular or open plan, and the 'jam' is the service core containing lifts, staircases and lavatories.

The size of the core is related to the height of the building, since this determines the number of lifts needed. Capitol Records has three lifts; the Australia Square tower has 17. The depth of the ring of offices is determined by methods of lighting and ventilation. In the late nineteenth and early twentieth centuries it was generally agreed that the effective limit of depth away from the window walls for offices to be lit and ventilated naturally was around 7.5 m (25 ft).[18] This figure is in part dependent on the ceiling height, which in day-lit offices of that period was typically 3 to 4 m. Modern methods for calculating the energy and environmental performance of offices have taken twice the ceiling height (i.e. typically 6 or 7 m) as the depth of this 'passive zone' around a building's perimeter (Figure 15). Space further away from the windows is assumed to require permanent artificial lighting and air conditioning.[19]

The band devoted to office rooms in the Capitol Records building is 7.75 m deep, and so could in principle have been naturally lit throughout, and perhaps (just) ventilated naturally. But this would have required open planning, or one ring of elongated cellular offices: as actually laid out there are *two* concentric rings of offices. The inner ring is for clerical workers, and borrows light from the outer ring of professional offices. The Los Angeles sun is strong, the building is exposed, and air conditioning was thought necessary from the start. In other circumstances and a different location a building of this form but with a slightly shallower plan and one row of offices might have dispensed with air conditioning.

36 Plan geometry, rectangular and circular

The Australia Square tower is also air-conditioned, and exploits this fact to lay out a band of offices, again two rooms deep, with a total depth of 12.1 m, well beyond the limit for natural lighting and ventilation. On a larger site, this dimension might have been increased yet further, allowing even more open-plan office area behind the peripheral ring of cellular offices.

The ratio of these dimensions of 'dough' and 'jam' results in different percentages of total floor area that is 'lettable' (i.e. excluding the area of core and circulation). This figure is of major economic concern to developers. In office buildings with circular plans, the ratio is controlled by two constraints, as we have seen. The first constraint is the diameter of the core, which increases with the height of the building. The second is the depth of the office ring, which cannot exceed 7 or 8 m if the building is to be naturally lit and ventilated, but can be increased where air conditioning is used.

For Capitol Records, whose offices are of a depth that *could* be naturally lit and ventilated, lettable area is around 87 per cent of total area. In Australia Square the ring of air-conditioned offices is deeper; but the core is also deeper since the building is taller. As a result, lettable area is close to 78 per cent of total area. For comparison: measurements on a small sample of *rectangular*-plan office buildings of the 1950s and 1960s, of varying heights and sizes, give figures between 62 per cent and 90 per cent for net useable or lettable area. The figure tends to fall as buildings get larger. There is no evidence therefore, at least on this basis, that circular office plans are more or less 'efficient' in these terms than rectangular plans.

Circular plans in general

There are some generic issues arising in the planning of all circular buildings that do not occur with rectangular plans. The curved walls and non-orthogonal corners of any smaller spaces around the periphery present difficulties for the placing of rectangular furniture. The skyscraper at 30 St Mary Axe in London, designed by Foster and Partners, whose tapering vegetable profile has earned it the nickname of the Gherkin, might be expected from the exterior to have circular floors. In fact the floors have the shape of six-armed crosses, with triangular voids between the rectangular arms. The positioning of walls and placement of furniture can all be orthogonal, and the layout problems that beset truly circular plans are avoided.

A second general issue is that circular plans are difficult or impossible to extend at later dates. This criticism was made of the Benthams' Panopticons. Jeremy's solution was to propose larger prisons consisting of several rotundas (as was done at Stateville). But these would have had to be guarded and supervised separately, where the several long straight cell blocks of the radial prison could all be supervised from a single central observatory. Capacity could be increased in the radial plan – up to some limit – by adding more cell blocks around the same central point, and each block could be extended at its far end – as indeed has happened in many actual prisons.

Finally it seems likely that construction costs would tend to be higher in buildings with circular geometry, because of the need for many specialised components, and/or more complex formwork for poured concrete. Perhaps these characteristics of inflexibility, difficulty of internal planning, and additional cost have contributed to the relative rarity of circular buildings in architectural history.

A 'morphospace' of buildings with circular plans

We can bring together the separate buildings discussed above and present them in a 'morphospace' of possible and actual 'jam doughnut' plans. The word morphospace has gained currency in theoretical biology in recent decades, to describe mathematical/graphical methods for the definition of natural forms, either the forms of complete animals and plants, or else the forms of separate organs.[20] Some of these forms are actually found in nature; others are less probable; still others may be completely unviable. We can transpose the idea and method to the study of building plans.[21]

TABLE 3 Morphospace of buildings with circular plans

Outer diam. (m)

	10	15	20	25	30	35	40	45	50
15	55.6								
20	75.0	**43.8** *Saxon Snell Ward*							
25	84.0	**64.0** *Panopticon 1787*	36.0						
30	**88.9** *Marina City*	**75.0** *Capitol Records*	**55.6** *Panopticon 1791*	30.6					
35	91.8	81.6	67.3	49.0	26.5				
40	93.8	85.9	75.0	60.9	43.8	23.4			
45	95.1	88.9	**80.2** *Australia Square*	69.1	55.6	39.5	**21.0** *Stateville Penitentiary*		
50	**96.0** *Camden Roundhouse*	91.0	84.0	75.0	64.0	51.0	36.0	19.0	
55	96.7	92.6	86.8	79.3	70.2	59.5	47.1	33.1	17.4
Inner diam. (m):	10	15	20	25	30	35	40	45	50

38 Plan geometry, rectangular and circular

The morphospace is presented in Table 3. Possible values for the overall diameter of plans of the 'jam doughnut' type are shown on the *y*-axis. Possible values for the diameter of the internal core (the 'jam') are shown on the *x*-axis. The values are rounded to increments of 5 m. The values in the table itself give the percentage of total floor area represented by the outer ring (the 'dough'). Readers can imagine that the same information might be presented as an array of circular diagrams, or even as a single animated diagram. The values in the table in bold correspond to real buildings discussed earlier, indicated by abbreviated names. Note that because of the rounding of the dimensions to 5 m intervals, some of the percentages depart slightly from the more accurate figures given in the text.

Where the nature of the building's function would tend to require the area of the ring to be maximised relative to the core, then 'more efficient' plans in these terms will be found at lower left, and 'less efficient' plans upwards and to the right. Thus the three 'inefficient' Panoptical prisons are close to the main diagonal, as is Saxon Snell's circular ward design. By contrast the two office buildings have higher proportions of lettable floor area, and are found nearer the *y*-axis, as is the parking floor plan of Marina City. If more examples of 'jam doughnut' buildings of these types were collected, including residential towers, we might expect their plans for this reason to be clustered towards the left-hand side of the morphospace, leaving the right-hand side relatively empty.

These kinds of criteria do not apply to the Camden roundhouse, since the dimensions of turntable and engine bays are fixed. The plans of the two circular German car parks are not shown, since in both cases the core is an empty or unused space, and the critical parameter, as discussed, is the ratio of the ramp area to the total area of parking spaces. Also their plans are divided in effect into more than two concentric rings.

Conclusion

The device of the morphospace allows the architect and the building scientist to take a strategic view of the field of possibilities for plans under some generic geometrical definition – in this case two concentric circles. Variations in the performance of the plans on different criteria across the theoretical space can be measured with suitable numerical indicators. These values can guide designers' choices, giving warnings of penalties in certain areas of the space, and benefits in others. I believe this kind of approach offers a rich field for future architectural research, to be conducted in the spirit that animated the work by Lionel March and collaborators on built form of the 1960s and 1970s.

Notes

1 M G Bevilacqua, 'The Helixes of Vittorio Bonadè Bottino: Symbolism, geometry and architectural types', *Nexus Network Journal* Vol. 17, 2105 pp. 487–506.
2 The analogy with patisserie is not perfect. Sometimes the central 'jam' is the more important part of the plan, at other times the peripheral 'dough'.
3 L Martin and L March, eds, *Urban Space and Structures*, Cambridge University Press, Cambridge 1972.
4 P Steadman, 'Why are most buildings rectangular?' *Architectural Research Quarterly (arq)* Vol. 6, 2006 pp. 203–207 (see this volume paper **1**).
5 For example H Halberstadt and A Halberstadt, *The American Train Depot and Roundhouse*, Motorbooks International, Osceola WI 1995.
6 J Bentham, *Panopticon: or, the Inspection-House*, Thomas Byrne, Dublin 1791; P Steadman 'The contradictions of Jeremy Bentham's Panopticon penitentiary', *Journal of Bentham Studies* Vol. 9, 2007 pp. 1–31; P Steadman, *Building Types and Built Forms*, Troubador, Leicestershire 2014, Chapter 9.

7 B Comment, *The Painted Panorama*, Harry N Abrams, New York, 2000.

8 J Semple, *Bentham's Prison: A Study of the Panopticon Penitentiary*, Clarendon Press, Oxford 1993.

9 P Steadman, *Building Types and Built Forms*, Troubador, Leicestershire, 2014 Chapter 3.

10 J Marshall, *On a Circular System of Hospital Wards*, Smith Elder, London 1878.

11 J Taylor, 'Circular hospital wards: Professor John Marshall's concept and its exploration by the architectural profession in the 1880s', *Medical History* Vol. 32, 1988 pp. 426–448.

12 H S Snell, 1885, 'Circular hospital wards', *The Builder*, 26 September 1885, pp. 443–445.

13 G Müller, *Grosstadt-Garagen*, Deutsche Bauzeitung, Berlin 1925.

14 D Klose, 1965, *Multi-Storey Car Parks and Garages*, Architectural Press, London.

15 The parking floors in Marina City are cantilevered, and have an overall diameter of 32.5 m. The apartment floors have a diameter (not counting the balconies) of 30.4 m.

16 G Baker and B Funaro, *Parking*, Reinhold, New York, 1958 pp. 90–91.

17 It is interesting to note that the overall diameter of Capitol Records (29.5 m) is very close to the diameter of the apartment floors at Marina City (30.4 m).

18 H W Corbett, 'The planning of office buildings' *Architectural Forum* Vol. 41, 1924, pp. 89–93.

19 N Baker, D Hoch and K Steemers, *The LT Method: Energy Design Tool for Non Domestic Buildings*, Commission of the European Communities, n.d.

20 D Raup, 'Computer as an aid in describing form in gastropod shells', *Science* Vol. 138, 1962 pp. 150–152; G R McGhee, *The Geometry of Evolution: Adaptive Landscapes and Theoretical Morphospaces*, Cambridge University Press, Cambridge 2007.

21 P Steadman, *Building Types and Built Forms*, Troubador Leicestershire, 2014, Chapters 6 and 12.

PART II

The history and 'evolution' of building types

3

THE CONTRADICTIONS OF JEREMY BENTHAM'S PANOPTICON PENITENTIARY

(*Journal of Bentham Studies*, Volume 9, 2007)

The eighteenth century political philosopher and penal law reformer Jeremy Bentham is the presiding genius of University College London, my own place of work. And when I say 'presiding genius' I mean that literally: Bentham's body – his 'Auto-Icon' – continues to sit in its glass-fronted box in the College's South Cloister, a taxidermised testimony to the philosopher's theory of representations.

In 1791 Bentham published his celebrated architectural scheme for a Panopticon penitentiary, in which the prisoners could be observed at all times. The Panopticon has cast a long shadow over the design of prisons and other institutional buildings ever since. There can be no doubt about the power and influence of the Panopticon as an image of the surveillance state. It is surprising therefore that, not only did Bentham himself fail to get his penitentiary built, but later prison designers came to regard the Panopticon principle as fundamentally unworkable. This essay explores the reasons.

The paper had its origin in a public lecture given at UCL in 2007. The text was then reworked for the Journal of Bentham Studies*, which is produced by the College's ongoing project to edit and publish Bentham's many manuscripts.*

The term 'Panopticon' has been used more or less loosely, since Jeremy Bentham first coined the word, to refer to any prison – or indeed any other kind of institutional building – which has a centralised plan and some sort of observation post at the middle.[1] But if we take the word to apply more narrowly to cylindrical prisons along the lines that Bentham himself imagined, then very few have ever been built. There were three panopticons erected in Holland in the late nineteenth century, all of which survive. Figure 1 shows the *Koepelgevangenis* (cupola prison) at Arnhem, designed by J F Metzelaar.[2] Perhaps the best-known true panopticons ever constructed were at the Stateville Penitentiary near Joliet in Illinois (Figure 2), where there were five rotundas within the one prison, built between 1916 and 1924. The architect was W Carbys Zimmerman. All but one have since been demolished. Stateville was the model in turn for a prison on the Isle of Pines in Cuba, opened in 1931. And that is about it.[3] Meanwhile hundreds of prisons were built across the world throughout the nineteenth century and well into the twentieth, on the general layout of Pentonville prison in London, whose plan has a series of straight cellblocks radiating from a central hall (see Figure 19).

FIGURE 1 *Koepelgevangenis* (cupola prison) at Arnhem, the Netherlands, 1886, architect J F Metzelaar. Photo from www.archivolt-bna.nl/.

FIGURE 2 Stateville Penitentiary, near Joliet, Illinois, 1916–24, architect W Carbys Zimmerman. From a 1930s postcard

All this is odd, since architectural historians and social scientists, most prominent among them Michel Foucault, have attributed enormous influence to Bentham's Panopticon.[4] They have seen it as the original model for a new kind of supervisory power relation across a whole range of nineteenth-century types of institution: not just prisons, but schools, hospitals, barracks and factories. In Foucault's own words:

> In the 1830s, the Panopticon became the architectural programme of most prison projects.[5]
>
> The fact that it should have given rise, even in our own time, to so many variations, projected or realized, is evidence of the imaginative intensity that it has possessed for almost two hundred years . . . Whenever one is dealing with a multiplicity of individuals on whom a task or a particular form of behaviour must be imposed, the panoptic scheme may be used.[6]

Janet Semple, author of the only monograph on the Panopticon, has said that Foucault "... and other revisionist historians, link the penitentiary with the evolution of the whole apparatus of social control developed in response to the needs of the emerging industrial capitalist society".[7]

In this paper I will not address directly these kinds of political and sociological claims. My focus is instead on the design of Bentham's building, taken on its own terms. Why – despite Foucault – was it so rarely copied, and why did radial prisons on the model of Pentonville succeed – at least numerically? I will suggest that there were many contradictions at the heart of the Panopticon's design, most of them stemming in truth from its central guiding idea – that of arranging prisoners in a circle, watched by an all-seeing eye at the centre. These contradictions were many of them resolved in the radiating plan of Pentonville.

First however it is necessary to provide some background to the intense discussion of prison reform going on in Britain, Europe and the United States towards the end of the eighteenth century, of which one product was Bentham's revolutionary proposal. Space allows only the

FIGURE 3 George Cruikshank, 'Newgate – Prison Discipline, City of London System', c.1818. From Joseph Adshead, *Prisons and Prisoners*, Longman, London 1845, frontispiece

sketchiest account, and so what follows is a simplification and generalisation of these complex debates. Conditions in most European and American prisons were appalling. The great reformer John Howard made a series of inspections of British gaols in the 1770s, and revealed the extent of the horrors in his celebrated and widely read report *The State of the Prisons* of 1777.[8] Inmates were left alone and unsupervised for much of the time. Different kinds of prisoner were held together in promiscuous confusion: men, women and children; hardened criminals and first-time offenders; prisoners on remand and debtors mixed with thieves and murderers. Not surprisingly, there was violence and intimidation, there was sexual depravity, and young detainees became corrupted.

Figure 3 reproduces George Cruikshank's cartoon of 'Newgate Prison Discipline' from as late as 1818.[9] One suspects that Cruikshank's picture, though grim enough, is somewhat more jovial and less ugly than the real thing. Howard describes how "[i]n some Gaols you see (and who can see it without pain?) boys of twelve or fourteen eagerly listening to the stories told by practised and experienced criminals, of their adventures, successes, stratagems and escapes".[10] Since there was little occupation for the inmates, and they had easy access to alcohol, the results were idleness, drunkenness and vice – the very things that the penal reformers saw as the causes of crime in the first place.

The prisons too were repositories of disease, the most dangerous of which was 'gaol fever', now known to be a form of typhus. Howard estimated that more died from this cause in 1773 and 1774 than went to the gallows.[11] The infection was even carried by prisoners into the courts. The authorities were greatly alarmed by one occasion at the Old Bailey in April

46 The history and 'evolution' of building types

1750 when those present noticed a particularly 'noisome smell'.[12] A week later two judges, a lawyer, several of the jury and more than forty others developed high fevers and died.

It is against this backdrop that one can understand the urgent efforts towards prison reform around the turn of the eighteenth and nineteenth centuries. The new institutions like Pentonville and the Panopticon might, in some of their features, seem brutal and cruel to us today. But we ought to judge them against what they replaced, and appreciate that they were the products of humane, pious and benevolent men (and a few women), many of them Quakers and Evangelicals. What were the solutions? In order to combat disease, the new prisons were to be clean, hygienic, dry and heated. There would be prison doctors and infirmaries. The Panopticon was intended to have central heating and forced ventilation, together with privies and running water in every cell, supplied from a giant cistern in the roof. Bentham also envisaged a basement kitchen with dumb waiters to carry hot meals to the cell floors.[13] At Pentonville all these things were realised in practice.[14] Indeed from the point of view of services and sanitation Pentonville was one of the most advanced London buildings of its time, along with the Reform Club and the Houses of Parliament.

Prisoners were to be kept occupied in useful labour, to equip them with trades on their release, and to make profits for the private prison contractor in the case of the Panopticon. In both Pentonville and the Panopticon the inmates were to work in their cells. Prisoners were to be separated into classes, by age, sex, and the type and seriousness of their offences. These distinct classes were to be confined in different blocks or wings of the same prison, or else segregated in specialised prison establishments. The *ne plus ultra* of this drive towards classification was solitary confinement, which would prevent all possibility of moral contagion and sexual promiscuity, and would of course also limit the spread of contagious disease. One important further motive for separating prisoners completely was the belief that in quiet seclusion they would be able to reflect on their sins, seek God's forgiveness, and repent. Hence the new term for the prison: the 'penitentiary'.

Bentham originally planned the Panopticon for solitary imprisonment, but changed his mind later as evidence emerged of the terrible cruelty of the practice.[15] At Pentonville too, prisoners were held in complete isolation in the early years – according to the so-called 'separate system' – despite the fact that in many cases this caused them to become torpid, sullen and embittered, and eventually drove some of them mad.[16] The corporal punishments of the eighteenth century were designed to break offenders' bodies; but solitary confinement broke their spirit.

However while such regimes lasted, some reformed prisons especially in America experimented with mixed programmes where convicts were kept in single cells at night, but were brought out to work and exercise in 'association' during the day. They were however obliged to remain silent at all times. This effort to prevent any speaking or other communication – the 'silent system' – was sometimes carried to extremes, even to the extent of making the prisoners wear hoods or masks. Above all in the penitentiary the prisoners were to be continually *watched*, to deter them from idling, talking or otherwise misbehaving. With all this in mind, let us look at the design of the Panopticon.

It is clear that from the outset Bentham imagined a circle of prison cells with the governor or inspector at the centre. Figure 4 shows what seems to be an early thumbnail sketch for the frontispiece of a projected book on the Panopticon.[17] The central oval depicts the ring of cells. The three words read 'Justice', 'Mercy' and 'Vigilance'. The text below is from the 139th Psalm: "Thou art about my path, and about my bed: and spiest out all my ways."

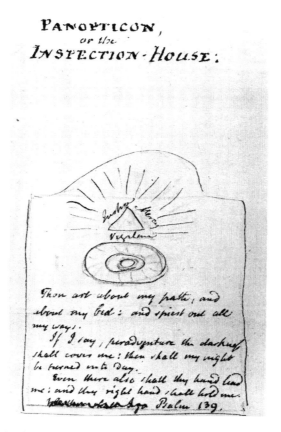

FIGURE 4 Sketch for the frontispiece [?] of Bentham's planned book *Panopticon: or the Inspection-House*, quoting the 139th psalm. Bentham papers, University College London, by kind permission of UCL Special Collections

Figure 5 shows a preliminary architectural scheme of 1787 on the way to the final design of 1791.[18] The drawing shows a half-elevation, a half-section, and a half-plan. In this early proposal there are four floors of cells, lit with large windows so that, viewed from the governor's tower at the centre, the prisoners are brightly lit from behind and their every move can be clearly seen. Bentham's wish however was that this process of observation be *one-way*. He wanted the governor, and his staff, and visitors to the prison, to be able to watch the convicts; but he did not want the prisoners to watch back. The idea was that every prisoner should be under constant apprehension that he *might* be observed, night and day, even if no-one was actually looking in his direction at that very moment. He would thus be constantly fearful of being discovered in any misdemeanour. As Miran Bozovic has pointed out, the prisoners would in time become so conscious of this threat of constant observation it would be as if they were *watching themselves*.[19]

So the governor's quarters were to be hung with blinds or curtains, through which he and his staff might look out through small peepholes. This meant however that the centre of the building would have been in more or less complete darkness.[20] Bentham struggled and struggled to achieve his goal of one-way vision, but as we will see he was ultimately defeated (he would have been very excited about CCTV). Also Bentham discovered that there was

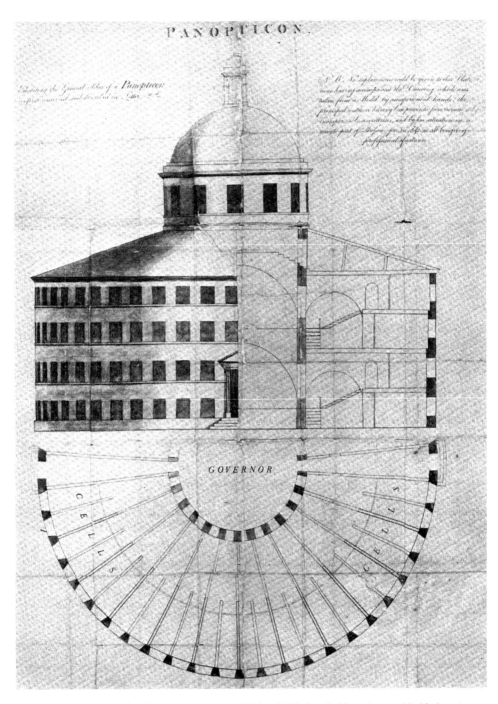

FIGURE 5 1787 design for the Panopticon, combining half-plan, half-section and half-elevation. From Jeremy Bentham, *Management of the Poor*, Dublin 1796, Plate 1

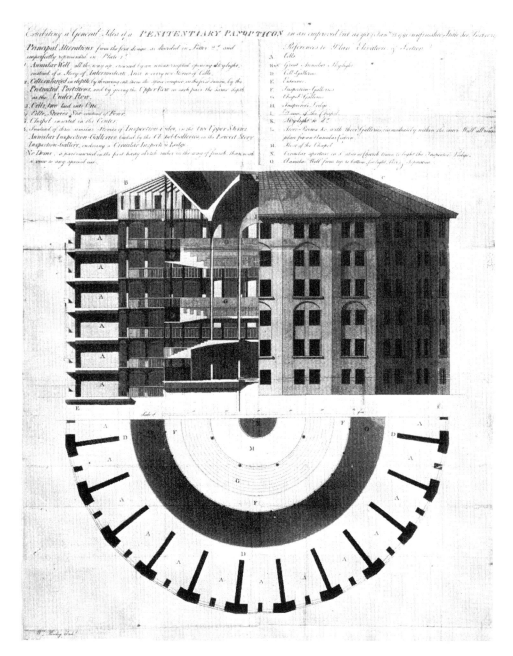

FIGURE 6 1791 design for the Panopticon by Jeremy Bentham, Samuel Bentham and the architect Willey Reveley. From Jeremy Bentham, 'Postscript, Part 1', 1843 Plate II

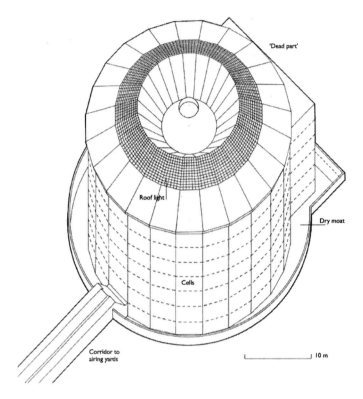

FIGURE 7 Axonometric (bird's eye) view of the 1791 Panopticon to show the six floors of cells, the roof-light and oculus, the 'dead part' and the corridor to the airing yards. Author's drawing

not enough room in the middle of the building to house all of the other functions needed by a prison: lodgings for the doctor and chaplain, a chapel, stores and so on. And if they *were* built at the centre, they would obviously block the all-important views of the cells.

In 1791 Bentham asked the architect Willey Reveley to draw up a revised design, which was intended to remedy some of these defects (Figure 6).[21] Jeremy's engineer brother Samuel Bentham also advised. There are cells now on six floors, and the building is lit from the top by a giant annular roof-light, as well as by the cell windows. Living accommodation for the governor and his staff has been removed from the centre, and the centre is partly – although not completely – empty. The geometry of this revised design is complicated, and so I have made some diagrammatic drawings to try to explain it.

Figure 7 is a bird's eye view of the Panopticon, looking like some gigantic pork pie. There is a basement in addition to the six floors of cells. The drawing gives a clear view of the roof-light, together with a central oculus to supply yet more light from the top. The building sits in a kind of trough or dry moat that serves to allow light and ventilation to the basement, and – with a surrounding wall – acts as an obstacle to any attempt at escape. The straight structure at lower left is a corridor leading to the exercise or 'airing' yards. The rectangular addition at upper right contains the governor's house and the administrative offices. Rather oddly, Bentham refers to this as the 'dead part' of the building.[22]

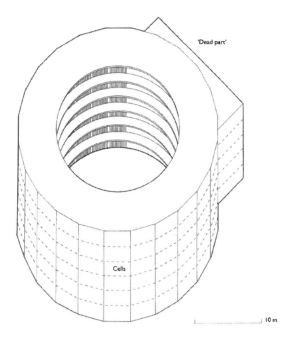

FIGURE 8 Axonometric view of the 1791 Panopticon with the roof and basement floor removed, to show the ring of cells and the cell balconies. Author's drawing

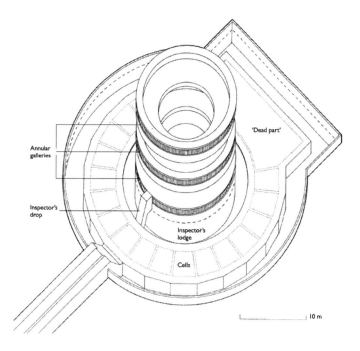

FIGURE 9 Axonometric view of the 1791 Panopticon with the roof, the cell floors and the 'dead part' removed, to show the inspector's lodge, the three annular galleries, and the central raked seating for divine service. Author's drawing

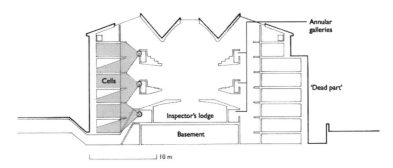

FIGURE 10 Cross-section of the 1791 Panopticon to show the cell floors, the 'dead part', the annular galleries, the 'annular well', the inspector's lodge, the two tiers of raked seating, and the 'inspector's drop' leading to the corridor through which access is gained to the airing yards. The shading shows the views of the cells obtained by warders in the annular galleries. Author's drawing

In Figure 8 the roof and the basement are removed, and it is possible to see the rings of cells with their barred fronts, and the galleries giving access to the cells. There would be space for twenty-four cells in the complete circle, but the governor's accommodation takes the place of five cells. This seems to be why Bentham calls it the 'dead part': it has no windows onto the interior. Finally in Figure 9 the drum of cells is removed and all that remains is the basement and a central tower. At the bottom is a circular room, referred to by Bentham as the 'inspector's lodge'. This is the prison's operational control centre. The lodge is lit from the roof by a second oculus that is not visible in this view. Flying above the inspector's lodge are three 'annular galleries' – with the vertical shading – around which the warders now patrol.

It is perhaps easier to understand how all these elements come together in a cross-section (Figure 10). On the left are cells and on the right the 'dead part'. On ground level at the centre is the inspector's lodge with its oculus. Around and above the lodge are the three levels of annular inspection galleries, set at heights such that the warders can see from each of them into two floors of cells, as indicated by the shaded angles of view.[23] Bentham specifies speaking tubes, running up the structural columns, through which the warders above can communicate with the inspector in the lodge below. There are also to be loudhailers through which the inspector can address the prisoners. Within the annular galleries are two further structures that have sloping rows of seats looking towards the centre. The purpose is to provide for religious services, preached by the chaplain from a central pulpit.

Notice that between the central tower and the cells is a gap – Bentham calls it the 'annular well' – about 2 m wide and rising the whole height of the building.[24] They are not shown in Figure 10, but there are staircases in this annular well and bridges crossing from the tower to the cell balconies. Figure 11 reproduces a delicately water-coloured cross-section by Reveley for comparison that includes the staircases and bridges, the iron columns supporting the galleries, the water tank in the roof and the chaplain in his pulpit. The inspection galleries are again designed so that the officers can look out, but so that the prisoners – at least in theory – cannot look in. The interiors of the passages are painted black, and the openings are covered with blinds in which small peepholes are cut.

Figure 12 is Bentham and Reveley's diagrammatic plan for the layout of a complete Panoptical prison with three rotundas.[25] The 'dead parts' all front onto the main access road,

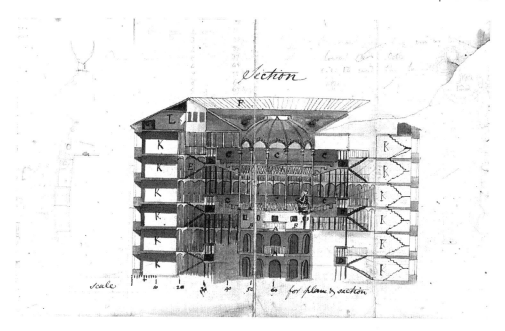

FIGURE 11 Cross-section of the 1791 Panopticon by Willey Reveley (with some differences from the published design of Figure 6). In addition to the features visible in Figure 10, this drawing shows the stairs and bridges crossing the 'annular well', the cast iron columns supporting the galleries and roof, the water tank in the attic, and the chaplain in his pulpit. Bentham papers, University College London, by kind permission of UCL Special Collections

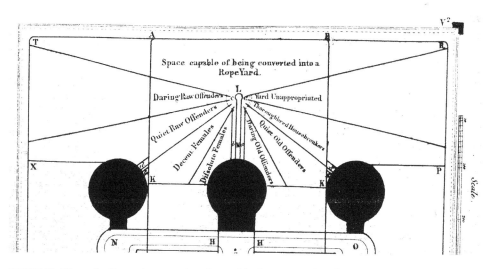

FIGURE 12 Plan of a Panopticon penitentiary with three rotundas, showing the access roads, airing yards and perimeter wall. From Jeremy Bentham, 'Postscript, Part I', 1843 Plate III

and the straight corridors lead out to the exercise yards at the rear. Around the whole site is an enclosing wall with two guard towers. Rather surprisingly however these towers look *outwards* and have no views over the prison grounds. Bentham was much more concerned with the threat of a mob breaking *into* the prison than with the possibility that the inmates might get out on their own initiative. He was motivated in this by the recent and painful experience of the Gordon Riots of 1780 – to which he alludes – when the rioters sacked Newgate Gaol and released its occupants.

The first thing to notice about the 1791 design is that there is now no single point, not even a single room, from which the governor and his guards can simultaneously see all the cells. From the centre, the galleries and raked seating always block parts of the view. In an important sense then, *this is no longer a true Panopticon*. There is no view out, except upwards, from the inspector's lodge. And from any given position in an annular gallery a warder can see, on each of two levels, the complete interior of just one cell, plus parts of six other adjoining cells, as the plan of Figure 13 illustrates. In architectural research a plot of the totality of what can be seen from a fixed position is known as an 'isovist'.[26] The shaded area shows the warder's isovist. The warder must circulate continuously to watch all the prisoners on his floor.

The inspection galleries were the architect Reveley's invention, not Bentham's, and it has to be said that they fundamentally undermine the central Panoptical principle. Bentham continued to toy with the idea of some kind of translucent 'inspection lantern' (Figure 14), sufficient to house just one observer, suspended somehow at the centre of the prison.[27] He seems to want to hang onto this idea as an alternative to Reveley's galleries. But such a lantern would have presented as many problems as it solved. How would the observer get into position without being seen; and having got there, how would he communicate to the prisoners or to his fellow officers about any breaches of discipline he might observe? More crucially, the

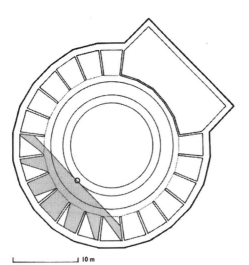
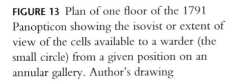
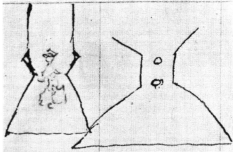

FIGURE 13 Plan of one floor of the 1791 Panopticon showing the isovist or extent of view of the cells available to a warder (the small circle) from a given position on an annular gallery. Author's drawing

FIGURE 14 Bentham's sketches for a central 'inspection lantern'. Bentham papers, University College London, by kind permission of UCL Special Collections

FIGURE 15 Interior of a rotunda at Stateville Penitentiary, Joliet, Illinois. Photo from Illinois Department of Corrections

idea of such a lantern implied of course that the entire remainder of the centre of the prison was empty, so that no other rooms or structures would block its view.

This actually *was* the principle on which the rotundas at Stateville were designed (Figure 15). There was a glazed lookout post at the centre, and nothing else. This was a huge waste of useless – and in the Stateville case poorly lit – space. Alfred Hopkins, a prominent American prison architect referred to the Stateville rotundas as '. . . the most awful receptacle of gloom ever devised. . .'[28] But there was an operational consequence that was much more serious, vividly described by a former Stateville inmate, Paul Warren.

> They figured they were smart building them that way. They figured they could watch every inmate in the house with only one screw in the tower. What they didn't figure is that the cons know all the time where the screw is . . .[29]

It is not of course sufficient for the warders just to observe. When they see trouble they have to *act*: they have to go rapidly themselves, or they have to send their colleagues to sort out the problem. Bentham was reluctant to acknowledge this point. He believed that whenever a prisoner misbehaved, a warder would see this, would issue an immediate warning by loudhailer, and the prisoner would desist. This seems overly hopeful. Suppose that despite the warning trouble persisted and even spread. In a Panopticon prison in which the cells have open fronts, it is in the nature of the situation that, once the warders emerge from their

56 The history and 'evolution' of building types

observation galleries, the prisoners *can see them coming*. The prisoners can never be taken completely by surprise in any wrongdoing.

The Panopticon design of 1791 had a further obstacle in the way of warders getting from the inspection galleries to the cells. There was the 2 m gap, the 'annular well', between them. To get to a trouble spot a warder would have had to run to a staircase, go up or down to a bridge, unlock the security gate on the bridge, and run round the gallery to the cell in question. One has the general impression that Bentham tended to think of his prison as a static device, where inmates stayed in one part and warders watched from another part. He talks about it as a 'machine': but it seems that despite this metaphor, Bentham did not think so clearly about the prison as a functioning institution, in which the different classes of occupants had on occasion to move about and interact.

Why did Bentham put the well between cells and inspection galleries? To give the warders a clear view of course. But the gap also acted as a kind of *cordon sanitaire* between guards and prisoners. Bentham wanted to separate the two groups with more than bars, not just for security, but because of the fear of possible infection carried by the inmates. He wanted members of the public to be able to visit and see the prisoners without fearing for their own safety. The Panopticon was a zoo, with the prisoners behind bars and the visitors gaping at them across the well.[30] Bentham gets himself into some rather absurd ideas as a consequence of this arrangement, about ways in which for example the warders might open and close the cell doors remotely, across the gap, using long poles.

The seats around the two ring-shaped structures in the middle of the Panopticon, as mentioned earlier, were intended for those attending divine worship. The seating was not however for the prisoners but for members of the public visiting the building on Sundays. The prisoners – at least some of them – were to watch from their cells. Reveley's coloured cross-section (Figure 11) shows that the position of the pulpit was not to be central, since Bentham appreciated that people seated behind the preacher would not be able to hear him clearly – something he tested by actual experiment.[31] Given Reveley's position for the chaplain's head, Figure 16 plots the extent of what he could see if he could turn his head and eyes through a full 360°. This is the chaplain's isovist. If the chaplain can see a point, then somebody whose head is at that point can see him. Anybody located within this isovist, that is to say, can see the preacher. Most people on the raked seats can see him, except those above his head. But he can only be seen by prisoners in three floors of cells opposite and perhaps just

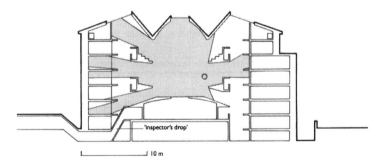

FIGURE 16 Cross-section of the 1791 Panopticon showing the isovist or extent of view available to the chaplain in his pulpit (the small circle), thus mapping the positions in the building from which he can and cannot be seen. Author's drawing

The contradictions of Bentham's Panopticon **57**

two floors of cells behind him. Bentham recognised this problem, and proposed that the prisoners on the floors without views be moved out onto the access galleries on the floors above or below for the duration of the service.[32] How this was to be organised, and the prisoners kept in order throughout, he did not say. He did however specify that when brought out of their cells, the prisoners should wear *masks* to conceal their identities. Here is another consequence of not leaving the Panopticon empty, but placing obstacles to vision at its centre.

One further aspect of Bentham's failure to think about how people might move around the prison is to be found in the design of the Panopticon's entrances. Bentham was reluctant to break the circular symmetry of the building with any ground-level entry points: so he devised a tunnel ducking under the cells at basement level (see Figure 10). This tunnel connected with the closed corridor giving access to the exercise yards, as we saw earlier. There was not really enough room to allow a staircase down from the inspection lodge to the tunnel. So Bentham ended up trying to justify what he called 'the inspector's drop'- a precipitous descent of 12 ft through a hole just 2 ft wide.[33] Not a place for corpulent warders: and it would not have been easy for them to get back up the steep ladder that Bentham envisaged.

This detail could doubtless have been improved with a bit more architectural thought. But it would still have remained a bottleneck, and a highly dangerous feature for the security of the whole prison. It is in the very nature of the Panopticon idea that *the prisoners completely surround the guards* – not generally a good idea in penal design. It would have needed only a few prisoners to seize this exit, together with another passage through the 'dead part', and they would have had all the officers trapped.

And there is yet another problem of security inherent in the circularity of the Panopticon. The guards at the centre may be able to see into all the cells. But they cannot see the external walls of the building, nor do they have clear views of the grounds outside. Should prisoners manage to get out of their windows – and remember these windows are large to provide sufficient light for observation – then it is possible that they could climb down on ropes or knotted sheets, without being spotted. When Lord Westmorland the Lord Lieutenant of Ireland was shown the plans of the Panopticon his comment was brief and dismissive: "[t]hey will all get out".[34] He was referring in part it seems to this feature of the design. Bentham was obliged to add the boundary wall around the site of the Panopticon to counter this objection. (Westmorland was also perhaps thinking about the fact that there were to be no shackles or leg-irons on the prisoners.)

It was an important aim in the design of the Panopticon, as in other reformed penitentiaries of the early nineteenth century, that the prisoners should communicate as little as possible. One final problem of the circularity of the Panopticon is that it makes this goal extremely difficult to achieve. Bentham's original intention was that the cells would be for single prisoners; but later as mentioned he changed his ideas. The cells in the 1791 design are planned for two, three or four occupants. Of course the occupants of a shared cell could communicate among themselves, even if a general silence was enforced. Bentham's idea was that these groups should be carefully selected so as to discourage criminal conspiracies.[35] Communication between prisoners in different cells was still to be strictly forbidden.

If however a convict moves to the very front of his cell, he can see into 12 neighbouring cells on his own floor (Figure 17). This is the prisoner's isovist. (He can also see into cells on floors above and below.) He has a better view than the warder. Bentham's answer was to paint a line on the floor of each cell a few feet back from the bars, and make it an offence

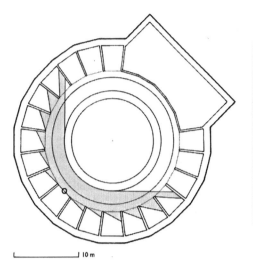 

FIGURE 17 Plan of one floor of the 1791 Panopticon showing the isovist or extent of view of adjacent cells available to a prisoner (the small circle) at the front of his cell. Author's drawing

FIGURE 18 The old south hall at Auburn Prison, Auburn, New York. By kind permission of Eastern Kentucky University Special Collections and Archives

for the inmates to step in front of it. This would obviously have been difficult to enforce. Furthermore, some prisoners can see into cells on the opposite side of the ring, across the central space, and communicate perhaps by waving or by other signs. Here Bentham's response was to propose sheets of canvas hung between the annular galleries. But these would have blocked the warders' views as well as the prisoners', and would have had to been taken down for religious services. Such problems were largely avoided in the notorious jails at Auburn (Figure 18) and Sing Sing in New York State, opened in 1819 and 1825 respectively, which were operated on the 'silent system'. The cells had open fronts with bars as in the Panopticon, but were arranged back-to-back in straight lines inside long halls. This meant that no cell had a view of the front of any other cell. At Auburn the walls projected a couple of feet in front of the doors, so making it quite impossible for prisoners to see into adjacent cells.

To summarise the difficulties arising then from the very essence of the Panopticon's circularity:

- The prisoners surround the warders. Should the prisoners manage to seize the two entrances, they have all the staff trapped.
- If all cells are to be seen from the inspection point, then the whole of the centre of the building must be empty, resulting in much wasted space (as at Stateville). Any other structures placed in the centre of the building (annular galleries, a chapel) will partially block the inspectors' views of some of the cells.
- If the fronts of the cells are barred, Bentham's desire for 'one-way vision' is enormously difficult to achieve. Once the warders come out of their hiding places, the prisoners can see them coming.
- The inspectors cannot see the outside walls of the prison building or the yards.

William Crawford was sent by the British Government to tour the prisons of the United States in the 1830s and report back. His findings had a considerable impact on the design of Pentonville. Comparing the radial plans of American prisons with circular plans of the Panoptical type, Crawford makes exactly these last two points.[36]

- Unless special precautions are taken, the prisoners can see into neighbouring cells, and into cells across the central space, and can communicate.

Let us now compare the Panopticon in these terms with Pentonville, the prison in north London whose outstanding architectural characteristic is that the cells are arranged in straight blocks radiating from a central focus. Pentonville was built by Captain Joshua Jebb of the Royal Engineers with the architect Charles Barry and completed in 1842. Figure 19 shows Jebb's isometrical perspective of the site. Pentonville is discussed here as an exemplar of the radial plan because it was the first of its kind in Europe and because it was much copied in Britain and other European countries: the Government deliberately intended it as a model for other gaols. During the nineteenth century around thirty radial prisons were built in Britain, some with different numbers of arms, but all following essentially the same layout. Across the world there have been over 300 radial prisons of this general type constructed to date.[37]

However Pentonville was not by any means the first prison on a radial plan. It was closely inspired in turn by a series of American gaols built by the emigré English architect John Haviland, of which the first was the Eastern Penitentiary in Philadelphia, completed in 1836. There is a strong case to be made for crediting Haviland with the design of Pentonville, alongside Jebb and Barry. William Crawford illustrated the Eastern Penitentiary in his *Report*; and Haviland subsequently supplied other plans to Crawford, Jebb and Lord John Russell,

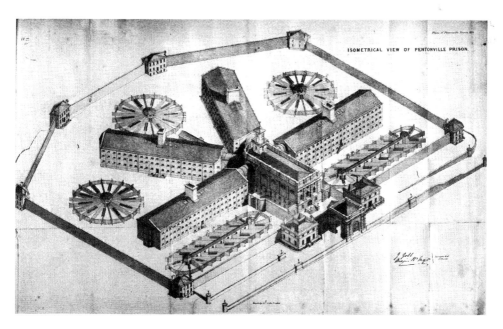

FIGURE 19 Isometrical perspective of Pentonville Prison, 1840–42, engineer Joshua Jebb. *Report of the Surveyor-General of Prisons*, London 1844

60 The history and 'evolution' of building types

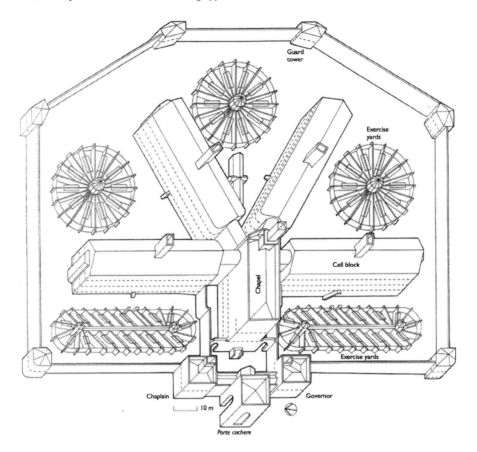

FIGURE 20 General axonometric view of Pentonville Prison. Author's drawing

secretary to the British Home Department.[38] Indeed R S Duncan, a former Governor, says explicitly in his history of Pentonville that the prison was built "... to the designs of John Haviland as approved by Jebb ..."[39]

Figure 20 shows the layout in detail.[40] There is a perimeter wall with guardhouses looking *inwards*. A grand entrance gateway is flanked by houses for the governor and the chaplain. The prison is entered through a corridor, with the chapel above. The kitchen, laundry, baths, other services and stores are in the basement. Notice a first point of comparison with the Panopticon in the overall organisation of the plan. The area from which Pentonville is controlled is pulled to the front of the site, and is not now surrounded by prisoners. The inmates would have much greater difficulty seizing the main entrance of Pentonville and trapping all the guards. They might capture individual wings, but not the whole prison.

The strange wheel-like structures in the grounds require some explanation. Pentonville, like Haviland's first American prisons, was designed as described for solitary confinement. The inmates slept and worked in their individual cells, which they left only to take exercise and to attend divine service. Elaborate precautions were taken to prevent prisoners from even seeing other prisoners on these occasions. The wheel shapes are made up from wedge-shaped exercise yards, one to a prisoner, supervised by guards in the central lookout huts. These are indeed truly Panoptical structures. Prisoners were brought to these yards one by one from the cells, with the guards using whistles or bells to coordinate the transfer process. The prisoners that is to say were separated in *time* as well as space.

Perhaps this system was excessively cumbersome.[41] In any case it seems soon to have been abandoned in favour of a regime whereby prisoners took exercise together but wearing caps with long peaks (known as 'beaks') to discourage talking (Figure 21). The prisoners had to hold on to the knotted ropes and keep them taut so that they would be spaced apart and walk alone, not in groups. During services in the chapel they were separated in wooden cubicles. Figure 22 shows the view from the pulpit. It was, as Philip Priestley says, a "segregated congregation".[42]

On entering the prison through the corridor beneath the chapel, one arrives at a central hall running the full height of the building. Here there was a series of glazed structures like bay windows from which the entire prison could be observed (Figure 23).[43] The cellblocks themselves have long central halls that rise to the roof. Access to the cells is given by open galleries. Two nineteenth-century authors Henry Mayhew and John Binny wrote a book about the prisons of London in which they described this panorama at Pentonville as being like "... a bunch of Burlington Arcades, that had been fitted up in the style of the opera box lobbies with an infinity of little doors".[44] The connotations of luxury and comfort conjured up by this comparison were perhaps unfortunate. But geometrically it is true that there is much in common between this type of radial cell block and the Victorian shopping arcade – the purpose in the arcade of course being to give the shopper an immediate and tempting view of every shop front on every level. It is no coincidence then that John Haviland, as well as designing prisons, also built some of America's first arcades.[45]

FIGURE 21 Prisoners exercising in masks or 'beaks' at Pentonville c.1860. H Mayhew and J Binny, *The Criminal Prisons of London,* Griffin, Bohn and Co, London 1862

62 The history and 'evolution' of building types

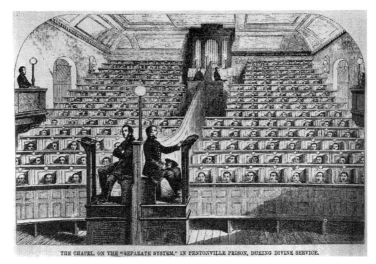

FIGURE 22 The chapel at Pentonville, as seen from the pulpit. H Mayhew and J Binny, *The Criminal Prisons of London*, London 1862

FIGURE 23 The central observatory at Pentonville. *Illustrated London News* No. 36 Vol. II 1843

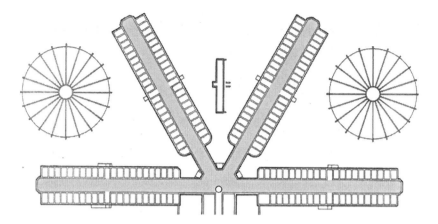

FIGURE 24 Plan of Pentonville showing the isovist or extent of view available from the central observatory (the small circle). The doors of all cells can be seen from this point. Author's drawing

Figure 24 shows the isovist – the field of view – available from the central observatory. Every cell door can be seen – if distantly and obliquely in some cases – from this vantage point. The guards cannot see a large part of the prison grounds outside the building from the observatory itself. But there are windows in the nearer parts of the wings from which this is possible; and the remaining external areas are of course covered by the peripheral guardhouses.

It will be appreciated that there are some key differences in this geometry of oversight at Pentonville from that of the Panopticon. It is not now possible to see *into* the cells from the centre, only to see the cell doors: and the fronts to the cells are solid, not barred. In the Panopticon Bentham enclosed the warders, and made peepholes in their observation galleries from which they could spy on the prisoners. In Pentonville the spyholes have migrated to the cell doors, with the result that the inmates can see very little of the halls: while the guards can move freely without being so easily watched. A warder can approach right up to a cell door and the occupant cannot see him coming. The most important geometrical consequence is that the huge empty space at the centre of the Panopticon can be collapsed into the relatively narrow halls of Pentonville.

The way in which the prisoners are supervised is now distinctively different. There are warders who patrol the halls and galleries, and who can look in, without warning, on the prisoners in their cells. And there are senior officers at the central observatory, who watch the patrolling guards, and can send reinforcements at any sign of trouble. In the Panopticon there was just one level of oversight or inspection: guards at the centre watched the prisoners directly. In the radial prison the supervision is two-level: staff at the centre watch the mobile guards, who in turn keep their eyes on the inmates. Bentham's ideal of continuous round-the-clock inspection is abandoned. But it seems that the extent of inspection offered by the radial arrangement was workable and sufficient for the control of the prison – as the success of the design would indicate. Sacrificing Bentham's central principle appears to have been a price that prison governors were prepared to pay for the other benefits brought by the radial plan.

The question remains as to whether it is reasonable or plausible to characterise the Eastern Penitentiary, Pentonville and all their radial progeny as 'Bentham-inspired' or 'Panoptical' –

64 The history and 'evolution' of building types

albeit in some rather broad and general sense – as Foucault and others have done.[46] This raises specific issues to do with architectural and intellectual influence that lie outside the scope of this paper. It is difficult to imagine that Jebb, who was deeply involved in penal reform and became the first Surveyor General of Prisons in England, would not have known something about the Panopticon. But it is also clear that he, with William Crawford and the British Government, looked rather to Pennsylvania, the 'separate system', and the work of Haviland.

Did Haviland owe anything to Bentham? What we do know for certain is that before he left for America Haviland was apprenticed in London to the architect James Elmes who built several small English gaols and in 1817 published *Hints for the Improvement of Prisons* in which he argued for the radial principle.[47] Norman Johnston in his recent study of the Eastern Penitentiary suggests that Haviland might have found precedents for the branching layout of the Philadelphia building in a series of provincial English and Irish radial prisons with which he would have been familiar via Elmes. These were built from the 1780s onwards, thus contemporaneous with the birth of the Panopticon, but before Bentham's work became widely known.[48] Further research might clarify these possible lines of connection. But no new documentary evidence will alter the fact that the radial prison was very different architecturally and operationally from Bentham's own cherished scheme, as this paper has shown.

Notes

1 Bentham set out his ideas for the Panopticon in a series of letters written from Russia to 'a friend' in England (in fact his father) in 1787. These were later supplemented by two much longer 'postscripts'. Both Letters and Postscripts were published as *Panopticon: or, the Inspection-House* (Thomas Byrne, Dublin 1791), and *Panopticon: Postscript* (T Payne, London 1791, 2 vols). They were then republished in 'Panopticon; or the Inspection-House', *The Works of Jeremy Bentham*, ed J Bowring, 11 vols, Edinburgh 1843, iii, pp. 37–172, along with 'Panopticon versus New South Wales: or the Panopticon Penitentiary System, and the Penal Colonization System, Compared', pp. 173–211. Both Letters and Postscripts are included in *The Panopticon Writings*, ed M Bozovic, Verso, London and New York, 1960. The political history of the Panopticon and Bentham's struggles to have it built are told in J Semple, *Bentham's Prison: A Study of the Panopticon Penitentiary*, Clarendon Press, Oxford, 1993.
2 The avant-garde Dutch architect Rem Koolhaas was commissioned in 1979 to make proposals to extend the life of this Arnhem Panopticon. The plans were not carried out. However the building was restored and renovated in 2000 by another firm Archivolt.
3 A few prisons with semi-circular plans were also influenced more or less directly by the Panopticon. These include the Edinburgh Bridewell (1791–95) by Robert Adam, who was shown the Panopticon drawings by Bentham himself; J M Gandy's female wing at Lancaster Castle Gaol (1818–21); and a prison built at Mataró near Barcelona in 1852, similar to the Edinburgh Bridewell. In the United States the Virginia Penitentiary at Richmond designed by Benjamin Latrobe and opened in 1800 had a horseshoe-shaped plan with cells facing inwards onto an uncovered courtyard. It seems possible that Latrobe saw some sketches for prisons by Thomas Jefferson who was familiar with the work of British prison reformers. All of these buildings departed significantly from Bentham's scheme in one way or another, but all had central observation points from which the interiors of all the cells could be seen – if with difficulty in the case of the Richmond gaol. The ill-fated Western Penitentiary in Pittsburgh (c.1820) by William Strickland, on the other hand, although described as a panopticon at the time, resembled Bentham's scheme only in being circular. See R Evans, *The Fabrication of Virtue: English Prison Architecture, 1750–1840*, Cambridge, 1982 p. 228 and N Johnston, *Forms of Constraint: A History of Prison Architecture*, Urbana and Chicago IL, 2000, pp. 52–53, 82–83 and 107.
4 M Foucault, *Surveiller et Punir: Naissance de la Prison*, Gallimard, Paris, 1975; trans. by A Sheridan, as *Discipline and Punish: The Birth of the Prison*, Allen Lane, London, 1977.
5 M Foucault, *Discipline and Punish*, p. 249.

6 Ibid., p. 205.
7 J Semple, *Bentham's Prison*, p. 152.
8 J Howard, *The State of the Prisons in England and Wales, with Preliminary Observations, and an Account of Some Foreign Prisons*, William Eyres, Warrington, 1777.
9 British Library.
10 J Howard, *State of the Prisons*, p. 16.
11 Ibid., p. 17.
12 See R Evans, *The Fabrication of Virtue*, p. 95.
13 See 'Postscript, Part I', sections ix, xxii and xxiii in J Bowring, iv., p. 87 and pp. 110–115; also R Evans, *The Fabrication of Virtue*, pp. 225–227 and Figure 114.
14 See R Evans, *The Fabrication of Virtue*, pp. 354–357.
15 'Postscript, Part I', J Bowring, iv. pp. 71–75.
16 R S Duncan, *Peerless Priceless Pentonville: 160 Years of History*, R S Duncan, London, 2000, p. 41.
17 Bentham Collection, cxix. folio 124, UCL Special Collections [hereafter UCL].
18 The original drawing was destroyed in a fire at the printers, and the engraver improvised this version. It was not included (although it continued to be numbered as 'Plate I') in the version of 'Postscript, Part I' in J Bowring, iv., p. 172, since it showed what Bentham by then thought to be an 'imperfect' plan.
19 Miran Bozovic, Introduction to Bentham, *Panopticon Writings*, p. 16.
20 'Postscript, Part I', J Bowring, iv., p. 80.
21 This drawing is reproduced as Plate II in 'Postscript, Part I', following p. 172. Reveley's original and other related drawings are in the Bentham Collection, UCL. They have been used as the basis of the author's own diagrams in the present paper.
22 'Postscript, Part I', J Bowring, iv., pp. 76–78.
23 Ibid., p. 70. The text refers to figures showing lines of sight from the inspection galleries into the cells; but these seem to be missing from 'Postscript – Part I'.
24 Ibid., pp. 69–70.
25 Ibid., Plate III, following p. 172. See also discussions in section xxi, pp. 105–106, and in 'Postscript, Part II', pp. 137–138.
26 M L Benedikt, 'To take hold of space: isovists and isovist fields', *Environment and Planning B: Planning and Design*, vi. (1979), pp. 47–65.
27 'Postscript, Part I', J Bowring, iv., p. 82. The sketch is in the Bentham Collection, UCL.
28 A Hopkins, *Prisons and Prison Buildings*, New York, 1930 p. 43; cited by G Geis, 'Jeremy Bentham' in H Mannheim, ed *Pioneers in Criminology*, Architectural Book Publishing Co. London, 1960, pp. 51–67. See p. 65.
29 P Warren, *Next Time is for Life*, Dell, New York, 1953 p. 139.
30 M Foucault in *Discipline and Punish* (p. 203) speculates as to whether Bentham found part of his inspiration in Le Vaux's menagerie at Versailles, which had an octagonal pavilion with the King's salon at the centre, surrounded by the animals' cages. Bentham certainly had zoos in mind when he proposed a mass-produced sculpture depicting foxes and wolves to be placed above the entrances to penitentiaries. The implication was that these were ferocious beasts, but ones that there was some hope of taming. He even pressed the prospects of the Panopticon as a tourist attraction: '[i]s it possible that a national penitentiary-house of this kind should be more at a loss for visitors than the *lions*, the *wax-work*, or the *tombs*?' ('Postscript, Part II', J Bowring, iv., p. 133) He does not however mention Le Vaux's building among his acknowledged architectural models for the Panopticon, which included the rotundas in Dublin and at Ranelagh Garden in Chelsea, and John Wood's Circus at Bath. Bentham's first inspiration was his brother Samuel's 'inspection-House' manufactory in Russia in which he employed unskilled peasants under strict supervision in the 1780s.
31 'Postscript, Part I', section vii, J Bowring, iv., p. 78.
32 Ibid., section vii, p. 79.
33 Ibid., section xvi, pp. 92–94.
34 See J Semple, *Bentham's Prison*, p. 120.
35 'Postscript, Part I', section v, pp. 71–72.
36 House of Commons, 1834 (593), Report of William Crawford, Esq. on the Penitentiaries of the United States Addressed to His Majesty's Principal Secretary of State for the Home Department.
37 N Johnston with K Finkel and J A Cohen, *Eastern State Penitentiary, Crucible of Good Intentions*, Philadephia Museum of Art, Philadelphia, 1994, p. 77.

66 The history and 'evolution' of building types

38 See N Johnston, *Forms of Constraint*, p. 90. Of all Haviland's designs, Pentonville most closely resembles his original scheme for the penitentiary at Trenton, New Jersey.

39 R S Duncan, *Peerless Priceless Pentonville*, p. 15.

40 For an extensive and thorough account of the design of Pentonville see Evans, *The Fabrication of Virtue*, Chapter 8, pp. 346–387.

41 R Evans, ibid., says (p. 361) that the circular structures 'were not constructed as designed'. However Duncan, *Peerless Priceless Pentonville* quotes (p. 46) what seems to be a contemporary account (but without citation) which describes three Panoptical solitary exercise yards and two communal 'rope yards' as being in operation at the same time. And P Priestley in *Victorian Prison Lives: English Prison Biography 1830–1914*, 2nd ed., Pimlico, London, 1999 quotes (p. 85) an account of the solitary yards by an Irish republican prisoner, O'Donovan Rossa, who actually experienced them. Priestley also gives contemporary descriptions of the system of moving prisoners.

42 P Priestley, *Victorian Prison Lives*, p. 91.

43 These glazed structures do not survive today; and the views down the cellblocks are now blocked by barred gates, new staircases, and wire netting stretched horizontally to prevent suicides. Observation (by human eye, not CCTV) is still however crucial, and when trouble erupts, extra guards are still summoned by whistle not by radio or phone.

44 H Mayhew and J Binny, *The Criminal Prisons of London*, Griffin, Bohn and Co., London, 1862, p. 120.

45 In New York (c.1827) and Philadelphia (1825–27). See J F Geist, *Arcades: The History of a Building Type*, MIT Press, Cambridge, MA, 1983, pp. 443, 445 and 536–538.

46 Michael Ignatieff is another who sees a direct continuation between the Panopticon and the 'horrors' of Pentonville. See *A Just Measure of Pain: The Penitentiary in the Industrial Revolution, 1750–1850*, Pantheon, New York, 1978.

47 J Elmes, *Hints for the Improvement of Prisons*, W Bulmer and Co., London, 1817.

48 N Johnston, *Crucible of Good Intentions*, p. 35.

4

SAMUEL BENTHAM'S PANOPTICON

(*Journal of Bentham Studies*, Volume 14, 2012)

Credit for devising the Panoptical 'inspection principle' for prison design is attributed, perhaps now irrevocably, to Jeremy Bentham. However Jeremy always insisted that the original conception came from his younger brother Samuel – "After all, I have been obliged to go a-begging to my brother, and borrow an idea of his."[1] Samuel was to have been an equal partner in the running of Jeremy's Panopticon penitentiary, and advised on its design. What is more, while Jeremy failed to get the penitentiary built in England, Samuel actually erected a 'school of arts' in Russia in 1807. This building could certainly be described as 'Panoptical'; however its geometry differed in crucial ways from Jeremy's two schemes.

In this paper I describe this remarkable Russian building, which has received only passing mention in the literature of architectural history and Bentham studies. The school admittedly in its short life had little influence outside Russia; but it anticipated the many 'radial prisons' built across the world in the later nineteenth century. Indeed Samuel's design avoided some of the contradictions that beset Jeremy's own penitentiary scheme of 1791, as outlined in the previous essay (3).

The paper was given at a conference on 'New Directions in Bentham Studies' held in London in December 2011.

The Bentham brothers in Russia

In 1785 Jeremy Bentham travelled to Russia to visit his brother Samuel, who was working for Prince Potemkin at Krichev, on the river Dnieper in the southern province of Mogilev, where the prince had an extensive estate.[2] Samuel Bentham had trained in Britain in the Navy's dockyards as a shipwright and engineer, and had then joined the service.[3] In 1780 he was sent, with financial support from his father, on a fact-finding tour of dockyards on the Continent, ending up in St Petersburg where he met Potemkin. Much impressed by his capacities and character, Potemkin made Samuel a lieutenant colonel and put him in command of a battalion stationed at Krichev with the purpose of training the men as sailors and shipwrights, and building ships for the Russian navy.

Potemkin also had a number of workshops at Krichev for making sailcloth, rope and other ships' fittings, as well as a distillery, a pottery and manufactories for working metal, wood and glass. Samuel was charged with their management, and recruited specialised craftsmen

68 The history and 'evolution' of building types

from Britain to direct the several operations. It has been said that Samuel's concern was with how these supervisors might best train and oversee a force of inexperienced local workmen. According to Simon Werrett however, he was in fact as much concerned with lack of discipline and application among the British craftsmen as among the peasant labourers.[4] In both cases the answer seemed to lie in the architectural design of new factory buildings.

The first sources of information about Samuel's invention of the Panopticon principle are the letters written by Jeremy to various correspondents, including their father, while he was at Krichev in 1786–87.[5] (Samuel also wrote down his ideas, but it seems those notes are lost. As he wrote to Jeremy in November 1787 after his brother had returned to Britain: "Inspection house papers I have mislaid or by mistake sent to you".[6]) In December 1786 Jeremy wrote to his friend Charles Brown:

> My Brother has hit upon a very singular new and I think important / though simple / idea in Architecture which is the subject of a course of letters I have just finished for my Father which it is not improbable may find their way to the press ... The architectural idea ~~consists in nothing but~~ / in the plan of what we / call an Inspection-house is that of a circular building so contrived that any number of persons may therein be kept in such a situation as either to be, or what comes to nearly the same thing to seem to themselves to be, constantly under the eye of a person or persons occupying a station in the centre which we call the Inspector's Lodge. You will be surprised when you come to see the efficacy which this simple and seemingly obvious contrivance promises to be to the business of schools, manufactories, ~~Hospitals and all sorts of~~ Prisons, and even Hospitals, if one may venture to say so to an adept.[7]

The letters to his father, to which Jeremy refers, did indeed 'find their way to the press', together with some very substantial 'postscripts', as *Panopticon: or, the Inspection-House* (1791), and again in *The Works of Jeremy Bentham* (Volume IV, 1843).[8] This is where the application of the Panopticon concept to prison design was worked out in detail, and where the famous architectural scheme of 1791 was published.

In April 1787 Jeremy drafted another letter from Krichev in Samuel's name, addressed to the prime minister William Pitt – but which was never sent – referring to "a particular kind of building contrived by me [Samuel] for the purposes of keeping persons of any description under the eye of an Inspector".[9] It seems that Jeremy had previously sent Pitt copies of the letters to his father. Now Samuel was intending to offer Pitt his services in the running of a national Panopticon penitentiary.

Given the respective characters of the two brothers, it makes sense that Samuel should have been the originator of the 'inspection principle'. Jeremy was the philosopher and theoretician, scholarly and reclusive. Samuel was outgoing, friendly and persuasive, had studied engineering and the sciences, and above all was gifted with a fertile mechanical creativity.[10] The list of his improvements, inventions and patents, most of them relating to the art of shipbuilding, runs to several pages.[11] In Russia he had impressed Potemkin with an 'amphibious carriage' convertible to a boat, built partly with his own hands, in which he travelled the country by road and river.

While in Potemkin's employ he also devised a new kind of ship for navigating the sinuous and shallow waters of the Dnieper and its tributaries. Christened by the brothers the 'vermicular', this consisted of a number of separate barges linked by universal joints, so that the whole composite craft could bend like a worm to negotiate even the sharpest turns.[12] Samuel built several such boats to carry timber and the products of the Krichev manufactories including parts of battleships for the Crimean fleet; and Potemkin commissioned an Imperial vermicular, in which the Empress Catherine was to have toured the south of the country. This was over 250 ft long, had a draught of just six inches, contained splendid apartments and bedrooms for the Empress, and was crewed by 120 oarsmen under the direction of Samuel himself, who stood at the stern with a megaphone. One can perhaps see, in these Russian boats of Samuel's, something of the bold eccentricity that also characterised the Panopticon.

When war broke out in 1787 between Russia and the Ottoman Empire, Potemkin sold the estate, and plans for the new workshop had to be abandoned. Samuel was ordered south to the Crimea where he distinguished himself in several naval battles. His own contemporary Panopticon notes seem to have been lost, as we have seen. The letter from Jeremy to Charles Brown quoted above refers to the projected building as 'circular', and Jeremy's prison designs of 1787 and 1791 were buildings with circular and polygonal plans respectively. Later, after his return to England, Jeremy wrote:

> The purpose to which this rotunda-form was destined to be employed by my brother, was that of a large workshop . . . partitions in the form and position of radii of the circle being employed in separating from each other such as required to be so separated; in the centre was the . . . Inspector's Lodge; from thence by turning around his axis, a functionary standing or sitting on the central point, had it in his power to commence and conclude a survey of the whole establishment in the twinkling of an eye.[13]

This would seem to imply that the building was perfectly circular (it had a 'rotunda-form'). On the other hand Samuel's widow Mary Sophia wrote in 1856: "The [planned] building consisted of a centre from which diverged several long rays, all of them, on all the stories, capable of inspection from the central part."[14] It is reasonably clear that she is talking here about the Krichev factory since she gives its date as 1787. The reference to 'long rays' suggests something quite different from the brothers' two circular prison schemes.

Samuel Bentham's School of Arts in St Petersburg

As it turned out, Samuel got a second chance to realise his Panoptical workshop.[15] In 1805 the Navy offered him the opportunity to return to Russia to build warships there for Britain, which he accepted. He negotiated an arrangement with the Russian Minister of Marine that for every British ship constructed he would produce another of similar design for Russia. Tsar Alexander however vetoed the use of timber for building foreign vessels: in an effort to please him, Samuel offered to construct a 'School of Arts' on the river Okhta in St Petersburg in which craftsmen and shipwrights were to be trained. The recruits were to work in the manufacture of equipment and supplies for the Russian navy including clothing, woodwork, sailcloth and navigational instruments. By September 1807 the building was nearing completion under Samuel's supervision; then the Tsar declared war on Britain and Samuel had to return home again.

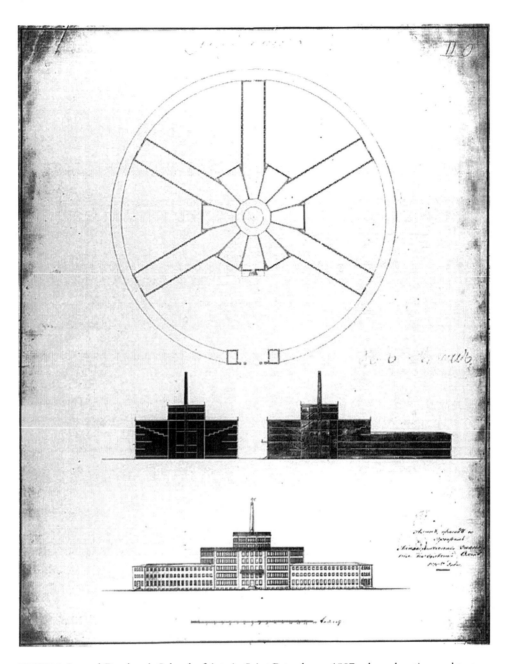

FIGURE 1 Samuel Bentham's School of Arts in Saint Petersburg, 1807, plan, elevation and two sections: Rossiiskii Gosudarstvennyi Arkhiv Voenno-Morskogo Flota [Russian State Naval Archive], St Petersburg, fond 326, opis' 1, delo 10043. The drawing is published on the website of the Bentham Project at University College London at www.ucl.ac.uk/Bentham-Project. Permission to reproduce the image was obtained by Professor Roger Bartlett of the School of Slavonic and East European Studies, UCL. The inscription reads 'Plan, façade and profile of the Panoptical Institution on the Great Okhta, 1810'

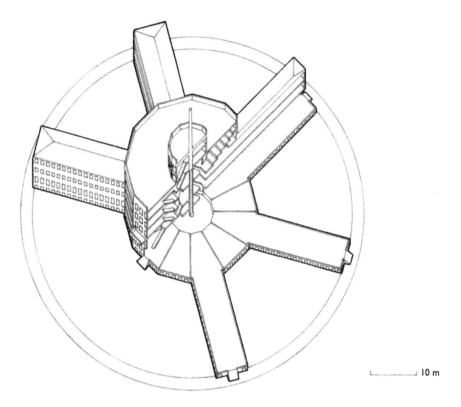

FIGURE 2 School of Arts in Saint Petersburg, cutaway bird's eye view: author's drawing

Figure 1 shows a drawing of the school dating from 1810 held in the Russian State Naval Archive, giving a plan, an elevation and two sections. Figure 2 is my own cutaway bird's eye view, constructed from these Russian drawings and detailed descriptions given by Mary Sophia Bentham in *The Mechanics' Magazine* (1849) and *The Civil Engineer and Architect's Journal* (1853).[16] Figure 3 reproduces a part-section from *The Mechanics' Magazine* article, which broadly matches one of the Russian sections, although there are several discrepancies.[17]

The flat roofs, plain regular fenestration and overall pyramidal form give the building a curiously twentieth century, even proto-Soviet aspect, despite its Imperial patron. It consists of a 12-sided drum at the centre, roughly 28 m [90 ft] in diameter, with five radiating wings, each of them 21 m [70 ft] long and 6.5 m [20 ft] wide. (These approximate dimensions come from the Russian drawing and differ from measurements mentioned by Mary Sophia in her texts – see note 17.) A portico and main entrance take the place of the missing sixth arm. The wings are on three storeys and – since their interiors are wholly visible from the centre – they are presumably open plan.

The drum is made up in plan of three concentric rings. The central ring is 5.5 m [18 ft] in diameter, on six storeys, plus a basement that according to Mary Sophia contained heating plant and the water supply. The ground floor contains an office for clerks. Above this is the 'principal inspection room'. 'Occasional inspection' is also possible from the next two floors. All three of these floors are in effect floating circular platforms. The topmost two floors serve as an infirmary that is separated from the remainder of the building.

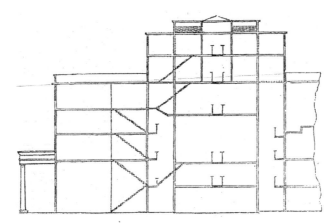

FIGURE 3 School of Arts in Saint Petersburg, part section: *The Mechanics' Magazine*, volume 50, 1849

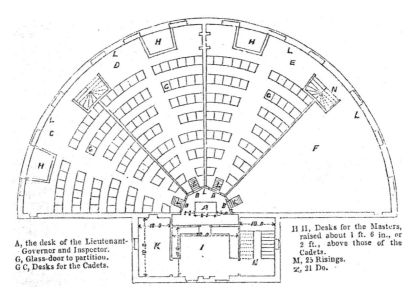

FIGURE 4 Samuel Bentham with Samuel Bunce, project for a school for naval cadets at Woolwich, 1790s, plan: *The Mechanics' Magazine*, volume 50, 1849

Around all these rooms is an annular space, 2 m [6 ft 6 ins] wide, which rises as a void through the five main storeys. It is surrounded by galleries, and crossed by stairs to the observation platforms. The third and outermost ring, 9 m [30 ft] wide, is divided into 12 wedge-shaped spaces, five of which form parts of the radiating wings. There are four storeys in this part, the topmost having a stepped floor – although in the part immediately above the entrance all the floors are flat. We might guess that most of the spaces on this level are auditoria of some kind. (None of the drawings is labelled with room functions.)

We can compare the design of this central drum with two other projects on the inspection principle that Samuel had worked on previously back in England, neither of which was built.

Mary Sophia describes the first of these in *The Mechanics' Magazine* article. This was a school for 'gentlemen cadets' at Woolwich, designed by Samuel in the 1790s.[18] Mary Sophia includes a plan (Figure 4). A friend of Samuel's, Colonel Twiss, had asked him to prepare the scheme, which was then worked up by the architect Samuel Bunce.[19] The building is semi-circular and divided into four radial parts. Three of the spaces are lecture rooms: each has 'Desks for the Cadets' and a 'Desk for the Master' at the narrow end of the room. The fourth space is left clear for 'fencing and dancing'. At the very centre is a small room with glass walls from which the Lieutenant Governor and Inspector can watch both masters and pupils at work. We can imagine that Samuel had essentially the same arrangement in mind for the top-floor classrooms at Okhta – assuming that is indeed their purpose – although these would have had tiered seating, rather than what were evidently flat floors (think of the dancing) at Woolwich. Also, going by the Russian drawing, the Okhta School would have had at least seven and perhaps nine classrooms.

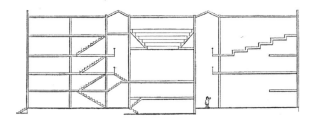

Fig. II.—Section.

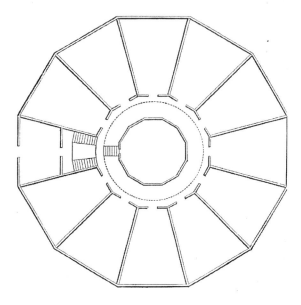

Fig. III.—Ground Plan.

FIGURE 5 Samuel Bentham with Samuel Bunce, project for a House of Industry, 1797, plan and section: *The Works of Jeremy Bentham*, ed J Bowring 1838–43, volume VIII

74 The history and 'evolution' of building types

In 1797 Samuel had collaborated with Bunce on a second Panoptical scheme: a standard design for a workhouse for paupers or House of Industry.[20] They proposed that 250 of these be built across Britain, each housing 2000 inmates. Figure 5 shows a plan and section. The building's form is that of a 12-sided drum on five storeys, divided internally into concentric rings, with inspection from central platforms and a void rising between these platforms and the outer ring of wedge-shaped rooms. Comparison of the respective sections shows that the form and arrangement of this House of Industry are almost identical to those of the main drum of the Okhta School, the only substantive difference being that the House of Industry lacks the infirmary on top. Inspection is from intermediate level floors in both cases, and the House of Industry even has some top-floor auditoria or classrooms with stepped floors. There are also close similarities in the fenestration of the two buildings, in continuous strips of windows with narrow iron frames. Robin Evans was particularly struck by the modernity of these facades, saying "Nothing quite like [them] would be seen again until the middle of the next century", and citing in comparison G T Greene's Naval Dockyard Boat Store at Sheerness of 1858–61.[21]

Supervision in the School of Arts

The key purpose of the geometry of the whole structure at Okhta is of course supervision of all the cadets, apprentices and their teachers working in the different spaces. The audiences in what I have suggested are raked lecture theatres are overseen by their instructors and from the centre. The students occupied in the radial workshops can all be observed from the 'principal inspection room' and from the platform on the floor above: notice in the Russian drawing how these floors at the centre are staggered in section in relation to the floors in the wings, so that two storeys in the wings are visible from each of the inspection platforms. Mary Sophia – who accompanied Samuel on this Russian trip – describes how she was allowed to enter the building when it was nearly finished: "From the central chamber a perfect view was obtained of all that passed within the walls on each of two floors, the rays inclusively."[22] Inspection "was effected by a very nice adjustment of the relative height of floors—one of the two principal floors being below, the other above the floor of the inspection room".[23]

At the very centre we find the building's most extraordinary feature. Here is a narrow cylindrical space, about 1 m in diameter, extending the full height of the building up to the level of the infirmary. Inside the cylinder is a chair for the Inspector of the School, ". . . suspended by a counterpoise, and regulated in its movements up and down by a simple and safe apparatus, easily managed by the inspector himself".[24] By pulling on the ropes, the inspector can propel himself vertically, to arrive unexpectedly at the different levels including the focus of all the classrooms on the top floor, and check that everybody is hard at work.

According to Mary Sophia – not perhaps an entirely unbiased witness – the pupils trained in the School were "found so useful, that the best of these youth were taken for service elsewhere by fifty at a time, even as early as 1808".[25] (How much this success was due to the architectural design is of course a matter for debate.) However the building did not survive for long. Samuel had specified that iron be used for the structural columns, but wood was substituted; and in 1818 the School caught fire and was destroyed.

The School of Arts in the historical literature

Since Mary Sophia's articles in the 1840s and '50s and her biography of Samuel of 1862, the School of Arts has been largely forgotten, and is hardly touched on in the modern literature of the brothers' Panopticon designs and the prisons they inspired. No doubt this neglect is due in part to the short life of the Russian building, the fact that it was a school not a penal institution, and the fact that it was geographically remote from developments in Europe. Also the Russian drawing of Figure 1 has only relatively recently been published in the west.

Janet Semple mentions the St Petersburg School briefly in her 1993 monograph on Bentham's Prison, but gives no description of its architecture.[26] Ian Christie's *The Benthams in Russia* only covers the period up to 1791. Simon Werrett in a fascinating paper on 'Potemkin and the Panopticon' gives due credit to Samuel for inventing the inspection principle, and argues for fuller consideration of the local political and cultural context of the Krichev workshop.[27] This, he says, would have essentially compressed the spatial structure of the Russian estate into a single building, with the noble at the centre and his peasant labourers surrounding him. There would have been further echoes, Werrett suggests, of the centralised architecture of the typical Russian Orthodox Church, both buildings privileging visibility and emphasising the omnipresence of God and the inspector respectively. Werrett touches briefly on the St Petersburg School of Arts; but he does not elaborate on its form or geometrical modes

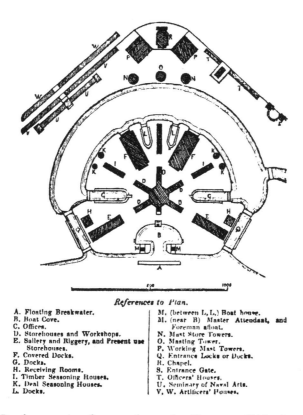

FIGURE 6 Samuel Bentham, project for a naval arsenal at Sheerness, 1812, plan: *Civil Engineer and Architect's Journal*, volume 16, 1853

76 The history and 'evolution' of building types

of oversight. What he does reveal is that the building did have some local influence: "Soon after its construction, the Tsar was building Panopticons across Russia, as the Okhta School of Arts was 'copied in several other private as well as Government establishments in that Empire'".[28]

Robin Evans mentions the School of Arts only fleetingly, and not even by name, in his 1971 paper on the brothers' Panopticons of 1787 and 1791.[29] In his influential book on English prison architecture, *The Fabrication of Virtue* (1982), Evans again gives the briefest of descriptions, saying that the school had "radiating wings on a central hub". He pairs it with a later un-built scheme for a naval arsenal at Sheerness that Samuel presented to the Admiralty in 1812 (Figure 6).[30] At the centre of this dockyard site is a building with a 12-sided central part and five radiating wings, very similar in plan to the Okhta School. The dimensions are nearly the same. Clearly Samuel has essentially repeated the Russian design. The centre contains offices, and stores and workshops occupy the wings.

We might guess that the internal room layouts of the two buildings would have been somewhat different however, since the Sheerness structure was not a school, and the officers were to watch over activities outside as well as inside the building. In a letter accompanying the plans Samuel emphasises the Panoptical virtues of the general arrangement of the site, and how

> the officers being all of them in the centre of the central building, and a higher part of that centre having a commanding view of the whole dockyard, every work, every transaction on the dockyard, may be inspected in different degrees of perfection from that central situation.[31]

There is no reference to Okhta in Norman Johnston's wide-ranging international history of prison architecture *Forms of Constraint*, although he does cite Jeremy's account of the projected Krichev factory, quoted earlier.[32] On this basis he describes that building as a "circular two-story textile mill, about one hundred feet in diameter". On the other hand he says in a footnote: "This building is sometimes described [presumably by Mary Sophia, although Johnston does not say] as though there were two-story wing buildings radiating from a central rotunda." This he adds is "unlikely".

[*In the original paper there were sections at this point on 'Failure of the Panopticon penitentiary' and 'Success of the radial prison'. These essentially repeat arguments of the previous paper (3), and so are omitted.*]

Did the 'School of Arts' anticipate the radial prison?

The question remains: to what extent did Samuel's School at Okhta anticipate the design of radial prisons like the Eastern State Penitentiary and Pentonville? In terms of overall form, with its five wings overseen from the central observatory, the answer is clearly yes. On the other hand, since it was a school not a prison, the requirements for oversight would have been rather less demanding. The wings at Okhta were open plan, while the wings at Pentonville are of course lined with closed cells. What is more the Okhta wings were on several floor levels and did not have full-height halls, so it was not possible to survey the entire building from one position.

Nevertheless the pattern of oversight of the Okhta wings and the Pentonville halls was broadly similar. All the cadets and their instructors could be watched at Okhta without a large waste of unused central space as in the circular Panopticon. On each floor there was one point at the very centre from which the inspector could see everyone – as Jeremy wanted and as was achieved in the collective (non-cell) spaces of Pentonville and the prisons that followed – and the inspector could move rapidly between different floors on his flying chair. The School of Arts also had a fan-shaped plan like those of the radial prisons, although security obviously did not have the same priority in the two cases.

Those later circular prisons that corresponded most closely to the Panopticon penitentiary schemes of 1787 and 1791 were built in the late nineteenth and early twentieth centuries. However what has been described as the 'première réalisation panoptique européenne', La Tour Maitresse in Geneva took its first inmates in 1825 and was thus contemporary with Haviland's Eastern State, and predated Pentonville. The architect was Samuel Vaucher-Crémieux.[33] Jeremy Bentham had close links at this period with liberal Calvinists in Geneva: indeed it was a Genevan pastor Etienne Dumont who, having met Jeremy in 1788, became his most enthusiastic disciple and promoter. Dumont went on to edit, rewrite, rearrange, translate and publish Jeremy's manuscripts; and so it was that many of the principal works on moral philosophy and legislative reform appeared first in French, only much later in English.[34]

Dumont had a particular interest in prison reform, and acted as a personal link between Jeremy and those responsible for the design and regime of the Tour Maitresse. When we look at the prison's plan however (Figure 7) we find not a drum-shaped building, but a semi-circular observatory with two radiating wings. These wings had open-plan workrooms on the ground floor and cells on the upper floor, whose doors only were visible from the centre. Can we detect the hand of Samuel hovering over this building? There is certainly an affinity here with the Okhta School of Arts.

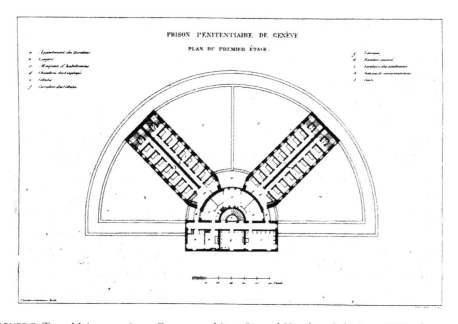

FIGURE 7 Tour Maitresse prison, Geneva, architect Samuel Vaucher-Crémieux, 1825, plan

Did the proposed Panopticon at Krichev have a radial plan?

A further and final question follows. Mary Sophia, as we have seen, wrote in 1856 that Samuel's planned workshop at Krichev had "a centre from which diverged several long rays, all of them, on all the stories, capable of inspection from the central part". Was she right about the 'rays'? Or was she confused, and perhaps projecting back in time from the Okhta building – which she knew personally – to what she was assuming her husband had planned for Krichev? There is one more source that I have not yet introduced, which I would suggest goes a long way towards answering this question. This is an article 'Arrangement of Buildings on Principles of Central Inspection', published in *The Builder* in 1847 under the name of 'The Late Sir Samuel Bentham', but whose author must surely once again be Mary Sophia. This paper says of the Krichev workshop, that Samuel

> . . . contrived a structure having a central chamber for offices, with rays diverging from it for workshops. The rays were of two stories, the central observatory but of one floor, but that of such a height, that being upon it, the inspector had full view over two floors of the rays, the floor of the lower workshop being below that of the observatory, the floor of the upper workshop above it.[35]

Mary Sophia – assuming she is indeed the author – goes on to describe how after Samuel returned to England in 1791, he had

> . . . complete models made on his principle of a prison for a thousand persons, in which, as the rays consisted of several floors, the upper ones were appropriate to services requiring the less constant inspection, but were subject to it at all times by means of a counterpoise apparatus affixed to the platform on which was the inspector's chair, so that at pleasure he could raise himself to any required height.[36]

The detailed and circumstantial character of these accounts suggests to me at least that Mary Sophia was not mistaken about the geometry of the projected Krichev building, and that its plan was indeed radial. What is clear furthermore from the description of the models, is that in the 1790s while Jeremy, helped by Samuel, was persevering with his cylindrical plans, Samuel was also continuing to develop and press for radial designs like those of Okhta and – as readers may now be convinced – Krichev.

A third passage in this paper is yet more revealing. It quotes a paragraph by Jeremy from his twenty-first Panopticon letter, "as indicating the origin of Sir Samuel's invention".

> In the Royal Military School at Paris, the bed-chambers (if my brother's [Samuel's] memory does not deceive him), form two ranges on the two sides of a long room; the inhabitants being separated from one another by partitions, but exposed alike to the view of a master at his walks, by a kind of grated window in each door. This plan of construction struck him, he tells me, a good deal, as he walked over that establishment . . . and possibly in that walk the foundation was laid for his Inspection-House. If he there borrowed his idea, I hope he has not repaid it without interest. You will confess some difference, in point of facility, betwixt a state of incessant walking, and a state of rest; and in point of completeness of inspection, between visiting two or three hundred persons one after another, and seeing them at once.[37]

This is of course the precise distinction between the mode of inspection from the centre (the 'state of rest') in all of the Bentham brothers' various buildings – although Samuel's inspectors could move vertically – and the mobile form of inspection along straight halls (the 'state of incessant walking') that typified the Eastern Penitentiary, Pentonville and all their successors. The irony is that Jeremy sees Samuel's change from mobile inspection to central inspection as an improvement. Had Samuel stuck more closely to what he had seen at the Royal Military School – and put peepholes in the place of the 'grated windows' – he really would have anticipated the key features of the radial prison.

Notes

1 *The Works of Jeremy Bentham* ed J Bowring, 11 vols, William Tait, Edinburgh, 1838–43 (henceforth 'Bowring'), X. p. 165.
2 For an account of Jeremy's journey, and the time that the brothers spent together at Krichev, see I R Christie, *The Benthams in Russia 1780–1791*, Berg, Oxford, 1993, especially p. 177 where the Panopticon is discussed.
3 For Samuel Bentham's biography see M S Bentham, 'Memoir of the Late Brigadier-General Sir Samuel Bentham, with an Account of His Inventions', *Papers and Practical Illustrations of Public Works of Recent Construction both British and American*, John Weale, London, 1856 pp. 41–79; and M S Bentham, *The Life of Brigadier-General Sir Samuel Bentham, K.S.G.*, Longman, Green, Longman and Roberts, London, 1862.
4 S Werrett, 'Potemkin and the Panopticon: Samuel Bentham and the Architecture of Absolutism in Eighteenth Century Russia', *Journal of Bentham Studies*, Volume 2 (1999), http://ojs.lib.ucl.ac.uk/index.php/jbs/article/view/10, accessed 17 July 2012.
5 See *The Correspondence of Jeremy Bentham* (henceforth 'Correspondence'), vol ix, ed I R Christie, Oxford University Press, Oxford, 1971 (*The Collected Works of Jeremy Bentham*, henceforth 'CW'), p. iii.
6 Ibid., p. 595, letter from Samuel to Jeremy Bentham, early November 1787.
7 Ibid., pp. 501–503, letter from Jeremy to Charles Brown, 18/29 December 1786. Passages struck through are deleted in the manuscript. Passages between '/ /' are inter-lineations.
8 'Letters and Postscripts' were published as *Panopticon: or, the Inspection-House*, Dublin, 1791, and *Panopticon: Postscript*, 2 vols, London, 1791. They were later republished in Bowring, IV as 'Panopticon; or the Inspection–House', pp. 37–172, along with 'Panopticon versus New South Wales: or the Panopticon Penitentiary System, and the Penal Colonization System, Compared', pp. 173–211. Both Letters and Postscripts are included in *The Panopticon Writings*, ed. M Bozovic, Verso, London and New York, 1995. The political history of the Panopticon and Bentham's struggles to have it built are told by Janet Semple in *Bentham's Prison: A Study of the Panopticon Penitentiary*, Clarendon Press, Oxford, 1993, Chapters 3 and 4.
9 *Correspondence* (CW) III pp. 534–536, draft letter to William Pitt.
10 For an attractive account of the private and family lives of the two brothers, and their contrasting characters, see C Pease-Watkin, 'Jeremy and Samuel Bentham: The Private and the Public', *Journal of Bentham Studies*, Volume 5 (2002), http://ojs.lib.ucl.ac.uk/index.php/jbs/article/view/22, accessed 17 July 2012.
11 Mary Sophia Bentham, 'Memoir of the Late Sir Samuel Bentham', pp. 77–79.
12 I R Christie, *The Benthams in Russia*, pp. 167–169.
13 Bowring, XI, p. 97.
14 Mary Sophia Bentham, 'Principal Inventions', p. 19. Mary Sophia talks here however of Jeremy visiting Samuel at 'Cherson' [Kherson], the port in the Crimea to which Samuel moved in late 1787.
15 Mary Sophia Bentham, 'Memoir of the Late Sir Samuel Bentham', pp. 65–66.
16 Mary Sophia Bentham, 'On the Application of the Panopticon, or Central Inspection Principle to Manufactories and Schools', *The Mechanics' Magazine, Museum, Register, Journal, and Gazette*, Volume 50 (January–June 1849), pp. 295–297. M S Bentham, 'The Panopticon or Inspection Principle in Dockyards and Manufactories', *The Civil Engineer and Architect's Journal*, Volume 16 (1853), pp. 453–455. There is one further, very mysterious drawing in *The Mechanics' Magazine* article, besides those reproduced here. Mary Sophia Bentham says that this is a plan of the Okhta School, but at a

80 The history and 'evolution' of building types

different scale from the section. The plan has three rings that seem to be in about the same proportions as in the Russian drawings. But otherwise the details seem not to correspond in any respect. Could this be a roof plan? A structural layout? I have no plausible interpretation.

17 Mary Sophia's drawing has a structure on the roof of the central tallest rotunda that appears to contain a water tank. This does not appear in the Russian design. Her drawing shows no basement (although she mentions one). However a half-basement is evident above ground in the Russian elevation and sections, although the part below ground is not visible in the sections. The relative diameters of the various cylindrical parts are not the same in the two sources. In fact the whole issue of scale is problematic. The Russian drawing has a scale in which the unit appears to be the *sazhen* or Russian fathom (appropriate for a naval building). Peter the Great had decreed that the *sazhen* should equal 7 English feet. But applying this scale to the drawing of the School results in dimensions that seem too small: for example storey heights come out at around 6 ft 8 ins. Mary Sophia's drawing has no scale, although she gives various key dimensions of the building in her text. These cannot be reconciled exactly with the Russian drawing. I have nevertheless worked to the *sazhen* scale in my Figure 2; but I suspect that the School was actually somewhat larger than my own scale (in metres) would indicate.

18 Mary Sophia Bentham, 'Manufactories and Schools', p. 298.

19 Bunce worked as an architect for the Navy Department.

20 Jeremy Bentham, 'Outline of a Work Entitled Pauper Management Improved', published in *Annals of Agriculture* in 1797, and reprinted in Bowring, viii pp. 369–439. The drawings of Figure 5 appear here facing p. 374.

21 R Evans, *The Fabrication of Virtue: English Prison Architecture, 1750–1840*, Cambridge University Press, Cambridge, 1982, p. 222, and note 78 p. 440. Evans says (p. 440): "It is tempting to suggest a connection, particularly as Samuel Bentham was a very active Inspector General of Naval Works between 1796 and 1805, and later (1812) designed a dock complex for Sheerness."

22 Mary Sophia Bentham, 'Dockyards and Manufactories', p. 454.

23 Mary Sophia Bentham, 'Manufactories and Schools', p. 297.

24 Ibid., p. 297. This space is just visible in the Russian cross-sections. The flying chair was not however in operation by the time the Benthams had to leave Russia.

25 Ibid., p. 297.

26 J Semple, *Bentham's Prison*, pp. 214–215.

27 S Werrett, 'Potemkin and the Panopticon'.

28 Ibid., note 69, *Correspondence* (CW), viii, p. 224. S Werrett also cites a letter from Admiral Chichagov to Samuel Bentham, 17 September 1807: British Library Add. MSS 33544 folio 316.

29 R Evans, 'Bentham's Panopticon: An Incident in the Social History of Architecture', *Architectural Association Quarterly* Volume 3, April/July (1971), pp. 21–37. See p. 33: "No Panopticon building was ever erected by Jeremy and only one, 'fleetingly', under the direction of Samuel."

30 R Evans, *The Fabrication of Virtue*, Chapter 5. The Sheerness scheme is also illustrated by Mary Sophia Bentham in 'Dockyards and Manufactories', p. 453.

31 Letter from Samuel Bentham to Bernal Osborne MP, Secretary of the Admiralty, quoted by Mary Sophia Bentham in 'Dockyards and Manufactories', p. 453.

32 (See note 13 above) N Johnston, *Forms of Constraint: A History of Prison Architecture*, University of Illinois, Urbana and Chicago IL, 2000, p. 50 and note 33.

33 R Roth, *Pratiques Pénitentiaires et Théorie Sociale: L'Exemple de la Prison de Genève (1825–1862)*, Librairie Droz, Geneva, 1981. Plans of the prison appear on p. 292.

34 See C Blamires, *The French Revolution and the Creation of Benthamism*, Palgrave Macmillan, Basingstoke, 2008.

35 'The Late Sir Samuel Bentham' [presumably the author is Mary Sophia Bentham: Samuel is referred to in the third person throughout], 'Arrangement of Buildings on Principles of Central Inspection', *The Builder*, 30 October 1847, pp. 515–516.

36 Ibid., p. 515.

37 'Panopticon Letter XXI', Bowring, IV p. 63.

5

THE CHANGING DEPARTMENT STORE BUILDING, 1850 TO 1940

(*Journal of Space Syntax*, Volume 5 Number 2, 2014, pp. 151–167)

Jeremy and Samuel Bentham's Panopticons [Papers 3 and 4] were architectural inventions. They were not completely without precedent in eighteenth-century prison design; but much of their geometry and detailed design was novel. By contrast the typical form of the department store building changed gradually in stages over a century, from its origins in other types of fashionable shop in the mid-nineteenth century, to the suburban store designs pioneered in the United States in the 1930s.

The nineteenth-century stores were sited in the centres of cities. They had deep plans, and obtained natural light and natural ventilation from large atria. From the 1940s stores moved to the suburbs and again had deep but artificially ventilated plans without windows, and large car parks. This essay follows the process, and identifies a series of causes: social changes especially the emancipation of women, changes in retail business practices, changes in transport technology especially the growth of car ownership, and changes in building construction notably the rise of air conditioning. Competition between the department stores and other types of retail business also played a major part.

I suggest at the end of the paper that the approach to explanation taken here might have application to processes of change in other types of building and institution. Those ideas are further developed in Chapter 11 of my book Building Types and Built Forms.

Introduction

Magnificent new premises were completed in 1874 for *Au Bon Marché*, then the biggest and most successful of all Parisian department stores.[1] The five-storey building, still in use today, occupies an entire block near the Jardin de Luxembourg in the centre of the city (Figure 1). It has great plate glass display windows along the four facades, cylindrical domed towers at the corners and a theatrical main entrance topped by a fifth dome on the Rue Sèvres. The corner towers serve to make the store visible from a distance along the adjoining streets. As built, the ground, first and second floors were devoted to sales, while the third floor and the fourth mansard floor were given over to kitchens, refectories and bedrooms for the hundreds of *demoiselles* who served in the shop. In the basement there was warehousing and a department for receiving goods and sending parcels. The interior was punctuated with a series of glass-roofed atria (Figure 2). The architects were Alexandre Leplanche and then Louis-Charles Boileau, with some possible involvement of the engineer Gustave Eiffel.[2]

FIGURE 1 *Au Bon Marché*, Paris: the part of the building constructed in 1869 on the Rue Sèvres, architect Alexandre Leplanche, showing the main entrance and the first of what were to be four corner towers. From Marrey, *Les Grands Magasins*

FIGURE 2 *Au Bon Marché*: the building of 1874 combining the section by Leplanche (at the south-east corner) and new parts by Louis–Charles Boileau architect and (possibly) Gustave Eiffel engineer. Author's axonometric drawing

FIGURE 3 Sears Roebuck store, Pico Boulevard, Los Angeles 1939, architect John Stokes Redden. Photo by 'Dick' Whittington

In 1939 the Sears Roebuck Company built a department store on Pico Boulevard, Los Angeles.[3] The building had two sales floors and car parking on the roof (Figure 3). It had an extremely deep plan, without roof lights, and there were no windows on the upper storey. More car parking was provided out front. The architect was John Stokes Redden.

The *Bon Marché* building stands at the high point of nineteenth-century department store architecture. The Sears building is an early example of the suburban store type that spread worldwide after World War II. How and why did the multi-storey top-lit atrium form first appear, and why was it transformed into the low-rise deep-plan form? What were the social, commercial and technological forces that drove the process? This paper offers some explanations, with a classification of the forces of change under four headings:

1 the influence of wider external developments in society and technology, especially transport technology, and building services;
2 changes in the nature of the activities carried on within businesses, and their consequences for built forms;
3 competition between activities and businesses, and competition in effect between alternative built forms for the same activities; and
4 functional failures in built forms, and their correction.

These causes can be found in combination, leading to a mutual interaction between and 'co-evolution' of activity and built form types.[4]

Changes in society and in transport technology

Let us start then with wider changes in society and in transport technology. (We will come later to changes in construction technology and building services.) Department stores emerged as a new type of retail business in the mid-nineteenth century.[5] They catered in the first place to rich bourgeois and aristocratic clients, so the stores' founders wanted to find sites in or near the districts where those clients lived, and from which they could easily travel by carriage or cab. In London this explains the concentration of stores along Oxford Street, following the westward movement of the city's moneyed elite towards the prestigious estates circling Hyde Park in Mayfair, Bayswater, Belgravia and Kensington.[6] In Paris the stores – several of them on Haussmann's new boulevards – clustered in the richest *quartiers* to the northwest around the Champs Elysées and the centre of financial power at the Bourse.[7] In New York they followed Manhattan's wealthy citizens up Broadway and Fifth Avenue as they moved north from the southern tip of the island, to reach Central Park by 1900.[8]

In the mid-nineteenth century ladies went shopping in pairs or groups, and might be served in their carriages by assistants rather than enter the premises themselves (Figure 4).[9] Or they might be 'walked through' the store to the appropriate counter by an attentive shop-walker. This 'carriage trade' survived into the 1900s, when the carriage owners started to buy cars. Meanwhile the second half of the nineteenth century saw major growth in the number and extent of horse-drawn omnibus and tram services in Paris, London and other cities.[10] Despite the implicit claim that omnibuses were 'for all', the fares were not easily affordable for the working classes, but they did allow the petit bourgeoisie to travel over longer distances to the shops. By the 1870s it had become socially acceptable for middle class women to travel unaccompanied. If the man of the family was using the carriage, his wife and children might take the bus. Figure 5 shows a happy bourgeois group going home from *Au Bon Marché*, an illustration used in the store's publicity. Harry Gordon Selfridge advertised his new Oxford Street store by putting posters on buses urging people to '. . . spend the day at Selfridge's' (and by implication 'Travel there by bus').[11]

By the middle of the century the centres of both Paris and London were ringed by mainline railway stations. The lines were not brought right into the hearts of the cities because of the price of land. So shoppers arrived at the terminals and transferred to buses or cabs; indeed these services in time became integrated with the railways in their organisation and finances. The trains brought yet more customers from the provinces to spend the day at the shops,

FIGURE 4 Whiteley's on Westbourne Grove, London in 1900, still catering to the 'carriage trade'; by permission of fotoLIBRA

FIGURE 5 Going home by omnibus from *Au Bon Marché*: illustrated card published by the store. By kind permission of *Bon Marché*, Paris

The changing department store building **85**

who would take a break at midday for lunch, and perhaps would fit in a matinée at the theatre. In Britain, shoppers came to London's department stores from as far afield as Bath and Cambridge – both cities with good shops of their own. As early as the 1870s William Whiteley, proprietor of the west London store that bears his name, estimated that a quarter of his customers came from outside the capital.[12] The author Gwen Raverat described her mother, two decades later, coming home to Cambridge 'famished and worn out' after a day of London shopping.[13]

Some department stores picked locations with half an eye to this provincial clientele, including Whiteley who set up on Westbourne Grove, well to the west of the Oxford Street stores but close to the new Paddington Station. In Paris *Le Printemps* and *Galeries Lafayette* are near the Gare St Lazare, and one of the *Félix Potin* stores was opposite the Gare Montparnasse. Many of the stores had large mail order operations delivering to the suburbs by van. (*Au Bon Marché*'s delivery vans are visible in Figure 1.) The railways allowed the range of these services to be greatly extended. Shoppers who came into town from a distance could have their purchases delivered to their homes. Mail order trade was especially important in the United States and other countries with widely scattered populations. The great Chicago department store Marshall Field's, like many of its competitors, ran a wholesale operation that until late in the century was bigger than the retailing business and supplied small shops across the middle west.

Railways were important to the stores for another reason: they transported much of the shops' stock from provincial manufacturers. Some of the goods sold were high-priced, handicraft items. But the nineteenth century saw a huge growth in the mass manufacture of what had previously been expensive luxuries, but could now be brought within the price range of a much bigger customer base.

During the last quarter of the century the stores broadened their appeal among the social classes. Real incomes rose generally in Britain and France, and respectable clerks and their wives had increasing amounts to spend. Some women had earnings of their own before marriage. Half-holidays on Saturdays allowed working people to spend the afternoon shopping. The growth of international tourism, encouraged by the century's world's fairs, brought yet more clients: by 1900 the stores had become 'sights' and were featured in guidebooks.

Social, legal and financial changes occurred in this period that began to transform the status of women, and gave them greater opportunities to spend their own (and their husbands') money. The department stores were an important catalyst in this process.[14] From the outset they cultivated a female clientele, and created for women something like the feminine equivalent of the gentleman's club. In the stores, women shoppers could meet their friends, they could relax, eat and drink, write letters and generally feel at home – indeed for many, the stores were much grander and more comfortable than their own houses. In the days before radio and the cinema, the stores could offer an occasional escape for bored or lonely suburban housewives. Not the least important of the facilities provided were ladies' cloakrooms and lavatories, which were rare elsewhere in public places in London and Paris. The department stores thus became some of the earliest institutions where women could spend time unaccompanied by men. Edward Filene described his Boston store as an 'Adamless Eden'.[15]

A few store proprietors like Harry Gordon Selfridge even believed that the stores contributed actively to the process of women's emancipation[16] – although Selfridge himself was a notorious womaniser. (It should be said that others argued the opposite: that the stores enslaved women in an acquisitive materialism.) The suffragettes were not entirely consistent

86 The history and 'evolution' of building types

in their attitude.[17] In Newcastle they protested against their lack of the vote by smashing shop windows. But they planned their campaign in the tearooms of Fenwick's department store.[18]

Changes in the activity of shopping itself

We have looked at some of the forces in the broader social and technological 'environment' of the department stores – in particular the new transport technologies of the nineteenth century – that encouraged their emergence in the first place. My second cause of change in the built forms of the stores lies in the activity of shopping itself.

Some of the major department stores were founded as such: but others grew from modest origins as much smaller and different kinds of retail enterprise. *Au Bon Marché* had started in 1852 as a *magasin de nouveautés* with a staff of just 12. These *magasins*, which appeared in Paris from the 1830s, sold fashionable clothes for women. Several other great Parisian stores had similar origins.[19] Most department stores in Britain grew in a comparable way from drapery shops, or in a few cases from what were known as 'bazaars' – premises shared among many independent small traders. Draperies dealt principally in cloth, for bed linen and furnishings, as well as for making up garments. In the United States the first department stores developed from 'dry goods stores' – dry goods meaning textiles, ready-to-wear clothing and in general things not sold in hardware stores or groceries.[20]

The early growth of many of these stores in all three countries was by accretion, with successful draperies, *magasins de nouveautés* or dry good stores acquiring adjacent properties and opening successive new departments, perhaps in the case of draperies adding millinery (ladies' hats), haberdashery (accessories), and so on. Whiteley's grew by stages in this way in Bayswater, as did Harrods – starting from a grocer's shop – in Kensington. Chicago's Marshall Field's started in dry goods and went through a long series of acquisitions and re-buildings.[21]

It has sometimes been argued that the success of the first department stores can be attributed to a series of radical innovations in business practice over their predecessors. The old-fashioned *magasin* or drapery, in this characterisation, was an austere, gloomy place in which the goods were kept in cupboards and little was on display. To enter the premises was a tacit commitment to make some kind of purchase. Items were brought out for individual customers to inspect. There were no fixed prices and it was customary to bargain. Every shop had its known clientele, who were afforded credit. The retailers' margins were high.

By contrast the department stores – it was said – used elaborate window dressings and bright lights to tempt clients inside, and faced them with a cornucopia of goods on show once they entered. Shoppers could browse indefinitely without buying. All prices were fixed and shown on tickets. Payment was in cash, but some stores allowed clients to return goods if they were dissatisfied, and gave refunds. Prices might be reduced on slow-moving lines in order to speed turnover.

There is much truth in all of this. However, as is often the case when history tries to draw sharp divisions, the transition was not so clear-cut. Some of these changes had begun a century earlier. There were draperies and fashion shops in London and Paris selling fixed-price, ticketed goods for cash from the late eighteenth century.[22] The sociologist Richard Sennett explains the business reasons.[23] These shops were growing in size and turnover. Haggling over prices wasted time, and in stores with many assistants, the owners were in any case reluctant to entrust such a delicate task to inexperienced juniors. The 'showrooms' and 'warehouses' that appeared in London at this same period selling luxury items like fine china, books or prints, encouraged browsing without obligation.[24] The wares were presented in elaborately decorated cases and shelves. Shopping was certainly a leisurely, pleasurable pastime for rich English and French men and women well before 1800, not least in the Parisian arcades of which the first were built in the 1780s and '90s. As for display windows, these were limited in the eighteenth century by the technology of glassmaking, but by the 1830s there were English shop fronts with panes measuring 4 or 5 ft across.[25] Draperies, 'showrooms' and the arcades pioneered the use of gas lighting from the 1810s.[26]

The department stores were *not* then the first types of shop to have these features. They had all these things certainly: but what was distinctively new was the sheer *scale* of their operations, and the huge variety of goods and services they offered. The 1874 *Au Bon Marché* had 52,800 m^2 of sales space and a staff of 2000. Besides fabrics and readymade clothes for women, men and children, it had departments for shoes, furniture, carpets, stationery and toys. When the owner Aristide Boucicault died in 1877 it was one of France's most successful businesses, and "... probably the largest retail enterprise in the world".[27]

By 1872 William Whiteley had more than 600 employees on site at Westbourne Grove and a further 2000 elsewhere. The total was to rise to over 5000 by the end of the century. Whiteley added food departments in the 1870s, much to the anger of local small grocers, and started to advertise his shop as 'The Universal Provider'.[28] In Chicago, Marshall Field's had grown by 1893 to 100 departments served by 23 elevators and staffed by 3000 employees.[29]

The great volumes of business carried on by the department stores led directly to their second special characteristic: despite the shops' luxurious image, many of the goods were *cheap*. This after all is what *bon marché* means in French. *Au Bon Marché* drew its first customers from the middle class, where other Parisian stores like *Le Louvre* for example served a more

FIGURE 6 *Au Bon Marché*: the reading room. Not much reading seems to be going on. By kind permission of *Bon Marché*, Paris

88 The history and 'evolution' of building types

exclusive, richer clientele. But in all cases they offered better value for money than their smaller competitors. Because of their size the department stores were able to buy in bulk and could strike hard bargains with their suppliers. Some took to manufacturing in their own right. Volumes were high, turnover was fast and prices could be kept low, encouraging yet further growth in sales. If they were well run, the firms were cash-rich, which meant they needed to borrow less. Again, because of their size, stores were obliged to introduce modern methods of management, stock control, cash handling and staff training, all of which led to further efficiencies.

Another way in which the department stores did genuinely differ from most of their predecessors was that, besides adding ever more lines of merchandise, they branched out into a variety of services, comforts and entertainments. The 1874 *Au Bon Marché* had a buffet, furnished like a theatre bar, which served fruit juices and cakes free of charge. There was a reading room with magazines and newspapers (Figure 6), a regular programme of concerts, and an art gallery.[30] Whiteley's in London, at this same date, was adding an estate agency, a cleaning and dyeing service, a hairdressing salon and a restaurant. Other stores put on fashion shows and exhibitions. William Whiteley applied to the Paddington magistrates for a licence to serve alcohol, telling them that many of his customers who came up from the country needed "a glass of wine and a biscuit to sustain their energies".[31] His application was refused, on the grounds that it might lead to immorality; but he did serve some nice fish lunches. It was all these extra attractions of course, along with the shopping, that further encouraged the customers to 'spend the day at the shops'.

Changes due to competition between the department stores and other types of shop

My third generic cause of changes in built form is competition between the businesses or institutions housed. We have already seen how the department stores took custom from smaller older types of shop business by competition on price, as well as by their glittering decor, the great variety of goods on offer, and the range of additional services and entertainments that they provided. There is certainly evidence that dowdy, inefficient, old-fashioned competitors lost custom and were bankrupted. This is the central theme of Émile Zola's 1883 novel *Au Bonheur des Dames* [*Ladies' Delight*] whose setting is the fictional department store of the title, which is nevertheless modelled very closely on *Au Bon Marché*.[32] When William Whiteley branched out into selling food, local small shopkeepers were incensed, as mentioned, and mounted a protest campaign against this unfair infringement of trade.[33] The department stores are also sometimes blamed for the decline in fortune of the shopping arcades, which – it is said – they out-competed in the market for luxury and fashion goods.

Once again, the reality was it seems rather more complex. Whiteley's for example attracted large numbers of shoppers from across a wide radius who actually, as it turned out, brought extra custom to neighbouring small shops. Before the emporium's arrival, Westbourne Grove had been known as 'Bankruptcy Alley'.[34] But the big new store turned round the street's fortunes and attracted rather than discouraged other new shop-owners. The effect was something like that played by the department stores positioned within modern shopping centres and malls as 'magnets' to pull shoppers past the smaller shops.

As for shopping arcades, it is true that very few were built in Paris after the 1840s when the department stores were rising to prominence. But this was a consequence of Haussmann's programme of reconstruction of the city and the creation of the boulevards. If we look internationally, we find that the greatest period for arcade building – but outside France – was between 1860 and 1910, coinciding exactly in time with the glory days of the department store.[35] The two types of business co-existed. It was only in the 1930s that arcades went into decline worldwide, for causes that one might speculate about: the rise of car ownership, the fact that the shops in arcades were small and could not be directly supplied by truck. On the other hand the collective business turnover of the arcades can never have been anywhere near that of the department stores.

The form of the typical top-lit department store

Because of their great size, the department stores of the 1860s onwards took very different built forms from those of older types of shop. They typically occupied one or more entire city blocks, so maximising the numbers of passing pedestrians; and they rose to the *de facto* height limit imposed by people's willingness to climb stairs, of five or six storeys. In practice the sales floors were rarely on more than four floors. The plan of the 1874 *Au Bon Marché* building measures some 75 × 110 m. It was clearly out of the question to light a building of this depth naturally with windows only. There was gas lighting, but this was supplementary, for evenings and dull days. The lighting instead was from the roof, in the case of *Au Bon Marché* via 15 glass-roofed atria of varying sizes (see Figure 2). As a result, no part of the shopping floors was more than 3 m from either a window wall or an atrium. *Le Printemps* of 1881, designed by Paul Sédille, had a single top-lit atrium forming the great 'nave' around which the form of the whole shop was organised (Figure 7).[36]

Valuable floor area was lost to these halls. But they had a compensating virtue, of giving shoppers extensive views throughout the building, from one storey to another. As the architect Boileau said of *Au Bon Marché*, the three sales floors in effect ". . . created a single vessel, or to put in another way, one space surveyable at a glance".[37] It has always been hard to persuade shoppers to move to upper storeys. This difficulty persists even today with the introduction of elevators, or escalators whose first application was in department stores. The designers of the department stores used the atria to give emphasis to highly visible staircases with invitingly shallow slopes (Figure 8). Even from ground level, shoppers could see something of what was on upper storeys behind the cast iron balconies. The shop-owners draped carpets and fabrics over the balustrades to tempt the clientele upstairs. Bridges crossing the atria at upper levels gave even better views.[38]

Earlier shop types lit from the roof

These atria were of unprecedented size for shop buildings. But their construction depended on improvements to the technology of glass roofs that had been going on over the previous hundred years. The department stores were not the first type of shop to be lit from the roof. Some of the eighteenth-century London 'showrooms' and 'warehouses' had roof lights.[39] This was because they occupied deep 'terrace' sites and were presumably unable to acquire adjoining properties on either side into which to expand. Instead they grew upwards and at the back. They could convert upper floors to sales space. Or they could build out over back yards or gardens.

FIGURE 7 *Le Printemps*, Boulevard Haussmann, Paris 1881, architect Paul Sédille: the great nave. From the Chevojon Agency archive, by permission of Carré Destinations

FIGURE 8 *Au Bon Marché*: one of Boileau's atria with shallow staircases and balconies. From the Chevojon Agency archive, by permission of Carré Destinations

FIGURE 9 James Lackington's bookshop 'The Temple of the Muses', Finsbury Square, London 1791: perspective of the interior by Ackermann showing the rotunda and galleries, and at the left the windows onto the street. From R. Ackermann ed., *The Repository of Arts*, London 1809 plate 17

This second option created deep plans, enclosed by adjacent properties, which could not have windows and so could only be day-lit with roof lights. If the sales areas were on several storeys, they had galleried light wells. One of the grandest of these buildings was 'The Temple of the Muses', a showroom for books opened by James Lackington in Finsbury Square in 1791 (Figure 9). It had a very large domed 'ware room' with galleries on four levels, lit from a cupola.[40]

The roof lights in these showrooms were still relatively small. Much larger glazed roofs were introduced from the 1820s into retail establishments in London and Paris known as 'bazaars'. The commercial principle of the bazaar as mentioned was that one proprietor rented space to many small dealers. Typically the tenants were accommodated on the open ground floor and upper balconies of large top-lit spaces. In effect these were market halls for fashion goods and novelties.

One example of this type, of particular architectural interest, was the Pantheon, built as 'assembly rooms' on Oxford Street by James Wyatt in 1772, and converted into a bazaar by Sydney Smirke in 1834.[41] It was a very large hall with a partly glazed barrel vault (Figure 10). There was an art exhibition and a toy bazaar on the galleries. Otherwise the shop sold fashion accessories and children's clothes. Refreshments were available, and there were plants and rare birds on sale in a conservatory. It is easy to see how some British department stores grew from these bazaars, the commercial difference being that in the stores all the goods were sold by a single organisation.

Bernard Marrey says of the Parisian bazaars:

> Up until then, in effect, the boutique could only display its merchandise in windows lit from the street front. Top lighting made it possible to exploit square meterage in

FIGURE 10 The Pantheon Bazaar, Oxford Street, London 1834: conversion by Sydney Smirke from assembly rooms designed by James Wyatt in 1772. With permission of London Metropolitan Archives

the interiors of blocks, whose commercial value was considerably less. Other things being equal, the department stores [and bazaars] paid prices for their locations which were much lower than those paid by traditional businesses. And if this lighting seems rather weak to us today, let us not forget that gas lighting was not then widespread, and that most roads and shops were still lit by candles.[42]

Finally among early shop types with roof lighting there are of course the shopping arcades, which originated in Paris in the 1780s around the same time as the bazaars, and spread to London, to many cities in Europe and to America by the 1840s.[43] (Arguably 'bazaars' might have been a better name for the arcades, given their formal resemblance to the linear vaulted bazaars of the Middle East.) The characteristic form of the arcade as we know is a double row of small shops either side of a passage covered by a glass roof. The shops have shallow plans, are usually without windows on their rear facades, and obtain their light from the passage. Sometimes there are shops on several levels, the upper levels reached by balconies. In other cases there are apartments or offices on the upper floors.

94 The history and 'evolution' of building types

In general the arcades were a means of opening up the interiors of large blocks and so increasing the length of available frontage in densely developed commercial districts. These sites were cheaper than those on the block fronts, as Marrey explains. In Paris, some arcades were built on land confiscated from the Church or the aristocracy during the Revolution. In certain English cities, arcades occupied long thin 'burgage plots' – previously occupied perhaps by inns or elongated courts – inherited from medieval town planning.[44] In all cases they tended to share party walls with other buildings, and had therefore to obtain their daylight just from the passage.

Towards the end of the nineteenth century arcades were built whose size begin to approach that of the department stores. In Moscow the Torgovye Ryadi complex of arcades actually *became* a department store.[45] Built in 1893 to house some 200 separate premises, it was nationalised after 1917 and renamed GUM. It required only a few architectural changes, and the absorption of many small firms into one (state) enterprise, to convert arcade into store.

There was another similarity between the arcades and the department stores: they both offered many kinds of diversion and entertainment besides shopping – although in the arcades these were housed not in the shops themselves but in adjacent premises under the same glass roof. In the Parisian arcades there were cafés, restaurants, bars, gambling rooms, museums, theatres, dance halls, eventually cinemas. The passages themselves, since they were sheltered from the weather, became places for promenading, loitering and smoking in public – the classic haunt indeed of the *flâneur* celebrated by Baudelaire and Benjamin.

There was however one marked difference between the amusements of the arcades and those of the department store. The arcades were dedicated first of all to the pleasures of the male sex. Many of the shops catered to men's tastes and desires: hats, gloves, shows, tailoring and male jewellery, books, tobacco and wines. The French *passages* were places of assignation and flirtation. Several, in both London and Paris, offered discreet prostitution in the upstairs rooms. The department stores on the other hand, despite the misgivings and fears of some men, were most definitely for the delight of women.

Functional failures in construction technology and their correction

For all these varied top-lit shop types – arcades, bazaars, the department stores themselves – one crucial technical issue was the detailed construction of their glass roofs, and specifically how they kept out the rain. At first there were many problems, but by the 1870s these had all been solved. Here is the fourth of my generic causes of change in built forms: the recognition of functional failures, and their correction.

The very earliest buildings with glass roofs were of course horticultural greenhouses: glass buildings for other purposes took over existing greenhouse technology. It was not too important if a greenhouse roof leaked onto the plants, nor if moisture condensing on the under-surface of the glass dripped down again. These problems were perhaps not too serious even in the arcades. Walter Benjamin says that the Passage du Caire 'in several places lacked glass covering' and umbrellas were needed.[46] But clearly, putting out valuable fragile goods for display and sale directly under glass roofs required something better.

Until about 1850 when cast iron came into general use, the glass was framed in timber. With both materials it was difficult to fix and waterproof the panes with putty.[47] Timber was liable to rot. Thermal movements in iron framing caused cracks to open up, and the putty had to be replaced. The iron itself rusted. It was not easy to get access for maintenance and cleaning, and grime accumulated on the glass. In Benjamin's words: ". . . the light that fell from above, through the panes between the iron supports, was dirty and sad".[48] The glass roofs of the late eighteenth and early nineteenth centuries had small thin panes that were easily broken. Bigger sheets became cheaper in Britain in the 1840s but their weight could distort the frames.

Over the century these failings were progressively overcome. The bigger horticultural glasshouses had ventilation systems that stopped condensation, as did the later arcades. Joseph Paxton, designer of the Hyde Park Crystal Palace, introduced methods of carrying rainwater away down grooved channels in the (wooden) glazing bars of the roofs. In the 1870s lead 'cames' – grooved strips of lead, as used in stained glass windows – were substituted for timber bars.[49] 'Patent glazing' invented in the 1890s also had grooved bars, and allowed for thermal expansion by overlapping the glass panes.

The innovation in design that took glazed roofs to another level of sophistication however was to have *two* skins of glass, one over the other, separated by a large ventilation and access space.[50] The top roof was of clear glass to admit maximum daylight, and steeply sloped to throw off rain and snow. The lower roof could be shallow in slope, even flat, and could be

FIGURE 11 *Au Bon Marché*: section by Boileau showing atria with two glass roofs one above the other. From *Encyclopédie d'Architecture* Vol. IX 1880 plate 660

96 The history and 'evolution' of building types

treated decoratively in stained or translucent glass. The weather-resisting structure above was concealed. Only minimal amounts of dust collected on the upper surface of the lower roof. The two skins created better thermal insulation, and the space between them allowed access for maintenance.

Figure 11 shows this form of roof construction in section at *Au Bon Marché*. Boileau gave the lower skin a decorative pattern of squares and rectangles, and gave the outer roof a steep double pitch that over-sails the lower roof and has its own gutters.[51] At *Le Printemps* the great nave, 12 m across, was again spanned by two separate iron structures, the lower arches carrying a stained glass barrel vault, and the upper roof supporting a pitched clear glass cover.[52] This fully mature technology meant that the department stores' roofs could be watertight while the atria were still naturally ventilated, and allowed ornamental treatments of the glass that were among the shops' greatest beauties (see Figure 7).

Changes in the technology of building services

The *Au Bon Marché* building of 1874 was equipped throughout with gas lighting.[53] *Le Printemps* of 1881 was lit entirely by electricity. This was the moment when the lighting of the great stores changed, with profound effects in due course for their built forms and internal organisation. (*Au Bon Marché* replaced all its gas lights with electric in 1888.)

Electric lighting was attractive to store owners for a number of reasons. Edison's and Swan's new incandescent bulbs could give a brighter light than standard gas fittings. They were clean and relatively cool, where gaslights produced soot and gave off carbon dioxide. And electricity was less dangerous. (Gas had been the cause of many department store fires in the nineteenth century.) At first electric lighting was more expensive, but this was not so important for large commercial organisations. And electricity offered possibilities for enchanting decorative displays as well as functional illumination. By 1900 electric lighting had become universal in the department stores.

Because lighting by electricity was less dirty and created less heat than gas lighting, it allowed for lower ceilings and brought about the introduction, in the United States, of the 'horizontal style' of department store, of which Louis Sullivan's Schlesinger and Mayer building in Chicago (later the Carson, Pirie and Scott store) was the first (Figure 12).[54] Here there were no atria and the floors had unbroken open plans.

Eric Mendelsohn had seen and admired Sullivan's building in 1924, and in the late 1920s and '30s designed stores in Germany for C A Herpich and Sons and the Schocken chain, again with low ceilings and a strong horizontal emphasis in the facades.[55] From the very first of these schemes, Mendelsohn turned the upper-floor windows into continuous high-level strips that allowed goods to be displayed against the lower parts of the walls. The horizontal glazing when illuminated at night became a dramatic means of advertising the stores. These buildings however had shallow plans and were naturally ventilated.

A kind of inertia in design thinking meant that many department stores continued to be lit naturally with central light wells on the nineteenth-century model, even when equipped throughout with electric lighting. One reason was that the atria performed a second important function in deep-plan stores, that of helping the ventilation. Warm stale air rose in the multi-storey voids and was vented through openings in the doubled glass roof structure. But if buildings with deep plans could be ventilated artificially, the atria would become redundant and could be filled in.

FIGURE 12 Carson, Pirie and Scott store (originally the Schlesinger and Mayer store), State and Madison Streets, Chicago 1899, extended 1903–04 and 1906, Louis Sullivan and D H Burnham Co, architects. Photo: Chicago Architectural Photographing Co. Richard Nickel Archive, Ryerson and Burnham Archives, The Art Institute of Chicago, digital file 201006_120810_005, with kind permission

Stores wanted increasingly to make this change because the atria represented such a large loss of potential sales area. As Kathryn Morrison says, by the 1920s architects were faced with a clear choice. They could either "... create stores with spectacular wells that provided customers with dramatic views of the establishment and admitted daylight to the interiors of sales floors, or they could adopt the American 'horizontal' system, and build open-plan floors". These "... had the advantage of a great deal of extra floor space, something that was becoming more valuable than either natural lighting or theatrical spectacle".[56]

Sales methods were beginning to change. More of the stock was being taken out of cupboards and put on show on racks or in glass cases. Customers were being encouraged to browse more freely among the goods. All this required more space both for the merchandise and the aisles. Peripheral windows on the upper floors and in particular glass curtain walls were coming to be seen as a liability. They created glare and caused fabrics to fade. Electric lighting was more controllable. If windows were replaced – at least in part – by solid walls

98 The history and 'evolution' of building types

as in the Mendelsohn stores, more goods could be shown around the edges of the open plan. Writing in 1928 the architect Howard Robertson asked whether large windows were even desirable in stores, since "wall space seems to be a greater desideratum than floods of natural light".[57]

The second technology that could make it possible to dispense with windows altogether was of course air conditioning. The first type of building to have air conditioning for the comfort of the occupants was the movie theatre, closely followed by the department store. By the 1920s several American stores were fully air-conditioned including Abraham and Strauss and Macy's in New York, and Filene's in Boston.[58] In France the established Parisian design tradition was broken for the first time by the architect Pierre Patout in an un-built scheme for *Galeries Lafayette* of 1932.[59] Patout reduced the fenestration to thin vertical strips of fixed glass blocks, and planned for full air conditioning.

All these were buildings with windows, albeit in some cases small ones. By the late 1920s the design press was talking however about the ultimate conclusion of this trend, the windowless store. Writing in 1935 the English architect C H Reilly was speculating on this possibility as something well into the future. "If daylight electric lamps were really perfect and cheap, and artificial ventilation too, [a] logical solution might be to exclude the daylight altogether, and have blank walls on the inside on which to hang things."[60] But this was already happening in America. In 1934 Sears Roebuck built a store with no windows above the ground floor at Englewood in Chicago, and in 1939 completed the windowless store in Los Angeles illustrated at the start of this paper (Figure 3).[61] No other company followed Sears' lead before World War II, but after 1945 the type was to become general in suburban and out-of-town locations.

Many of the older stores – even in Paris – filled in their grand top-lit naves, wells and rotundas. At *Au Bon Marché* little is left of the former glories of the atria other than a few of Boileau's roof lights, still visible on the third floor. The grand staircases have gone, replaced by escalators. *Le Printemps* survives but not its great nave. Bernard Marrey ends his book on the *grands magasins* with a lament for the sad fate of these spectacular interiors, victims of twentieth-century building services and the high price of retail floor space.

> The great halls, which evoked by analogy the image of modern cathedrals of commerce, could not be justified any more, now that electricity could supply daylight (at a cost, it is true, that is ever more difficult to measure), and that ventilation ducts, at least in theory, could supply air to the shops.[62]

Shopping by car, and a new form for the suburban department store

The Sears Roebuck building of Figure 3 brings us back to our first theme, the effects on built form of wider changes in transport technology. It is no accident that we find this particular example of the type in Los Angeles, the place where car ownership grew faster than any other city in the United States, in the 1910s and '20s.[63] It was the automobile that created the unprecedented low density and dispersed morphology of LA, which has always had one weak centre in the original settlement of Los Angeles – today's 'downtown' – but which otherwise was formed from an archipelago of widely scattered small towns, connected together at first by electric railways, and then by road.

There were department stores established in downtown LA in the early years of the century, whose architecture was comparable with nineteenth-century European and East Coast store buildings. Shopping in these stores, in Richard Longstreth's words, "became at once a frequent pastime and ritual indulgence among millions of consumers, especially middle-class women".[64] By the mid-'20s many of these women drove or were being chauffeured in their own automobiles. The streets of old Los Angeles were narrow however, and carried trams and light rail as well as car traffic. In 1920 there was a serious crisis of congestion – the first in the USA – and the City Council instituted a ban on kerbside parking. There was a huge outcry, the takings of the stores dropped disastrously, and the ban was rescinded after just 19 days. This episode however marked the beginning of a process that led to branches of the downtown stores, and later the flagship stores themselves, migrating to the satellite towns of the metropolis like Hollywood and Pasadena.[65] Here they could find large cheaper sites to which access was easier for car drivers, and where new buildings could be erected on one or two storeys so that the difficulties of getting shoppers upstairs would no longer apply.

Many of these new suburban stores retained a prestigious luxury image and catered to a rich clientele among Angelenos. Sears Roebuck, a mail order company based in Chicago, entered the retail business at this time and took a different approach.[66] Sears had recognised how completely the car had changed shopping behaviour, and that ". . . the outlying store . . . with lower land values, could give parking space; with lower overhead, rent and taxes, could lower operating costs, and could with its enlarged clientele created by the automobile offer effective competition to the downtown store".[67] Sears's strategy in the 1930s was accordingly to select non-retail locations well outside established urban centres. The Pico Boulevard store is about a mile and a half away from the old township of Santa Monica. Sears built large plain buildings where the methods pioneered by chain stores, including self-service, were used to sell large quantities of basic goods at competitive prices. Sears always invested heavily in advertising, in particular through its mail order catalogue, and this in turn attracted shoppers to its retail stores.

Air conditioning and an almost total reliance on artificial lighting allowed for very deep plans. The fact that the great majority of the customers arrived by car, and there were few if any passing pedestrians, meant that traditional display windows served little purpose and could be dispensed with. Also the store could be moved back from the street line allowing parking in front as well as at the back and sides. A tower or an illuminated sign on a pylon could make the store's location visible to passing drivers.

Internally the new built form allowed for a radical reorganisation. Typically the services were pulled to the periphery, since it was no longer necessary or desirable for the sales areas to have windows and they could be central. The offices – and perhaps a café or restaurant – could be naturally lit on the edge of the plan, or on the roof. At the same time delivery trucks could be driven right up to the building and unloaded directly into the ground-level stock rooms. The middle of the plan was unobstructed and the sales areas could be flexibly arranged and rearranged. Figure 13 shows a diagram by William Snaith, a post-War store designer, of 'the proper interrelationship of trucking, bulk and impulse merchandise, entrances and parking' in a single-storey plan of this type.[68] By comparison with the nineteenth-century stores, the plan is turned inside out, and all of the design effort is transferred to the interior. Similar principles were adopted in most post-War suburban stores, and were extended and elaborated in the new out-of-town shopping malls.

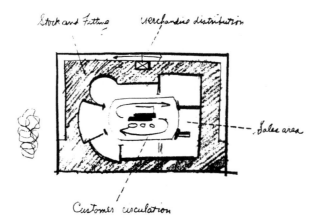

FIGURE 13 Basic arrangement of services and circulation surrounding sales areas in a post-War deep-plan store, sketched by the designer William T Snaith. From Hornbeck ed., *Stores and Shopping Centers*

Conclusion

Changes in the built forms associated with particular activities are historically contingent, and are brought about by many local social, economic and technical factors specific to the periods in question, as we have seen in the case of the department store. Some of the broader trends discussed here, for example developments in transport technology, and the move to air conditioning and artificial lighting, have nevertheless had comparable effects on the built forms of other types of business and institution over the same timeframe, such as offices, warehouses and factories. The rise of car ownership and the use of motor trucks have brought about similar moves towards low-rise deep-plan built forms on large suburban sites. Taking a wider view still, I have proposed a four-way categorisation of forces for change, exemplified here with the case of retail. I would suggest that this has potential as an abstract scheme for analysis of the history of many building types.[69]

Notes

1. The history of *Au Bon Marché* as a business is recounted by Michael B Miller, *The Bon Marché. Bourgeois Culture and the Department Store, 1869–1920*, Princeton University Press, Princeton NJ 1981. Bernard Marrey describes the process of design and construction, with many illustrations, in *Les Grand Magasins des Origines à 1939*, Librairie Picard, Paris 1979 pp. 59–83. *Au Bon Marché* still trades in the building today. The exterior is little changed but the interior is much altered, as described below.
2. The name of Eiffel has often been associated with the design of the building, but his involvement is questioned by Robert Proctor, 'A Cubist history: the department store in late nineteenth-century Paris', *Transactions of the Royal Historical Society* Vol. 13, 2003, pp. 227–235; see p. 231.
3. See Richard Longstreth, *City Center to Regional Mall: Architecture, the Automobile, and Retailing in Los Angeles, 1920–1950*, MIT Press, Cambridge MA 1997 p. 252 and Figure 173.
4. For a discussion of the effects of these four forces on built form types more generally, see Philip Steadman, *Building Types and Built Forms*, Troubador, Leicestershire 2014, pp. 367–373.
5. See John William Ferry, *A History of the Department Store*, Macmillan, New York 1960 for separate histories of many American and British businesses. B Marrey, *Grands Magasins* provides a history of French stores up to 1939.

The changing department store building **101**

6 See Kathryn Morrison, *English Shops and Shopping*, Yale University Press, New Haven CT 2003 p. 160 Figure 159.

7 See B Marrey *Grands Magasins* pp. 249–256.

8 Mona Domosh, 'Shaping the commercial city: retail districts in Nineteenth Century New York and Boston', *Annals of the Association of American Geographers* Vol. 80 No. 2, June 1990 pp. 268–284.

9 Alison Adburgham, *Shops and Shopping 1800–1914*, Barrie and Jenkins, London 1964 p. 93.

10 See *Dickens's Dictionary of London*, Charles Dickens, London 1879, pp. 168–189; and Alfred Martin, *Étude Historique et Statistique sur les Moyens de Transport dans Paris*, Imprimerie Nationale, Paris 1894.

11 Gordon Honeycombe, *Selfridges: Seventy-Five Years. The Story of the Store 1909–1984*, Park Lane Press, London 1984 p. 181.

12 Richard S Lambert, *The Universal Provider: A Study of William Whiteley and the Rise of the London Department Store*, Harrap, London 1938 p. 73.

13 Gwen Raverat, *Period Piece: A Cambridge Childhood*, Faber and Faber, London 1960 p. 95.

14 There is a sizeable feminist literature on women and the department store. See *inter alia*: Christopher P Hosgood, '"Doing the shops" at Christmas: Women, men and the department store in England, c.1880–1914' in Geoffrey Crossick and Serge Jaumain, eds, *Cathedrals of Consumption: The European Department Store, 1850–1939*, Ashgate, Aldershot 1999 pp. 97–107; Lisa Tiersten, 'Marianne in the department store: Gender and the politics of consumption in turn-of-the-century Paris' in Crossick and Jaumain, *Cathedrals of Consumption* pp. 116–126; William R Leach, 'Transformations in a culture of consumption: Women and Department Stores, 1890–1925', *The Journal of American History* Vol. 71 No. 2, September 1984 pp. 319–342; Mona Domosh, 'The feminized retail landscape: Gender, ideology and consumer culture in nineteenth-century New York City' in Neil Wrigley and Michelle Lowe, eds, *Retailing, Consumption and Capital*, Longman, Harlow 1996, pp. 257–270; and Erika Diane Rappoport, *Shopping for Pleasure: Women in the Making of London's West End*, Princeton University Press, Princeton NJ 2000.

15 Bill Lancaster, *The Department Store: A Social History*, Leicester University Press, London and New York 1995, p. 171.

16 Honeycombe, *Selfridges* p. 24.

17 Rappoport, *Shopping for Pleasure* pp. 215–217.

18 Lancaster, *The Department Store* p. 192.

19 Miller, *Bon Marché* p. 21, p. 25.

20 See Ferry, *History of the Department Store*. The term 'dry goods' originated in colonial New England, where merchants imported two principal commodities, rum ('wet goods') and calico ('dry goods').

21 Ibid., pp. 124–137, and pp. 204–221.

22 Dorothy Davis (*A History of Shopping*, Purnell Book Services, London 1966 p. 187) gives the example of Flint and Palmer's drapery and haberdashery, which operated on Old London Bridge in the mid-eighteenth century. Miller (*Bon Marché* p. 23) says that *Le Petit Dunkerque*, a Parisian fashion shop, adopted a fixed pricing policy at the end of the century.

23 Richard Sennett, *The Fall of Public Man*, Cambridge University Press, Cambridge 1977 p. 142. Sennett sees this as just one example of a general trend towards impersonal, anonymous interactions among strangers in the nineteenth-century city.

24 Claire Walsh, 'The newness of the department store: A view from the eighteenth century' in Crossick and Jaumain, *Cathedrals of Consumption* pp. 46–71.

25 Mary Eldridge, 'The Plate-Glass Shop Front', *Architectural Review* Vol. 123, March 1958, pp. 192–195.

26 For gas lighting in the arcades, see Johann Friedrich Geist, *Arcades: The History of a Building Type*, MIT Press, Cambridge MA 1983.

27 Miller, *Bon Marché* p. 40.

28 Lambert, *Universal Provider* pp. 72–73; Ferry, *History of the Department Store* pp. 204–209.

29 Lloyd Wendt and Herman Kogan, *Give the Lady What She Wants! The Story of Marshall Field and Company*, And books, South Bend, Indiana 1952 p. 167, pp. 217–218.

30 Miller, *Bon Marché* p. 168 and p. 171.

31 Lambert, *Universal Provider* pp. 72–73.

32 Émile Zola, *Au Bonheur des Dames*, Paris 1883; translated in 1886 as *Ladies' Paradise* and again in 1957 by April Fitzlyon as *Ladies' Delight*, John Calder, London.

33 Lambert, *Universal Provider* p. 76.

34 Ibid., p. 61.

102 The history and 'evolution' of building types

35 See Geist, *Arcades*, in particular pp. 124–129. Also Steadman, *Building Types and Built Forms* pp. 364–366.

36 See Marrey, *Grands Magasins* pp. 96–109.

37 L C Boileau, 'Magasins du Bon-Marché, à Paris', *Encyclopédie d'Architecture*, Deuxième Série, Vol. IX 1880 p. 183; my translation.

38 Some analyses of visibility in these department store atria, as well as in shopping arcades, using 2D and 3D isovists, are given in Steadman, *Building Types and Built Forms* pp. 330–333.

39 See Morrison, *Shops and Shopping* pp. 34–40 for a history of these buildings.

40 Ibid., p. 38.

41 Ibid., p. 92 and pp. 95–96.

42 Marrey, *Grands Magasins* p. 20; my translation.

43 Geist, *Arcades* is the most comprehensive history. See also Margaret MacKeith, *The History and Conservation of Shopping Arcades*, Mansell, London and New York, 1986.

44 MacKeith, *Shopping Arcades* pp. 65–66.

45 Ibid., pp. 61–62.

46 Walter Benjamin, *The Arcades Project*, trans. Howard Eiland and Kevin McLaughlin, Belknap Press of Harvard University Press, Cambridge MA 1999 p. 33.

47 See MacKeith, *Shopping Arcades* pp. 80–82 for a general discussion.

48 Benjamin, *Arcades Project* p. 150.

49 Raymond McGrath and A C Frost, *Glass in Architecture and Decoration*, The Architectural Press, London 1937 pp. 176–178; also MacKeith, *Shopping Arcades* p. 146.

50 For a discussion see Robert Bruegmann, 'Central heating and forced ventilation: Origins and effects on architectural design', *Journal of the Society of Architectural Historians* Vol. 37, October 1978, pp. 143–160; see pp. 151–152 and Figure 15.

51 Marrey, *Grands Magasins* Figures 70 to 73, pp. 81–83.

52 Ibid., Figure 98 p. 105.

53 *Encyclopédie d'Architecture* Vol. IV 1885, pp. 31–33.

54 Carl W Condit, *The Chicago School of Architecture*, University of Chicago Press, Chicago IL and London 1964 pp. 162–166.

55 Regina Stephan, 'Department stores in Berlin, Breslau, Chemnitz, Duisburg, Nuremberg, Oslo and Stuttgart, 1924–1932' in Regina Stephen, ed., *Eric Mendelsohn Architect 1887–1953*, Monacelli Press, New York 1979 pp. 72–109.

56 Morrison, *English Shops and Shopping* p. 173.

57 Howard Robertson *Architect and Building News*, 10 February 1928, pp. 227–230.

58 Sze Tsung Leong, with Srdjan Jovanovich Weiss, 'Air conditioning', in Chuihua Judy Chung *et al.* eds, *Harvard Design School Guide to Shopping*, Taschen, Koln 2001 pp. 92–107; see p. 109.

59 Marrey, *Grands Magasins* pp. 237–241.

60 C H Reilly, 'Criticism. 3. The Modern Store', *Architectural Review* May 1935, pp. 217–219; see p. 218.

61 Longstreth, *City Center to Regional Mall* pp. 252–253.

62 Marrey, *Grands Magasins* p. 246; my translation.

63 For the spatial development of Los Angeles, see Robert M Fogelson, *The Fragmented Metropolis: Los Angeles, 1920–1950*, MIT Press, Cambridge MA 1967. For the effects of cars on the city, see Scott L Bottles, *Los Angeles and the Automobile: The Making of the Modern City*, University of California Press, Berkeley and Los Angeles CA 1987.

64 Richard Longstreth, *The Drive-in, the Supermarket, and the Transformation of Commercial Space in Los Angeles, 1914–1941*, MIT Press, Cambridge MA 1999 p. 25.

65 See Longstreth, *City Center to Regional Mall* Chapters III to V.

66 Ibid., pp. 119–120 and pp. 251–254.

67 R E Wood, vice-president of Sears, quoted in James Worthy, *Shaping the American Institution: Robert E Wood and Sears Roebuck*, University of Illinois Press, Urbana and Chicago IL 1984 p. 83.

68 William T Snaith, 'How retailing principles affect design' in James S Hornbeck, ed., *Stores and Shopping Centers*, McGraw-Hill, New York 1962 pp. 2–10; see p. 6.

69 For an extended discussion in relation to nineteenth- and early-twentieth century hospitals, schools, offices and prisons, see Steadman, *Building Types and Built Forms* Chapter 11, 'Building types and how they change over time'.

6

EVOLUTION OF A BUILDING TYPE

The case of the multi-storey garage

(*Journal of Space Syntax*, Volume 2, Number 1, 2011, pp. 1–25)

The form of the department store (Paper 5) could be described as undergoing an 'evolution' between 1870 and 1940, using that word in its pre-Darwinian sense, of a process of change or development of any kind. In the case of the multi-storey garage, we find something more closely resembling a Darwinian evolutionary process – although there are great dangers in drawing too simplistic a biological analogy. Many designers, only a few of whose names are recorded, worked on various solutions to the problems posed by this wholly novel building type when it first appeared in the 1920s and '30s. These garage designs were in commercial competition, in changing economic, social and technological environments.

Some garage sub-types proved to have advantages and multiplied, while others failed and died out. In this paper a few simple quantitative measures are used to compare the relative 'fitness' of these competing designs. The analysis uses historical data. It also makes comparisons, on a common basis, of a range of specially designed theoretical garage buildings. I suggest that the process of garage evolution has some affinities with what is known by Darwinists as 'evolutionary radiation', where a new unoccupied environment is colonised by a single species that rapidly evolves into a variety of different forms.

Where analogies of the evolution of artefacts with organic evolution go seriously wrong, is to imagine in effect that the process is one of blind trial and error. In this way the knowledge, intentions and skills of individual designers are underplayed and overlooked. Those contributions are not ignored here: credit is given where possible to some successful inventors of new garage sub-types.

The paper was given originally at the Design History Society conference on 'Design and Evolution' held at the Technological University Delft, Holland, in August/September 2006.

The emergence of the multi-storey garage in the early 1900s

In the years immediately before World War I an entirely new type of building appeared in American cities: the multi-storey parking garage.[1] Car ownership grew rapidly in the US in the early part of the century, from under half a million in 1910 to more than 8 million by 1920.[2] The first automobiles were expensive and fragile, with open tops, and paintwork that was not as weather-resistant as today's finishes. They were generally kept indoors, and put into storage for the winter.[3] At first old buildings were converted for the purpose. Some of the earliest purpose-built garages were erected by private motoring organisations such as

104 The history and 'evolution' of building types

the Massachusetts Automobile Club, whose three-storey building was opened in 1902. Automobile dealers kept their stock in garages. Other garages were built in wealthy residential areas where the new car owners were concentrated, or near expensive hotels. In some of these structures, cars were stored on floors above ground.

By the early 1920s larger cities were already experiencing traffic congestion in their central streets, exacerbated by kerbside parking. In Chicago the situation in the Loop was such that proposals were being made to raise all sidewalks to upper levels so as to free up more road space.[4] Los Angeles, which had more cars per person than any other city at this period, experienced a serious crisis in 1920 that resulted in a temporary ban on street parking downtown.[5] It was in this context that a new market appeared for multi-storey buildings devoted to daily or short-term parking, by commuters or shoppers. Seven large high-rise garages were built for example in LA between 1923 and 1928.[6]

Some of the earliest parking buildings raised the cars to the upper levels with modified freight elevators. Garages were also built with ramps. The ramp buildings were of a great variety of different designs: with straight or helical ramps; with the ramps placed inside the building, on the exterior, or in central courtyards; with split-level floors connected by half-length ramps – each generic layout found in several variants. I will go into more detail later. In Europe, few multi-storey garages were built before World War II, one notable exception being the giant *Autorimessa* in Venice, designed by Eugenio Miozzi and completed in 1934. The subject nevertheless attracted considerable pre-War interest among European engineers, of whom the most prominent was Professor Georg Müller, 'the pioneer of the modern garage' and author of *Grosstadt-Garagen*, the first book on the subject, published in 1925.[7] Many theoretical designs were proposed, and numerous patents were taken out. Müller lists 35 US and six European patents up to 1924, the first of them awarded in 1913.

The elevator garage survived until the 1960s, but soon after that almost completely vanished from both Europe and America. Out of the great diversity of pre-War types of ramp garage, many were also abandoned by the late 1950s; and the majority of garages then operating in America were designs with split-levels and so-called D'Humy ramps.[8] Why did this happen? In this paper I argue that we have here a particularly clear-cut and instructive example of the evolution of a building type, under the pressures of a changing economic and technological environment.

A case study in the evolution of a building type

Multi-storey garages are not, it must be admitted, the most interesting or challenging type of building from an architectural point of view. True, they have on occasion attracted the attention of leading names, as for example Paul Rudolph's sculptural Temple Street garage in Newhaven, Connecticut, or Louis Kahn's project for cylindrical fort-like parking towers in Philadelphia. In general though, as *The Architectural Record* remarked, "Parking garage operators . . . assign 'architecture' to the outer six inches of their buildings."[9] The very simplicity of garages however makes them an ideal subject for a semi-quantitative evolutionary analysis. Evidently, they have just one basic function: to provide space in which to park cars on upper floor levels (as well as on the ground). Some means are needed to get the cars to these positions, and to retrieve them again, in both cases as rapidly as possible. (Although there can be further considerations relating to access, as we shall see.) In general, these being utilitarian structures, many of them run for profit, the costs of both construction and operation need to be kept low. These various requirements could possibly be combined into a single objective function, capable of mathematical optimisation – although no attempt is made to do so here.

The word 'evolution' should however be used cautiously in relation to buildings.[10] There has been some interest among architectural researchers in computer-based 'evolutionary design methods', where candidate designs are varied at random, evaluated, selected, varied again and so on in a cyclic process, loosely analogous to natural evolution, but speeded up in the laboratory of a computer simulation.[11] The purpose is to arrive at the design for some particular individual building. In this paper, by contrast, I consider a process of gradual change in the form and internal arrangement of a *type*, taking place over decades, and involving thousands of real buildings actually tested in use and in the marketplace.

One of the dangers of applying biological analogies simplistically to the 'evolution' of building types is that the deliberate intentions of individual architects and engineers are thereby underrated and overlooked. If types of building can be said to evolve at all, this is most definitely *not* – at least in modern design practice – through 'random variations'. The many designers of multi-storey car parks have had very definite (although not always completely rational) ideas about how their particular schemes could provide advantages over other designs. This said there *is* nevertheless a sense in which all these designers have worked collectively, through the first half of the twentieth century, to explore a world of slightly differing possibilities for car park architecture. At times they have, in effect, searched this world unsystematically, even 'blindly' – although after a while the comparative merits of some of the alternatives have become generally known.

The fact that different designs were in direct economic competition was recognised very early. As the *Architectural Record* put it: "Because the parking garage business is still in its infancy, commercial garages must necessarily be extremely efficient from the economic standpoint if they are to compete with future buildings of improved character . . ."[12] And there *is* a sense in which external factors in the 'environment' of car parks, such as the cost of labour, the design of cars, and the changing preferences and concerns of car drivers have acted, at different times, to make certain designs of building more useable, efficient or profitable than others. In these limited senses then, the use of concepts borrowed from evolutionary biology has some validity. We will come back to these evolutionary issues at the end of the paper.

Elevator garages, and parking by attendants

Meanwhile let us look in some more detail at the history of high-rise car parks in the twentieth century. Today it is general practice for drivers to park their own cars. This was not the case in the United States in the 1920s and '30s and even for some time after World War II. The early elevator garages were worked by attendants who moved the cars on and off the lifts. (Later the process was completely automated.) Up to the 1950s it was normal also for attendants to park the cars in ramp garages. Once having parked a car, an attendant would slide to ground level down poles like those used by firemen. To get to the upper levels to retrieve a car, he would ascend by paternoster or 'manlift' (Figure 1).

It seems that Americans' reluctance to park their own cars in this period was partly to do with lack of driving skills and the failings of automobile technology. Early, low-powered models had difficulties on stiff inclines. It was believed that women in particular were daunted

FIGURE 1 Garage attendants ascending by paternoster and descending by slide pole; from Baker and Funaro, *Parking* 1958

by the prospect of negotiating steep slopes and sharp turns. Two American authors writing in 1958 say for example that, with the introduction of automatic gear shifts, "Women drivers no longer fear gear-changing or running backwards down ramps".[13] Parking by skilled attendants had the minor advantage that bays and aisles could be made somewhat smaller than for customer parking. By contrast with the States, attendant parking was never popular in Europe. Dietrich Klose says in his book *Multi-Storey Car Parks and Garages* that this was because ". . . the [European] motorist does not like to part with his car, and . . . because rapid handling is impeded by the multiplicity of car types with different controls".[14]

In summary then, we can distinguish four classes of high-rise garage according to the means of access and how cars are parked:

- elevator garages, attendant parking;
- elevator garages, automatic;
- ramp garages, attendant parking;
- ramp garages, customer parking.

As mentioned, elevator garages were being built in the USA in the 1920s and '30s, as for example the Pure Oil garage in Chicago, and the Kent garages in Chicago, New York and Cincinnati.[15] Typically, these buildings had half a dozen stalls clustered around each elevator on every level. The Kent Garage in New York accommodated 12 cars per lift per floor.[16]

In some cases, one elevator could carry several cars. Hill's Garage in Los Angeles for example, which opened in 1928, had three elevators each of which carried three automobiles.[17] Cars were either driven from elevator to stall, or were pushed on dollies. The result was buildings with small footprints, which could be fitted onto expensive and constricted central sites. But in order to get sufficient car places served by one or a few elevators to make the operation economic, it was necessary to build very high – up to 24 storeys at the highest. This increased the cost of construction.

Even more important, it meant that the process of parking and retrieving cars was extremely slow. This had the knock-on effect that, at peak times, a queue could develop at the entrance, and extra 'reservoir' space had to be provided at ground level for cars waiting to be parked. When picking up their cars at peak times, drivers could wait 20 minutes or more. One further weakness was that the elevators themselves were costly to maintain, and liable to occasional electrical or mechanical failure, in which case the cars were trapped. All these problems led to the general demise of the simple elevator type garage by the late 1930s. According to Jakle and Sculle in their book *Lots of Parking*, all of Manhattan's elevator garages went bankrupt in the Depression.[18] (On the other hand an article in the *Architectural Record* in 1958 mentions that two pre-War elevator garages were still operating in the 1950s, the New York Kent Garage and the Park-O-Mat in Washington DC.[19]) Müller in his book shows a number of theoretical schemes for elevator car parks with circular or octagonal plans – but these it seems were never built.[20]

After the Second World War a new generation of elevator garages emerged, and a number of manufacturing companies were formed, some of them quite successful for a period. Their success depended on significant changes in design and methods of operation. One common feature was extensive automation, so that it was no longer necessary to employ large numbers

FIGURE 2 Zidpark elevator garage, Upper Thames Street, London 1961; from Klose, *Multi-Storey Car Parks and Garages* 1965

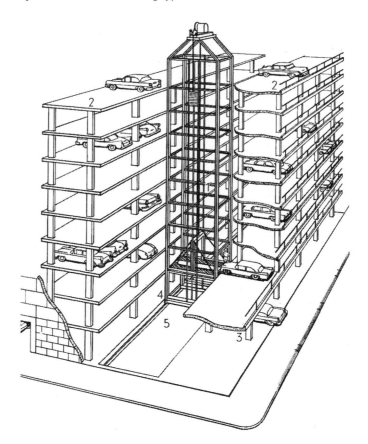

FIGURE 3 Principle of the 'pigeon hole' type garage, with a central elevator tower moving horizontally along a void between the car stalls; from Klose, *Multi-Storey Car Parks and Garages* 1965

of attendants – an important consideration given post-War increases in labour costs. The Zidpark system resembled the pre-War elevator garages, but with many elevators and their associated stalls, packed close together. Car drivers left their vehicles in the lifts at ground level. On each upper level there were four stalls associated with each lift, the cars being moved sideways into the stalls on dollies. The whole process was automatic, and was operated from a central control panel. Figure 2 shows a Zidpark garage built in Upper Thames Street, London in 1961.

In other systems such as those of the US-based Bowser Parking System and Pigeon Hole Parking companies, the key innovation was the introduction of elevators capable of moving vertically *and horizontally* at the same time along an elongated central shaft or slot in the building, with parking places ranged – like pigeonholes, precisely – on either side (Figure 3). In this way, one elevator could serve a much-increased number of stalls on each level. Like the pre-War mechanical garages, such buildings were specially suited to restricted downtown sites. The Autosilo company of Heidelberg developed a very comparable type of pigeonhole system for the European market. The basic idea was not entirely new. Müller illustrates several proposals, and one actual completed building in Paris dating from the 1920s (Figure 4), with

FIGURE 4 Elevator garage with moveable bridges for transferring cars from the elevator to the stalls, Paris, 1920s; from Müller, *Grosstadt-Garagen* 1925

FIGURE 5 Pigeon Hole garage serving a hotel in Harrisburg, Pennsylvania, 1950s; from Baker and Funaro, *Parking* 1958

FIGURE 6 The control panel of a Bowser garage; from Klose, *Multi-Storey Car Parks and Garages* 1965

car parking bays on several storeys either side of a central top-lit hall, fixed elevators, and light moveable bridges to carry the cars along the hall.[21] The post-War systems differed by virtue of having the lift itself move laterally, and under automatic control.

Bowser and Pigeon Hole came to be the main competing manufacturers of elevator garage systems in America. The first Pigeon Hole installation was built in 1950; the first Bowser garage in Des Moines, Iowa, in 1951. In the Pigeon Hole system the elevator tower moved on rails (Figure 5). In the Bowser system it was suspended from an overhead gantry. As Baker and Funaro say in their book *Parking*, this lateral movement was "... the all-important difference between these elevator systems and those which proved unsuccessful in the Thirties".[22] Bowser had attendants driving the cars from elevator to stall, and had cars packed two deep on one side of the elevator shaft, the back rows being offered to all-day parkers at lower rates. (The penalty was that it was still sometimes necessary to move the cars in front to retrieve those behind.) Pigeon Hole moved the cars automatically on dollies. Figure 6 shows the control panel for a Bowser garage. The structures of these buildings could be just

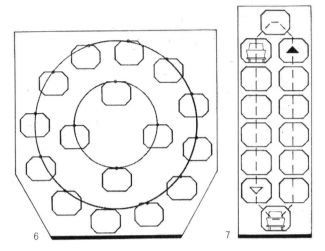

FIGURE 7 Diagrams to show garages based on the Ferris wheel and paternoster principles; from Klose, *Multi-Storey Car Parks and Garages* 1965

minimal steel cages, and the stalls could have restricted widths and heights compared with those needed for driver parking. One general problem with mechanical garages, on the other hand, was that the stall sizes were fitted inflexibly to particular car dimensions, whereas stall dimensions could, to an extent, be adjusted in large ramp garages with wide structural spans, when fashions in car size changed.

Yet further types of automatic parking system were developed by other companies using the principle of the paternoster or the Ferris wheel. Here the parking stalls were moved to meet the cars, rather than the other way round. An endless chain of stalls or cages was moved past the point at which the cars were loaded and unloaded (Figure 7). Westinghouse had been experimenting with a prototype Ferris wheel design as early as 1937. Such systems seem not to have met with much success, presumably because of the time taken for parking and retrieving cars in large installations. Klose says in 1965, "Up to now, such parking facilities have only been built as minor units."[23] Little more is heard of them.

This question of parking and retrieval times undoubtedly proved critical in the final showdown between elevator garages and ramp garages that took place in the 1960s. Table 1 is reproduced, with some adaptation, from Klose and gives operating statistics for 15 multi-storey garages around the world. The figures were supplied by the builders and operators and should therefore perhaps be treated with a little caution. The overall picture is however clear enough. The table gives basic data in each case on number of floors and number of car places ('capacity'). The columns of special interest here however relate to the 'intake' and 'delivery' rates, i.e. the maximum rates at which cars can enter and leave the garage. These are given both as numbers of cars per hour, and as percentages of the total capacities of the buildings. Seven of the garages are elevator types (E) and eight are ramp types. Of the ramp garages, parking in two is by attendant (RA) and in six by the customers (RC).

The percentage intake rates for ramp garages with customer parking (RC) lie in the range 69 to 182 per cent, while those for elevator garages (E) lie in the range 24 to 67 per cent (the one exception being the London Zidpark with a rate of 108 per cent). That is to say,

TABLE 1 Statistics for 15 garages worldwide

Parking facility	System	Capacity (no. of car places)	Number of floors	Intake rate (cars/hr)	Delivery rate (cars/hr)	Intake as % of capacity	Delivery as % of capacity
Farmers Trading Co., Auckland NZ	RC, straight ramps	550	6	1000	740	182	135
Henry Ford Hospital, Detroit	RC, split levels	870	5	600	600	69	69
Downtown Center, San Francisco	RC, helical ramps	1374	11	1200	1500	88	109
Pershing Square, Los Angeles	RC, helical ramps	2150	3	–	4000	–	186
Shillito Garage, Cincinnati	RC, various ramps	1469	7	1260	2938	86	200
Parkade, Calgary, Canada	RC, ramped floors	475	5.5	480	480	101	101
Star Ferry Concourse, Hong Kong	RA, straight ramps	423	3	258	205	61	48
Parking garage, Miami	RA, split levels	560	4	120	120	21	21
Facility No. 1, Denver	E. Bowser	480	11	210	210	44	44
Facility No. 1, Chicago	E, Bowser	718	14	200	180	28	25
Facility No. 5, Chicago	E, Bowser	420	8	100	100	24	24
Temperance Street, Toronto	E, Pigeon Hole	396	8	180	236	45	60
Autolift, Vienna	E, Wertheim	300	14	120	–	40	–
Upper Thames St, London	E, Zidpark	464	7	500	500	108	108
Speed Park, New York	E, Speed Park	270	8	–	67	–	24.2

RC = ramp garage, customer parking; RA = ramp garage, attendant parking; E = elevator garage. Adapted from Klose, *Multi-Storey Car Parks and Garages* 1965 p. 38

112 The history and 'evolution' of building types

the customers are able to park their own cars in ramp garages much faster – typically of the order of three times faster – than cars can be parked in the elevator garages. The comparative rates for retrieving cars are similar to those for their delivery. This is even more important, since at elevator garages, returning drivers must sit and wait idly for their cars; while as Baker and Funaro cannily point out "... if a customer is busy fetching his car, he will not notice how long it actually takes him to reach it".[24]

Meanwhile the parking and retrieval rates for the two ramp garages with attendant parking (RA) are comparable with those for elevator buildings. These rates in general depended directly on the number of attendants employed. It was always possible to increase the delivery rates by taking on more staff – but this in turn raised labour costs.

Customer parking in ramp garages therefore scored over other systems of operation in terms of typical speeds of delivery and retrieval. Another advantage, as we have seen, was that – since entry of customers to the garage was continuous – there was no need to provide extra reservoir space at the entrance. On top of this there was the question of costs. Customer parking by definition avoided almost all of the labour costs associated with attendant parking, and all of the capital and maintenance costs of the complex machinery involved in the automated systems. Elevators (and stairs) were still needed in tall garages, but only for the customers themselves, not their cars. The delivery and retrieval rates quoted for the London Zidpark garage in Table 1 are fast – faster indeed than many of the ramp garages. But these are achieved at the cost of providing 16 car-carrying elevators in a building with 464 places on just seven floors.

All this confirms the conclusions of Baker and Funaro, writing in the late 1950s: "Operating costs of mechanical garages will be higher than self-parking ramp garages, but lower than ramp garages with attendant parking."[25] They add that, in their opinion, "... the increasing cost of labor will soon make attendant parking unprofitable and inefficient in all but a very few special areas where land costs and receipts are both exceptionally high".[26]

These comparisons of entry rates, delivery rates and costs have demonstrated then, at least in broad terms if not with quantitative data in every respect, why elevator garages and attendant parking largely faded into history in the late 1960s. We are left with the question of the comparative merits of different detailed arrangements for ramp garages, where the cars are parked by the customers.

Ramp garages, with parking by customers

Customers want to get to empty spaces as quickly as they can, of course. But the situation is now slightly different from attendant parking. When cars are parked by attendants, there must be some sort of system like those for checking coats in cloakrooms: that is to say the attendants must keep a record of where all the customers' cars are parked so far, and which places remain empty. When parking new cars, they can then go directly to the nearest vacant positions. A customer who parks his or her own car does not have this information, and must search for a place. He or she will be able to do this the more effectively, if the entry route provides a tour of the park, level by level. When the customer comes out again however, there is no need for a tour, and he or she will want to go directly to the exit. Notice that in Table 1, in two of the customer parking ramp garages (RC) the rate of exit from the park is faster than that of entry, for just this reason. (In a third case however, the garage in Auckland NZ, it is *slower* to get out than get in, which is perplexing.)

Both on the way in and on the way out, the flow of cars will be smoother if streams of traffic do not cross, and if cul-de-sacs are avoided, where drivers are obliged to reverse. There may be advantages to one-way traffic, where this is feasible, in creating simpler, less obstructed movement patterns. In some designs the car stalls are arranged alongside the ramps ('adjacent parking') so that cars being manoeuvred in and out of stalls block the traffic flow; while in others the ramps are free of parking (they are 'clearway ramps'). These are some of the ways in which the various arrangements of ramp car park may be made more or less efficient and smooth running. Klose summarises the "optimal solution for the self-parking motorist": "On arrival, the motorist is taken past all the parking stalls; there is no oncoming traffic, and the departing cars can leave via the exit ramp, rapidly and without hindering the parking manoeuvres of other cars."[27]

Books on car park design tend to present the variety of possible ramp layouts in a bewildering array of isometric diagrams, festooned with directional arrows and dotted movement paths. In some types the three-dimensional geometry is indeed complex. At heart however there are just a few basic organising principles. The plan for the remaining part of this paper is to make a measured comparison, on a common basis, of 14 theoretical designs of garage, each representative of a different ramp system. Together these cover the great majority of sub-types appearing in the literature up to the 1960s. More details are given in the Appendix.

The various features will be explained as we proceed, together with some of the history of each generic design. All these notional buildings (with one exception) are on four storeys and have a simple rectangular plan with the same overall dimensions, 32 × 75 m. They have capacities between 350 and 450 cars, not untypical of the immediate post-War period (compare Table 1). Axonometric drawings of all 14 garages, labelled A to N, are presented in Figure 8. The designs are compared numerically on three basic criteria, whose significance should by now be clear:

- the length of a complete tour of all car spaces;
- the mean distance of car spaces from the entrance and from the exit;
- the mean floor area per car space.

This last measure is intended as a proxy for construction cost, in the absence of real data (albeit a rather rough proxy, for reasons to be discussed). In the different designs, the number of car spaces varies somewhat, because of the exigencies of the ramp layouts. The total floor area can also differ because of the presence of internal voids or externally attached ramps.

Comparison of theoretical designs of ramp garage

In order for the comparison to be as fair as possible, common standards have been set for key dimensions throughout. The size of every car space has been fixed at 2.5 × 5 m, which was normal in post-War European practice – although bay sizes in American garages tended to be larger.[28] The bays can in principle be laid out at different angles to the aisles. When set at 45°, the stalls in adjacent rows can be fitted together into parquet-like or herringbone patterns. (The arrangement is compatible only with one-way traffic.) It is easier to manoeuvre in and out of angled bays, and the aisles can be made narrower than with 90° parking. On the other hand a series of laborious analyses made in the 1950s seemed to show that the arrangement which packs the most spaces into the smallest floor area is 90° parking – partly

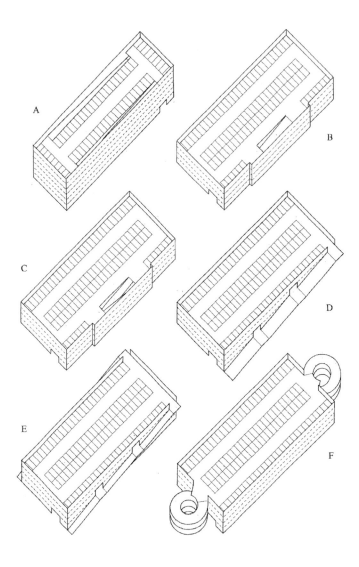

FIGURE 8 *(above and facing page)* Axonometric drawings of 14 theoretical designs of ramp garage, A to N (see text for explanation)

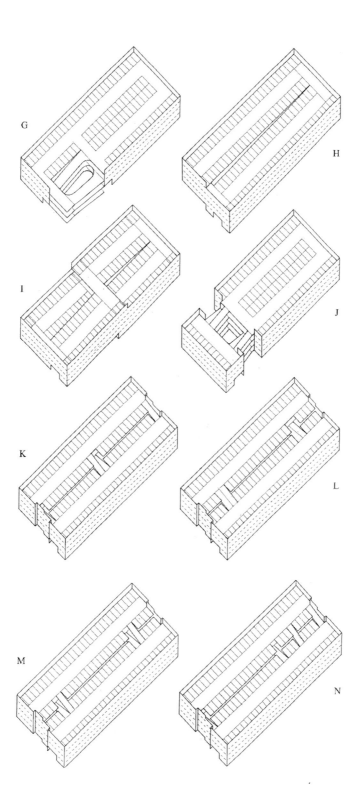

116 The history and 'evolution' of building types

because angled bays waste space at the ends of the rows.[29] In the theoretical buildings the parking is therefore laid out at 90° to the aisles throughout.[30]

In all but one of the buildings the basic layout on each floor is in four rows of parking stalls, served by two aisles whose width – for two-way circulation – is 6 m. This gives the standard overall building width of 32 m. Most authorities recommend maximum gradients for access ramps of between 10 and 15 per cent. (In the earliest ramp garages the gradients were often shallower, for reasons already explained.) For the present experiments we assume a maximum gradient of 12.5 per cent. Given a 2.5 m floor-to-floor height, this gives a straight ramp of 20 m length (in plan) for a full storey, and 10 m length for a half-storey. These dimensions fit nicely with the car bays. In some designs there are straight ramps that run the length of the building. The 75 m-plan dimension allows for such a longitudinal ramp to rise the full three storeys – hence the decision to make all the buildings this length. In every case the entrances and exits are at the ends of the building (sometimes at the same end).

One basic difference between the sub-types of ramp garage is in the nature of their floor plates. These can be simple flat floors on each level, as in designs A to G. The floors themselves can be given a continuous gentle slope, and can serve as both ramps and parking surfaces, as in designs H and I. Or the floor levels can be split and connected with half-length ramps, as in designs J to N.

Scheme A has two straight one-way ramps on either side of the garage. These are very shallow and rise only one storey in the building's entire length. Cars entering take one of the side ramps to the first floor, return along the central aisle, take a second ramp to the second floor, and so on. Cars leaving go down the matching ramps on the opposite side of the building. The arrangement is compatible only with two long rows of parking bays per floor (plus two short rows at the ends), giving a plan width of 22 m. In order to compensate in the analysis, this building (alone) has been increased from four to six floors, so that the total number of parking spaces is comparable with other designs. Such shallow ramps are characteristic of some of the very earliest ramp garages of the 1920s and '30s. Müller for example illustrates a garage built for postal vehicles in Budapest in the early '20s (Figure 9) with long straight single-storey ramps either side of a central void.[31]

The designs of garages B and C again have straight longitudinal ramps, but much shorter than in A. Scheme B has two-way ramps. Scheme C has separate one-way up and down ramps, sloped in opposite directions. Such ramp systems were also found in early garages. *The Architectural Record* gives illustrative examples of both types (but without identifying the actual buildings).[32]

Schemes D and E have long straight ramps like garage A, but now on the exterior. In garage D cars enter from the ramp through doors at 'landings' on the successive levels, and exit via the same doors. Garage E is essentially the same, but with two one-way straight ramps on either side of the building, one for entry and the other for exit. Figure 10 shows a particularly handsome version of this arrangement, designed by Paul Schneider-Esleben and built in Düsseldorf in 1953.[33]

Schemes F and G have flat floors accessed by helical ramps. Scheme F has two separate one-way ramps attached externally at the opposite ends of the building, one for entering and one for leaving. The Venice *Autorimessa* has ramps of this kind (Figure 11). In scheme G there are again two helical one-way ramps, one for entry and one for exit, but now fitted into a rectangular area within the body of the building. Each rises two floors in a full turn, and the two ramps are intertwined. The positioning is such that the points of entry and exit are on opposite sides of the ramps.

The case of the multi-storey garage **117**

FIGURE 9 Garage for postal vehicles in Budapest, with long straight shallow ramps, early 1920s; from Müller, *Grosstadt-Garagen* 1925

FIGURE 10 Garage with single straight external ramp, designed by Paul Schneider-Esleben, Düsseldorf 1953; from Vahlefeld and Jacques, *Garages and Service Stations* 1960

FIGURE 11 Spiral ramp in the *Autorimessa* garage, Venice, designed by Eugenio Miozzi, 1934; from Vahlefeld and Jacques, *Garages and Service Stations* 1960

FIGURE 12 Rupert Street car park, Bristol, designed by R Jelinek-Karl in 1960. The garage has a continuously sloped floor with an oval plan. From Klose *Multi-Storey Car Parks and Garages* 1965

FIGURE 13 D'Humy ramp in a garage built by the Ramp Buildings Corporation in the early 1920s; from Müller *Grosstadt-Garagen* 1925

Schemes H and I have the gradually sloped floors that are sometimes referred to by the rather curious name of 'non-dissipative ramps'. In effect the entire structure is a wide access ramp, on which the cars are also parked. The maximum slope generally recommended for such floors is 5 per cent: the two designs meet this standard. One can think of these buildings as very tightly wound helical roads with 'kerbside' parking. As Louis Kahn says of his own cylindrical designs, which are of this general type, ". . . the street wants to be a building". Scheme H consists of a simple single two-way helix. Figure 12 illustrates the Rupert Street car park in Bristol, which is of this type but has an oval 'racetrack' plan. The designer was R Jelinek-Karl, and the garage was built in 1960. In scheme I two helices interlock, and movement is one-way up on one helix, and one-way down on the other. Cars can move between the helices at the central cross-aisles.

Finally, buildings J to N are split-level designs, in which the ramps are all half-length and rise half a storey. These are D'Humy ramps, named after their inventor Fernand E D'Humy of Englewood, New Jersey, who received his first patent in 1919 and took out three more in the early 1920s. D'Humy was responsible for other inventions in lighting, the telegraph, and dirigibles; but it was his parking ramps that brought him a modest immortality. The Ramp Buildings Corporation of New York was set up in 1920 to exploit D'Humy's designs.[34] Figure 13 shows a D'Humy ramp in a garage built by the company, dating from this period.[35] (Notice the Model T Fords.) In our scheme J, the levels are split across the building, and the ramps are in the centre of the plan and aligned longitudinally. In schemes K, L, M and N the levels are all split longitudinally, and the ramps run crossways. The different positioning and direction of these ramps is critical, as we shall see.

Total floor areas including ramps have been measured for all 14 schemes. In order to analyse the buildings' access patterns, to clarify them visually, and to help measure distances, a special representation has been devised. The patterns are depicted as networks in the graph-theoretic sense, with edges corresponding to the aisles and ramps, and vertices corresponding to their junctions. These networks have been drawn with the edges at their true lengths to scale, and according to a convention inspired by the so-called 'justified graphs' used in space syntax studies of buildings by Hillier and Hanson.[36] For the pattern of entry to a garage, the ground-level entrance point is placed on the left of the diagram. Aisles and ramps are then drawn 'stretched out' horizontally towards the right, connected in the order that they are reached via the shortest routes.[37]

The total distance travelled from the entrance to any point in the network (the 'metric depth' of that point) can then be measured on a horizontal scale. For clarity in the diagrams, branching 'parallel' routes in the network are separated vertically by using curved joining lines – but the vertical distances involved here are not be counted in the length measurements. Junctions and (straightened out) 90° turns are both shown as hollow circles. Ramps are shown in heavier line than aisles. From these 'justified' network diagrams it is very straightforward to calculate the mean distances of all car spaces from the entrance (since those spaces are regularly distributed along the aisles), as well as the lengths of complete tours. In some cases the networks for both entering and leaving the garage are the same, because of symmetries in the plan. In other cases the presence of one-way aisles and ramps, and the positioning of ramps, can mean that the routes and mean depths from the entrance are not the same as those from the exit – in which case two different diagrams are drawn, for distances going in and coming out.

Figure 14 gives diagrams in this format for all 14 buildings. From these visualisations of the overall structure of the circulation patterns it is easy to see where a layout provides a continuous uninterrupted tour of the building (the network consists of a single unbranching route); where a tour involves going up and reversing back down cul-de-sacs (the network is tree-like); or where a tour or route to the exit involves crossings (the network contains cycles).

Comparative performance of the theoretical garage designs

Table 2 gives numerical results, for all 14 buildings, for the mean distances of all car places from entrance and exit (m), the length of a tour (m), and the mean floor area per car space (m^2). All of these values should ideally be low – as we have seen – in an efficient, cost-effective design. The table shows that tours of the garages are shortest where they follow a simple helical path around the longitudinal and cross-aisles. This is the case, naturally, for the two helical sloped floor schemes, H and I, as well as for two of the split-level garages, J and N. Routes to the exit are shortest on average when drivers can get quickly from any car space to a ramp that then descends directly to the ground – whether this ramp is straight (as in schemes D and E) or helical (as in schemes F, G and, in effect, scheme N). (In the case of designs D, E, F and G however, the routes to these exit ramps involve crossings that could cause delays.)

The mean floor area per car space is lowest in the sloped floor garages H and I and in the D'Humy ramp garages K, L, M and N. Earlier it was suggested that this value could be a rough indicator of construction cost. It is likely however – at least in the context of later twentieth-century construction practice – to underestimate the relative costs for garages with helical ramps, since these require more complex formwork for the *in situ* concrete. The split-level garages are simple to build, since they have flat floors, and the D'Humy ramps themselves are just tilted rectangular slabs. Indeed in the 1960s the Tishman Research Corporation of New York developed a system of prefabricated pre-cast concrete units for D'Humy ramp garages, for which they claimed costs per car place competitive with rival methods.[38]

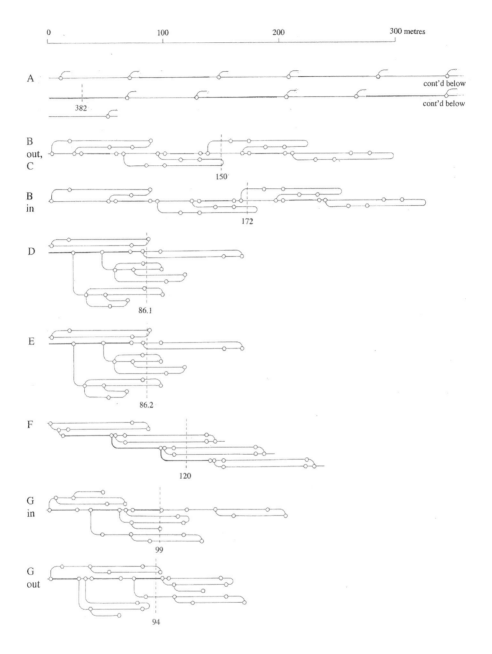

FIGURE 14 Network diagrams to show the circulation systems of all 14 theoretical garages A to N. The entry (or exit) is shown at extreme left in each case, and aisles and ramps are stretched out horizontally with their lengths to scale. Hollow circles show junctions and 90° turns. Ramps are shown in thicker line. Mean depths of all car places from the entry (or exit) are shown with broken lines. In cases where shortest distances from the entrance and exit are not the same, two networks are shown, for routes in and out

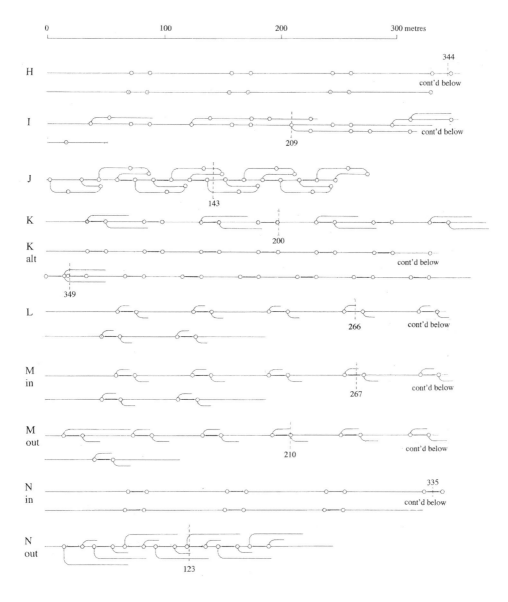

TABLE 2 Statistics for the 11 theoretical designs of ramp garage

Garage type		Capacity	Mean depth (m) on entry	Mean depth (m) on exit	Length of tour (m) on entry	Mean area / car place (m²)
A:	Long straight ramps each rising one floor;) in one side, out the other (6 floors)	372	382	382	969	26.6
B:	Two-way internal straight ramps	384	172	150	808	25.4
C:	Opposed internal one-way straight ramps	384	150	150	778	25.4
D:	External straight ramp to all floors; in and out same side	434	86.1	86.1	820	23.2
E:	Two external straight ramps to all floors; in one side, out the other	428	86.2	86.2	816	23.5
F:	Two external helical ramps; one in, one out	448	120	120	835	24.0
G:	Two internal intertwined helical ramps, rising one floor in half a turn	354	99	94	788	25.6
H:	Sloped floor with two-way traffic	448	344	344	692	21.4
I:	Sloped floor with one-way traffic	436	306	209	748	22.0
J:	Split levels with central longitudinal D'Humy ramps	352	143	143	713	25.0
K:	Split levels with lateral D'Humy ramps, 1	432	200	200	956	21.8
L:	Split levels with lateral D'Humy ramps, 2	432	266	266	814	21.8
M:	Split levels with lateral D'Humy ramps, 3	432	267	210	862	21.9
N:	Split levels with lateral D'Humy ramps, 4	432	335	123	669	21.8

The lists below show how all 14 garages are ranked on the three most important measures:

Measure	Low										High
	K										
Mean area per car (m^2)	H L M I D E F J B G A										
	N						C				
Mean depth (m) on exit	D E G F **N** J B K I M L H A										
			C								
Length of entry tour (m)	**N** H J I C G B L E D F M K A										

No outstanding winner emerges, way ahead of the field, from this analysis. The two schemes with external straight ramps D and E have short distances to the exit – the shortest of all designs – but have long tours, and what is more, these tours have many crossings. The two schemes with sloping floors, H and I, score well on floor area per car, and on length and simplicity of the entry tour; but the mean distance to the exit is very long in both cases.

The scheme with what is undoubtedly the best overall performance however in these terms is the split-level design **N** with D'Humy ramps. In this layout, two widely spaced ramps on each floor provide for the entry tour, while two closely spaced ramps, offset towards the exit end of the building, create a fast – in effect helical – route out. It is this special disposition of the ramps that gives scheme N the edge over the other split floor designs. It has the shortest tour, the equal second lowest floor area per car, and the fifth shortest mean distance to the exit – and even this, only some 40 m longer than the best scheme. In D'Humy ramp garages in practice it is actually possible to pack even more cars onto a given site area than in the examples here, since the floors can be slightly overlapped so that the bonnets [American: hoods] of one row of cars hang over the bonnets or boots [American: trunks] of the cars below. This comparative 'efficiency' of D'Humy ramp garages had been already recognised by the 1920s.[39] As we saw earlier, split-level car parks of this general kind had come to dominate the field, at least in the United States, by the late 1950s. Our experimental comparison shows why this happened.

This exercise has of course been limited and to an extent artificial. The comparative results would differ somewhat with altered assumptions about dimensional standards and detailed layout. More importantly, two considerations, not taken account of here, would affect the suitability in practice of the different designs to different circumstances. The first is the size and shape of the given site, and its relationship to adjoining streets. There is a basic modular dimension in car park layout, given by the width of one aisle plus the depths of the two rows of stalls to which the aisle gives access. Ricker refers to this as the "unit parking depth", Chrest *et al.* as the width of one "parking bay".[40] In our designs here the module is 16 m, repeated twice to give the 32 m width of each building.

It will be clear that the actual dimensions of any given site will determine the possible number of unit parking depths that can be fitted in, and will constrain the directions in which the aisles run. In awkward cases, this might lead to inefficiencies in the use of space. The site might further determine the positions of exits and entrances, and so lead to a choice of ramp positions that might not be optimal on other criteria. In such situations, as Baker and Funaro say, "Figures of average space per car are often unimportant, and even deceptive."[41] Our theoretical buildings have been designed with no concern for these exigencies of siting.

124 The history and 'evolution' of building types

The second factor ignored here is the special character of the customers for whom the garages might cater. We have assumed some kind of general non-specific parking demand. In reality the users might be office workers leaving their cars all day, shoppers parking for a few hours, theatre-goers parking for the evening, hotel guests leaving their cars overnight, or passengers at airports leaving their cars for many days. The patterns in time in which these users would typically arrive and depart would vary accordingly. Car park designers during the later twentieth century have worked to tailor buildings more carefully to these distinctive markets and their peak demands. We have emphasised the problem of customers searching the garage for empty spaces. But, for example, when a garage caters to the same group of office workers every day, they get to know the layout, and the ramp system does not have to be quite so legible and easily navigable as for drivers to whom the garage is unfamiliar.

Another trend over the last fifty years has been a general increase in garage size. As Chrest *et al.* say, "in the past" – i.e. in the mid- twentieth century – an average American car parking structure served 300 to 500 cars, and a 1000 car garage was "huge".[42] At the start of the twenty-first century, structures for 1000 to 3000 cars are not unusual, and garages have been built for up to 12,000 cars. In these much larger garages, new types of ramp layout have become possible. The basic helical sloped floor design (our scheme H) for example can be doubled end-to-end, or extended laterally into three or four unit parking depths.

Different performance criteria begin to apply. In the experiments reported here, *distances* measured in garage layouts have been taken as reasonable proxies for *times* taken entering and leaving. In the 1940s Ricker pioneered actual time-and-motion studies in different types of garage, using a stopwatch and taking movies.[43] And in the late 1960s the Transport and Road Research Laboratory in England developed a theoretical model that related together aisle and ramp design, angle of parking, one-way or two-way movement, type of user, and overall plan layout, with which it was possible to predict rates of traffic flow, in particular at times of peak demand.[44] The issue of peak flow has since come to be a central concern in car park design.

When garages are made extremely large, there is a real danger of drivers getting disoriented, or being unable to find their cars again. So legibility of layout – irrespective of any signing – becomes another key design objective. Some layouts can be preferable on grounds of security, as for example when drivers can oversee large parts of each parking floor without obstructions.

For all these reasons, the simple results of the comparative experiment reported here would not apply to larger garages, or garages for some more specialised market niches, built later in the twentieth century. An equivalent approach could no doubt be carried out to compare such designs, but space here does not allow. Even so, it is worth noting that the discussion of different generic garage layouts and their merits in today's leading design handbook concentrates almost exclusively on different sloping floor and split-level types – more basic forms of which beat the competition in the analysis presented above.[45]

The evolution of the multi-storey garage as an instance of 'evolutionary radiation'

To go back to the analogies with natural evolution introduced at the start of the paper: the case of the multi-storey garage has some loose affinities with what is known by Darwinists as *evolutionary radiation*. The most celebrated biological example is the variety of slightly differing species of finch that Darwin himself discovered on the Galapagos Islands, and that provided him with crucial evidence for the theory of natural selection. It seemed that one species of seed-eating finch had originally migrated from the mainland, to find an environment with little direct competition from other bird species, and a variety of available sources of food. In the car park analogy, this novel environment is the completely new demand for car storage buildings arising in the 1920s.

The original Galapagos species of finch evolved over time into as many as 14 distinct species, adapted differently in bodily form – especially in the shape of the beak – to eating cactuses and insects as well as seeds, and to living at ground level as well as in trees. The equivalent in the evolution of garages is the variety of different detailed designs of ramp and elevator building that emerged between the World Wars. In both cases, biological and architectural, the 'empty' environment provokes a flowering of diversity.

The separate species of Galapagos finch were able to coexist, since they were no longer in competition for the exact same habitat and food supply. This is the phenomenon of *adaptive radiation*, into different ecological niches. What is different in the case of garages is that most of the designs were in direct competition for a general market in short-term parking provision in cities. This is why many of them were abandoned. There *were* nevertheless some separate commercial niches (the same word and concept in economics as in biology) in which certain specialised designs could flourish in relative isolation. Elevator garages were particularly adapted to small central sites onto which ramp garages could not be squeezed. Indeed the elevator garage survives in similar special niches today – despite its general disappearance otherwise – in locations with extremely high land values, and for all-day or all-night parking where the speed of retrieval of cars is not critical, as in some residential areas of Tokyo, or associated with city centre hotels.

The initial variety of garage designs in the 1920s and '30s was *not* evolved through 'artificial selection', but was produced rapidly through the inventiveness of many designers. It turned out nevertheless that some designs possessed greater 'fitness' for the parking environment, and competition began to select for them. Over time this general economic and social environment changed – as already described – in costs of labour, in costs of construction, in the willingness or not of drivers to park their own cars – in ways which at successive periods favoured one species of garage over another. Elevator garages went extinct, were reborn, and went nearly extinct for a second time. Attendant parking disappeared, as did some of the ramp types. The split-level garage beat much of the competition. As Jakle and Sculle put it, "Parking garages evolved considerably to the midpoint of the twentieth century, but never teleologically. Economic ebbs and flows opened entrepreneurial opportunities as well as closing them with what seemed great suddenness."[46]

To take this type of analysis further it would be necessary to have statistics for the entire populations of the different designs, for successive decades of the twentieth century. For garages such data would be very laborious to collect. There are other building types where population data are more or less complete however such as shopping arcades, which might be used for comparable evolutionary analyses – in the case of arcades, as they first emerged as a new type in eighteenth-century Paris, and eventually lost the competition with department and other variety stores and became extinct in the early decades of the nineteenth century.[47] With garages we can at least say something about the dates at which separate *species* originated and disappeared, if not about the total numbers of individuals within each species.

There were temporal changes in the economic and social environment of multi-storey garages. There were also differences between parts of the world at the *same* point in time.

126 The history and 'evolution' of building types

Attendant parking was never popular in Europe, as it was in the USA. I have not gone deeply into the complex subject of construction costs: but it is clear for example that varying costs of building labour between different countries have altered the relative competitiveness of *in situ* concrete as a structural material, in ways that will have been relevant to the capital costs of ramped garages. The multi-storey car park environment changed again in the second half of the twentieth century, and is likely to continue to alter in the future. New designs may be evolved gradually from old ones; or quite unprecedented novelty may be introduced overnight. This is one of the many differences between biological evolution and the evolution of artefacts. Another is that, when a natural species goes extinct it is lost forever, whereas extinct types of building can come back from the dead.

Appendix: Types of garage listed in different publications cited

The 1929 *Architectural Record* article illustrates actual garages corresponding to my types B and C, a single D'Humy ramp design, and garages with internal helical ramps comparable to my scheme G although much more wasteful of space.[48] (It also shows a plan for a multi-storey garage within the core of an office building.) This 'park at your desk' idea was revived in the 1950s. Baker and Funaro illustrate a design by Leroy L Warner for the Cafritz building in Washington D C, with parking at the centre of the plan and offices around the periphery.[49] [*This illustration is reproduced in Paper 2 in this volume, Figure 13. The building still exists.*] Interestingly the *Architectural Record* compares these types for their 'efficiency', i.e. floor area per car space, on the basis of theoretical plans with standard dimensions of 100 × 200 ft. The standard plans are not however illustrated.

An article in *Architectural Forum* in 1953 simply mentions four generic types: 'straight ramp, staggered floor or split ramp, spiral ramp and sloped floor'.[50] The 1958 *Architectural Record* article gives isometric drawings of 13 types.[51] These include straight ramp designs comparable to my schemes A, B and C; sloped floor schemes equivalent to my H and I; two garages with variants of the type of internal helical ramp in my scheme G; three D'Humy ramp garages comparable to my schemes J to N; and a D'Humy ramp design with three staggered floors. This last type is however intrinsically larger than the garages compared here.

Comparing the types analysed here with those listed in textbooks of the 1950s and '60s, I include seven out of 11 generic layouts shown by Ricker,[52] eight out of the 14 layouts shown by Vahlefeld and Jacques[53] and all nine layouts shown by Klose.[54] Ricker has several designs with lateral straight ramps that differ slightly from those compared in this exercise; another three-level staggered floor scheme; and a design with a semi-circular ramp rising one floor in 180°, otherwise similar to my scheme F. The types omitted here but included in Vahlefeld and Jacques's enumeration are mostly buildings arranged around central courtyards or atria (their Figures 4, 8, 9, 13 and 14). Such buildings have their inspiration perhaps in courtyard office buildings or palazzi, with the car ramp taking the place of the grand central staircase. They provide good natural lighting; but tours and mean distances to entry and exit are necessarily longer than in deep-plan buildings without courts. Also excluded is a garage with long straight ramps each rising one floor (their Figure 2) that has some affinities with, but is not identical to, my scheme A. Klose shows sloped floor garages with attached rapid exit ramps, both straight and helical.[55] These would improve exit rates over my schemes H and I, although on the other hand they would increase construction costs.

Notes

1 As so often with the identification of the supposed point of origin of innovations, there are earlier precedents, of a kind. Multi-storey stables were built for horses in the nineteenth century, near London railway terminals, with access by ramps to upper levels. In America, livery stables were converted to garages in the 1910s and '20s.

2 United States Department of Commerce, Bureau of the Census *Historical Statistics of the United States from Colonial Times to 1970*, Part 1, A73, G152-G155, 'US motor vehicle registrations, 1900–1975', US Government Printing Office, Washington DC 1975.

3 J A Jakle and K A Sculle, *Lots of Parking: Land Use in a Car Culture*, University of Virginia Press, Charlottesville VA and London, 2004.

4 W J Showalter, 'The automobile industry: An American art that has revolutionized methods in manufacturing and transformed transportation', *The National Geographic Magazine* Vol. 44, 1923 pp. 337–413.

5 S Bottles, 'Mass politics and the adoption of the automobile in Los Angeles', in M Wachs and M Crawford eds, *The Car and the City: The Automobile, the Built Environment, and Daily Life*, University of Michigan Press, Ann Arbor MI, 1992, pp. 194–203.

6 R Longstreth, *City Center to Regional Mall: Architecture, the Automobile, and Retailing in Los Angeles, 1920–1950*, MIT Press, Cambridge MA 1997.

7 G Müller, *Grosstadt-Garagen*, Deutsche Bauzeitung and Klasing & Co, Berlin 1925. German authors went on to make a speciality of this minor branch of architectural literature, as several sources used here show.

8 E R Ricker, *Traffic Design of Parking Garages*, The Eno Foundation for Highway Traffic Control, Saugatuck, CT 1948: revised edn 1957 p. 110.

9 'Garages (standards for design and construction)', *Architectural Record* Vol. 65, February 1929, pp. 178–196: see p. 181.

10 P Steadman, *The Evolution of Designs: Biological Analogy in Architecture and the Applied Arts*, Cambridge University Press, Cambridge 1979; revised edn, Routledge 2008.

11 See for example J Frazer *An Evolutionary Architecture*, Architectural Association, London 1995.

12 'Garages (standards for design and construction)' p. 182.

13 G Baker and B Funaro, *Parking*, Reinhold, New York 1958 p. 116.

14 D Klose, *Multi-Storey Car Parks and Garages*, Architectural Press, London 1965 (adapted by J I Elliott and C R Fowkes from original German edition, Verlag Georg, Munich 1953) p. 33.

15 Baker and Funaro, *Parking*.

16 Jakle and Sculle, *Lots of Parking*.

17 Longstreth, *City Center to Regional Mall*.

18 Jakle and Sculle, *Lots of Parking*.

19 'Commercial parking garages', *Architectural Record* Vol. 124, September 1958, pp. 181–188.

20 Müller, *Grosstadt-Garagen*.

21 Ibid., p. 70.

22 Baker and Funaro, *Parking* p. 187.

23 Klose, *Multi-Storey Car Parks* p. 29.

24 Baker and Funaro, *Parking* p. 121.

25 Ibid., p. 117.

26 Ibid., p. 164.

27 Klose, *Multi-Storey Car Parks* p. 36.

28 Baker and Funaro (*Parking*) recommend a bay to fit most fifties American models of car, with dimensions of 9'0" × 19'0" (2.7 x 5.8 m). Ricker (*Traffic Design of Parking Garages*) recommends 8'6" × 18'0" (2.6 × 5.5 m).

29 See for example the tables in Baker and Funaro, *Parking* pp. 170–179.

30 The idea that 90° parking is always the most efficient in space became accepted wisdom among garage planners. It has however been questioned more recently, as by M S Smith 'Functional design' in A P Chrest, M S Smith, S Bhuyan (1996) *Parking Structures: Planning, Design, Construction, Maintenance and Repair*, Chapman and Hall, New York, 2nd edn 1996 pp. 6–54. Smith shows that angled bays can in certain circumstances save space, since the one-way aisles can be narrower than two-way aisles.

31 Müller, *Grosstadt-Garagen* p. 59.

32 'Garages (standards for design and construction)' p. 183.

128 The history and 'evolution' of building types

33 Illustrated in R Vahlefeld and F Jacques *Garages and Service Stations*, Leonard Hill, London 1960 p. 139.

34 Jakle and Sculle, *Lots of Parking* p. 128.

35 Another early example of split levels with half-storey ramps was the Mutual Garage on Olive Street, Los Angeles, opened in 1924. See Longstreth, *City Center to Regional Mall* p. 47.

36 B Hillier and J Hanson *The Social Logic of Space*, Cambridge University Press, Cambridge 1984. See in particular Chapter 4.

37 The lengths of ramps have been measured in plan, not as actual distances up and down the sloping surfaces. Since this approximation is made for all 14 cases, it should not greatly affect the comparative results.

38 Klose, *Multi-Storey Car Parks* pp. 106–110.

39 'Garages (standards for design and construction)'.

40 Ricker, *Traffic Design of Parking Garages*; Chrest *et al.*, *Parking Structures*.

41 Baker and Funaro, *Parking* p. 115.

42 Chrest *et al.*, *Parking Structures*.

43 Ricker, *Traffic Design of Parking Garages*.

44 P B Ellson, *Parking: Turnover Capacities of Car Parks*, TRRL Report 1126, Transport and Road Research Laboratory, Crowthorne, UK 1984.

45 Chrest *et al.*, *Parking Structures*.

46 Jakle and Sculle, *Lots of Parking* p. 133.

47 J F Geist, *Arcades: The History of a Building Type*, MIT Press, Boston MA 1983; first published as *Passagen*, Prestel-Verlag, Munich 1969; M MacKeith *The History and Conservation of Shopping Arcades*, Mansell, London and New York 1986. An analysis of the development of the arcade as a type using these sources is given in P Steadman, *Building Types and Built Forms* 2014 pp. 364–366. The word 'extinct' is used here to mean that after some date no new examples of a type were built. Old examples of course could continue in use.

48 'Garages (standards for design and construction)' p. 183.

49 Baker and Funaro, *Parking* pp. 90–91.

50 'Garages grow up', *Architectural Forum* Vol. 98, February 1953, pp. 120–141: see p. 126.

51 'Commercial parking garages'.

52 Ricker, *Traffic Design of Parking Garages* pp. 102–114.

53 Vahlefeld and Jacques, *Garages and Service Stations* pp. 21–23.

54 Klose, *Multi-Storey Car Parks* pp. 30–31.

55 Ibid., p. 37.

PART III
Built form and urban form
Geometry, energy and density

7

WALL AREA, VOLUME AND PLAN DEPTH IN THE BUILDING STOCK

(with Stephen Evans and Michael Batty)

(Building Research and Information, Volume 37, 2009, pp. 455–467)

'Allometry' is the study in biology of systematic differences in form between organisms of varying sizes. These might be members of different species, or members of the same species at successive stages in their growth from infant to adult. The changes in form occur in order to preserve certain geometrical relationships important to the physiological functioning of the creatures, as for example the ratio of the surface area of the body to its volume, which can be significant for heat loss. Ranko Bon was the first person to demonstrate allometric relationships in the forms of buildings, in work carried out at Harvard University in the 1970s.

Bon compared residential buildings of a range of sizes and showed that the relationship of wall area-to-volume displayed an allometric character. If the forms of large residential buildings (hotels, blocks of flats) were simple magnifications of the forms of small residential buildings (individual houses), the value of this ratio would vary significantly with size. Instead the value remains relatively constant. This is because for all such buildings there is a limit on their maximum depth in plan, so that they can be lit and ventilated naturally. Bigger buildings as a result become elongated either horizontally (in terraces or slabs) or vertically (in towers), in order to stay within this limit on depth. Bon showed this effect with empirical data for some forty randomly selected buildings of increasing sizes.

Bon's findings are confirmed in this paper, using data on wall area, volume and plan depth for some 3 million building blocks in London. Within this broad pattern, some variations in plan depth are found for London boroughs with major differences in the proportions of non-domestic buildings of different types.

Depth and allometry in building geometry

The advent of large-scale three-dimensional virtual models of cities has opened up new opportunities for research on urban built form. In this paper we describe some geometrical analyses from the Virtual London model, which was developed primarily so that future changes and plans might be visualised for a range of activities involving general dissemination and public participation.[1] The model uses the Ordnance Survey's digital MasterMap for its topographic base, and remotely sensed light detection and ranging (LiDAR) data on a 1 m grid spacing for the heights of buildings or parts of buildings.[2] The model currently extends out to London's M25 orbital motorway, and comprises some 3.2 million 3D blocks.

FIGURE 1 The Virtual London model, showing a detail along the River Thames

Figure 1 shows part of the model covering an area in the financial quarter of the city including the River Thames.

One geometrical property of building stocks that has been studied in the past on relatively small samples is the ratio of volume to surface area – or else the ratio of volume to external wall area, ignoring roofs. The first person to make such an analysis was Ranko Bon, who was a member of the Philomorphs, an interdisciplinary seminar at Harvard in the 1960s, which also included the palaeontologist Stephen Jay Gould and the geographer Michael Woldenberg. The Philomorphs were interested, among other morphological topics, in extensions of the biological concept of *allometry* to social systems, cities and buildings. These topics were covered in a special issue of the journal *Ekistics* in 1973.[3] Allometry describes the ways in which organisms change shape as they increase in size during development, in order to preserve certain geometrical properties important for physiological function. The ratio of surface area-to-volume is one of these properties, since it affects heat loss or gain through the skin. Allometric effects can also be seen in comparisons of the adult forms of animals of different sizes, between different species and genera.

In general one should be cautious about drawing analogies – which can be treacherous – between animal physiology and the functioning of buildings.[4] Individual buildings do not 'grow' (although they can be extended). The forms of animals are in many ways more flexible than those of buildings. One can speak figuratively of the 'metabolism' of buildings, but one must be clear exactly what is meant in terms of physical processes.

The forms of many buildings are limited by a general requirement for natural light and natural ventilation; but in other cases these constraints are broken with the use of artificial lighting and air conditioning. There can be allometric relationships – as Bon showed – between the lengths of circulation routes in buildings and the floor areas they serve; but again the circulation of people is hardly the same as the circulation of the blood, with which architects have sometimes drawn analogies. All this said however, there can be no doubt that allometric relationships exist between the volumes and surface areas of buildings, at least under certain conditions, as Bon showed and this paper will confirm.

Wall area, volume and plan depth   **133**

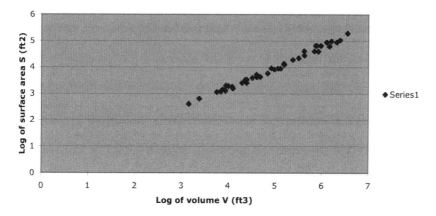

FIGURE 2 Measurements of wall area W and volume V for a sample of 40 residential buildings, re-plotted on a log-log scale from data in Bon, *An Introduction to Morphometric Analysis*, 1972

Bon took a sample of 40 residential buildings of greatly varying dimensions, from Neolithic and Egyptian huts to grand hotels and high-rise apartment blocks, taking in mobile homes, modern houses and mansions along the way.[5] These were selected at random from R. Martin Helick's atlas, *Varieties of Human Habitation*.[6] It is important to emphasise that these were all *detached* buildings. The same is not true for our London measurements, a fact that has significant consequences for the results, as we will explain. Bon measured volume V and exposed wall area W in each case. The latter he defined as the "exterior wall surface area of the actual living compartments generalized to a plane, not including non-habitable spaces, such as attics".[7]

The basic allometric relation between wall area and volume is

$$V \sim W^\alpha$$

where α is the allometric coefficient. Figure 2 shows Bon's plot of log V against log W. The strong linear correlation and the value of α confirms that there is indeed a marked allometric effect: the ratio of wall surface to volume increases faster than the simple increase in surface area associated with an increase in the volume of a rectangular building of unchanging shape. The forms of larger buildings are not in general simple magnifications of the forms of small buildings. Instead the bigger structures become flattened and elongated, in either the horizontal direction into slabs, or in the vertical direction into towers. Recently Steadman has replicated Bon's empirical results theoretically, by means of an 'archetypal building' from which many built forms of varying sizes can be generated.[8]

Why precisely should this allometric effect occur? It is found because Bon's examples are all residential buildings in which the great majority of 'habitable' rooms – living rooms, kitchens, bedrooms – are day-lit via windows. (There may also be some artificially lit corridors, small storerooms, or bathrooms in the interior.) The windows also serve of course to provide natural ventilation and views of the exterior. This means that the plans of these buildings *must in no place be more than two habitable rooms deep*; for if they were three or more rooms deep, the rooms in the centre could not have windows. The plans might be one room deep, and this is indeed found in larger detached houses. But such plans are less common in medium-sized and small houses and flats, for reasons we will come to shortly.[9]

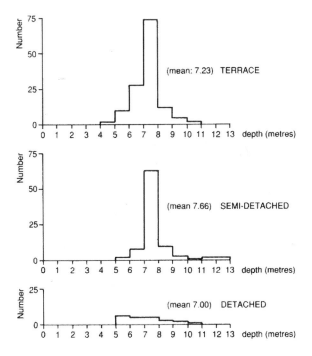

FIGURE 3 Statistics from a representative survey of 300 dwellings in Cambridge (UK) made by Brown and Steadman, 'The morphology of British housing', 1991, showing distributions of overall plan depth (metres) for terrace, semi-detached and detached houses

Now the fact is that most habitable rooms in modern dwellings have dimensions in plan of around 3 or 4 m. (Obviously there are many exceptions.) This we may assume has something to do with the typical space requirements of domestic activities and their associated furniture and equipment. In dwellings that are two rooms deep, this would imply a total plan depth of around 7 or 8 m. In the 1980s Brown and Steadman made a survey of a random sample of 300, mostly nineteenth- and twentieth-century houses and flats, in Cambridge, England.[10] They measured their depths in plan in every case (ignoring minor back extensions) and obtained a mean value for the whole sample of 7.4 m. Breaking down the sample by house types, they found mean depths of 7.2 m for terrace houses, 7.7 m for semi-detached houses, and 7.4 m for flats as illustrated in Figure 3. These they showed were the consequences of placing pairs of habitable rooms with dimensions of 3 to 4 m, back to back. Detached houses were somewhat shallower, with a mean of 7.0 m, because some were, at least in part, just one room deep.

As more day-lit rooms are added on the same floor level, so a building must become elongated in order to preserve the two-room depth. The architect Roger North recognised this fact as long ago as the seventeenth century in his writings on the design of country houses. He says that for a small house, a square plan will serve, but in a "great pyle" the plan "must be spread for air and light".[11] We can understand the relationship between volume, wall area and plan depth by considering a simple rectangular block as in Figure 4. The depth is d, the length l, the number of storeys n and the storey height h. Supposing we ignore the short end walls, in which case total wall area

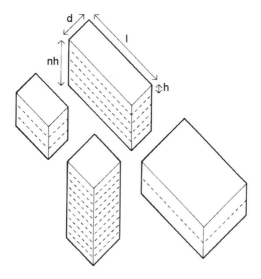

FIGURE 4 A building block with depth *d*, length *l*, number of storeys *n* and storey height *h*, with dimensioned instances

$W = 2nlh$

Volume $= dnlh$

Thus:

$V/W = (dnlh)/(2nlh) = d/2$

On this basis the ratio of volume-to-wall area for a long block is dependent simply on plan depth, and is not affected by changes in the length or height of the block.

On the other hand, for small buildings the areas of the end walls can be significant. Consider a freestanding block where $l = 5$ m, $h = 5$ m and $d = 7$ m. This could be a small detached house. When the areas of the side walls are included as well as the back and front walls, then $V/W = 1.46$. Let us now add more houses of the same size to form a terrace. The value of V/W rises progressively, as shown in Table 1, until when the terrace is long, V/W approaches 3.5. Note that the depth of 7 m is maintained throughout.

A block of this kind could be extended indefinitely in length in a straight line; or it could be cut up and rejoined into patterns of branching wings or courts. It could also be enlarged of course by adding more floors. This is how the ratio of wall area-to-volume can remain more or less the same while residential buildings change their forms, as they increase in size.

TABLE 1 V/W for terraced rows with increasing numbers of houses

No of houses	1	2	3	4	5	6	7	8	9	10	100
V/W	1.46	2.06	2.39	2.59	2.73	2.84	2.92	2.99	3.03	3.07	3.45

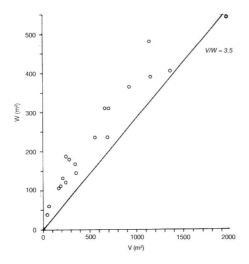

FIGURE 5 Measurements of wall area W and volume V for the sample of small residential buildings in Bon *An Introduction to Morphometric Analysis*, 1972 (compare Figure 2). This graph shows actual values for the smaller buildings. The heavy line marks a value of 3.5 for the ratio V/W, implying a plan depth of around 7 m. These dwellings are generally shallower than 7 m

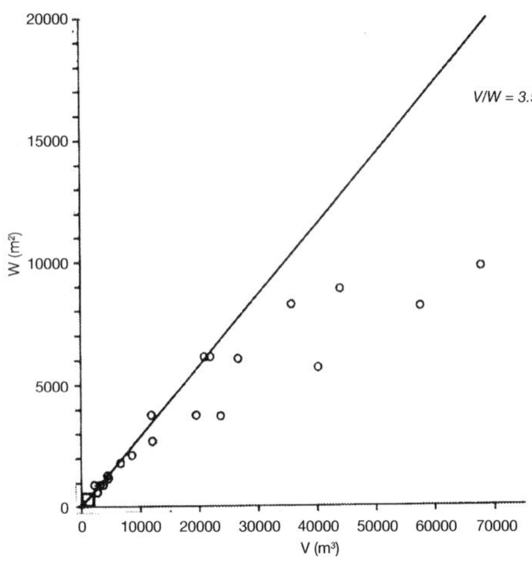

FIGURE 6 Measurements of wall area W and volume V for the sample of large residential buildings in Bon *An Introduction to Morphometric Analysis*, 1972 (compare Figure 2). This graph shows actual values for the larger buildings. The heavy line marks a value of 3.5 for the ratio, implying a plan depth of around 7 m. Some of these dwellings are deeper than 7 m

The relationship between V, W and $d/2$ is evident in Bon's data when his actual values are plotted. Two graphs at different scales show the smaller buildings in Figure 5 and the larger buildings in Figure 6 respectively. A line corresponding to a value of 3.5 for the ratio V/W, implying a plan depth of around 7 m, is superimposed on both graphs. See how buildings in the middle of Bon's size range lie near this line. The huts and small houses have values of below 3.5. This does not necessarily mean that their plan depths are less than 7 m, although this *could* be the case especially in the smallest examples. It reflects the fact that these are small detached buildings where the areas of the side walls are significant, as demonstrated. Notice by contrast in Figure 6 how several of the apartment blocks and hotels lie below the V/W = 3.5 line. This *must* mean that they are deeper than 7 m in plan, going up to around 14 m at the extreme. Such big buildings are likely to have central corridors, and possibly also internal windowless bathrooms and kitchens.

The characteristic depth of medium-sized houses and flats is *not* however determined by the maximum distance to which daylight can penetrate these domestic buildings from the two sides (depending on the sizes of windows, the level of lighting required at the centre of the plan, and some other factors). The depth is constrained by the requirement for daylight *together with* typical domestic room sizes. The absolute limit of depth for day lighting is greater, as we shall see shortly.

This argument explains then why many domestic buildings are not much deeper in plan than 7 or 8 m. We also find however that most dwellings tend not to be much shallower

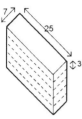 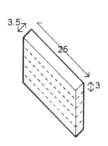 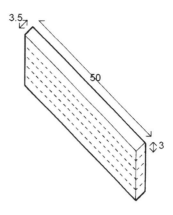

FIGURE 7
A five-storey building block with depth 7 m, length 25 m and storey height 3 m. The value of V/W (discounting the end walls) is 3.5

FIGURE 8
A five-storey building block with depth 3.5 m, length 25 m and storey height 3 m. The value of V/W (discounting the end walls) is 1.75

FIGURE 9
A five-storey building block with depth 3.5 m, length 50 m and storey height 3 m. This has the same volume as the block in Figure 7

than this, and are not in general just one room deep. Why should this happen? We can see the reasons by considering some worked examples of simple rectangular blocks. Figure 7 shows a five-storey block with $d = 7$ m, $l = 25$ m and $h = 3$ m. (The height and length are arbitrarily chosen and do not affect the comparisons that follow.) The combined area W of the long walls is 750 m² and the volume V of the block is 2625 m³ giving a value for V/W of 3.5 (half the plan depth).

Figure 8 shows a thin block just 3.5 m deep, each floor consisting of a single row of domestic rooms. Otherwise all dimensions are as in Figure 7. Now V/W takes the value of 1.75. The ratio of volume-to-wall area can have important practical consequences for the rate of heat loss from buildings per unit volume, via the walls. It can also affect the buildings' capital costs. In order for the 3.5 m-deep block to provide as much volume as the 7 m-deep block of Figure 7, it must be made twice as long (50 m), involving a doubling of W to 1500 m², as in Figure 9. The same volume, that is to say, is contained within roughly twice the area of expensive exterior wall, through which heat may be lost. Roger North recognised this problem when he spoke of the costs of 'too much spreading' in mansions with plans that are just one room deep. Not only is there a great 'charge of walls', in North's phrase, but also a need for 'long entrys and passageways'.[12] Imagine circulation routes running along the deep and shallow blocks of Figures 7 and 9. The route in the shallow block must be approximately twice as long as that in the deep block, serving the same floor area.[13]

Thus different 'generic functions' of architecture, acting in opposite directions on the built forms of typical medium-sized dwellings, tend to produce the regularities in plan depths observed by Brown and Steadman.[14] Day lighting and room sizes tend to keep the buildings from being made much deeper than 7 or 8 m, and capital and running costs, and the costs of circulation space, tend to keep them from being made much shallower.

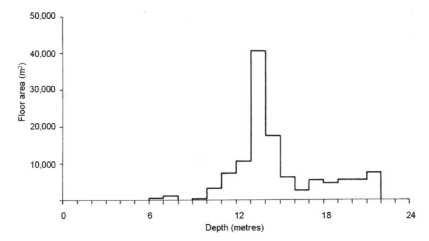

FIGURE 10 Plan depths of 19 office buildings in Swindon (UK), from a survey reported in Steadman et al., *An Approach to the Classification of Building Forms*, 1993. The graph shows the total floor area (m²) in the sample with the given plan depth (m)

Moving now to non-domestic buildings, we find that similar considerations apply, although typical values for plan depth are greater. Figure 10 plots values for the depth in plan of 19 office buildings in Swindon, Wiltshire.[15] The graph shows total areas of floor space in these buildings in blocks or wings of different depths. Notice how the distribution has two peaks, at 14 m and 22 m respectively. The lower value corresponds to day-lit buildings, and the higher value to buildings that are air-conditioned and which rely in their central zones on permanent artificial lighting.[16]

It has been observed since the nineteenth century that 7 m is about the furthest distance from window walls that day light sufficient for office work will penetrate (the exact distance depending again on many factors including window sizes, ceiling heights, the colours of interior surfaces, and whether or not there are obstructions outside the windows). In the American literature on office planning of the 1880s and 1890s, for example, it was frequently said that space more than 20 to 25 ft (6 to 7.5 m) from windows would be difficult or impossible to let.[17] This rule of thumb continues to be applied today. For example, the LT Method for calculating energy use in commercial buildings divides their plans into two zones. There is a 'passive' perimeter zone, whose depth is twice the floor-to-ceiling height (i.e. typically 6 m) assumed to be day-lit. And – where this exists – there is a 'non-passive' core zone, further than this distance from the windows and assumed to be artificially lit and ventilated, which would in many cases also need to be cooled.[18]

Going back to the Swindon office buildings of Figure 10, the peak in plan depth of 14 m could correspond then to two rows of day-lit cellular offices of around 6 to 7 m depth, flanking a central 2 m corridor – or else to a fully day-lit open plan. (Notice in Figure 6 how Bon's largest residential buildings, the apartment blocks and hotels, also have plans up to 14 m deep at a maximum). In Figure 10 it is possible to see a very small proportion of floor area with 7 to 8 m depth, corresponding to office buildings or wings of buildings which – perhaps because of the constraints of their sites – receive daylight from one side only, and comprise just one row of rooms plus a corridor.

Building depths from the Virtual London block model

The Virtual London model makes it possible to calculate volumes V and external wall areas W of buildings – both domestic and non-domestic – on an unprecedented scale. The volumes of building blocks can be calculated relatively simply by multiplying the areas of their footprint polygons by mean heights derived from the LiDAR data. Measurements of exposed external wall areas are more complex, since it is necessary to distinguish these from unexposed party walls shared by adjacent building blocks.

The relatively straightforward procedures for calculating topological relationships within a geographical information system (GIS) can help to solve this issue. Different types of topological relation can be expressed as lists of features (e.g. an area is defined by the arcs comprising its border). In this way, the walls of the building footprints can be categorised as 'children' of their 'parent' polygons. The walls can be assigned heights, and by spatially analysing the polygons that they adjoin, it is possible to determine if they are walls that face onto a courtyard, or onto the street, or are party walls (walls which divide terraced or semi-detached properties). Sometimes these party walls divide properties of different heights, in which case there is an area of the party wall that rises above the roofline of the lower property and becomes 'exposed'. The exposed areas of these walls are also taken into account when making the calculations.

TABLE 2 Numbers of building blocks, domestic and non-domestic, in the six boroughs

Borough	Domestic	Non-Domestic	All
City	2414	2577	4991
Camden	38683	12956	51639
Hackney	43756	12233	55989
Islington	39850	11504	51354
Tower Hamlets	34650	15287	49937
Westminster	37859	16165	54024

The Ordnance Survey MasterMap data can be combined with the Generalised Land Use Database (GLUD), which contains classifications of land cover. For building footprints these draw a basic distinction between domestic and non-domestic buildings. Measurements of V and W and values for V/W are given here for six selected boroughs within London. Three of these – the City of London, Westminster and Tower Hamlets – cover between them much of the capital's financial and major office districts, and are the most densely developed. The remaining three – Hackney, Islington and Camden – are predominantly residential with some retail, commercial and industrial uses. Table 2 gives total numbers of blocks, domestic and non-domestic, broken down by borough. For each borough, results have been grouped into ten approximately logarithmic sized bands by volume. Table 3 gives the V/W results for domestic and Table 4 for non-domestic. Notice that these statistics relate to *building blocks*, each of which corresponds to a single ground polygon in the map. These blocks might or might not correspond to 'buildings' understood in some architectural or constructional sense. Many are just small parts of buildings. This is critical to what follows.

The value V/W can give an indication of the mean plan depth of the building blocks in question, as explained. It might be asked, why could plan depths not be measured directly

140 Built form and urban form

TABLE 3 Depth ratios V/W for the domestic stock

Size band (m³)	Westminster	City	Hackney	Islington	Tower Hamlets	Camden
0 to 3	0.037	0.080	0.104	0.113	0.022	0.076
3 to 10	0.300	0.360	0.439	0.411	0.485	0.344
10 to 30	0.603	0.467	0.829	0.726	0.785	0.738
30 to 100	1.030	0.897	1.152	1.191	1.158	1.110
100 to 300	2.112	1.438	2.427	2.326	2.438	1.887
300 to 1000	3.317	2.954	3.412	3.396	3.530	3.201
1000 to 3000	4.358	4.213	3.689	3.775	3.709	3.628
3000 to 10,000	5.559	5.101	4.585	5.220	4.935	4.784
10,000 to 30,000	7.104	7.179	5.917	7.857	5.967	6.750
30,000 +	11.229	11.247	6.893	16.152	11.139	13.762
Overall	**4.355**	**5.847**	**3.453**	**3.503**	**3.755**	**3.534**

on the Virtual London model? The depth of a theoretical rectangular block is given by definition; but the problem with real buildings is that they can take many shapes in plan where depth is not so easily defined. Imagine a simple L-shaped block. The depths of the wings themselves are known, but plan depth is undefined in the rectangular zone where the two wings meet. Where buildings have non-orthogonal, curving or indented outlines in plan, the problem becomes yet more difficult.

One feasible approach is to draw contour lines within the plan, offset at some constant distance from the window walls. It is then possible to measure the floor area within x metres of the perimeter. This is the approach taken in effect by the LT Method for defining passive perimeter zones. Where the plans of buildings are represented in a GIS, the method can readily be automated. Figure 11 shows examples of analyses of building blocks in Swindon, with offset contours at 1 m spacing. The distribution of floor area between successive contours gives a profile that can be seen as in some sense characterising plan depth.

TABLE 4 Depth ratios V/W for the non-domestic stock

Size band (m³)	Westminster	City	Hackney	Islington	Tower Hamlets	Camden
0 to 3	0.239	0.056	0.105	0.180	0.117	0.131
3 to 10	0.410	0.256	0.503	0.449	0.428	0.390
10 to 30	0.777	0.479	1.107	0.856	0.882	0.814
30 to 100	1.207	0.906	1.298	1.283	1.115	1.233
100 to 300	1.671	1.602	1.895	1.839	1.909	1.814
300 to 1000	3.593	3.088	3.047	3.282	2.933	3.339
1000 to 3000	4.871	4.918	4.195	4.210	3.780	4.279
3000 to 10,000	6.056	6.004	5.010	5.429	5.223	5.390
10,000 to 30,000	7.402	7.774	6.447	7.011	6.674	7.091
30,000 +	12.086	14.180	12.911	12.802	17.148	13.598
Overall	**7.284**	**10.061**	**4.964**	**5.709**	**7.012**	**6.524**

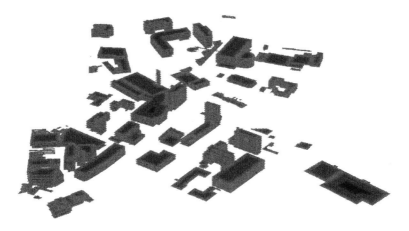

FIGURE 11 Buildings in Swindon (UK) modelled in the ArcView GIS, with internal plan contours offset from the window walls at 1 m spacing. The 1 m bands are coloured in darker shades with increasing distance from the windows

Here however we stick with the simple ratio V/W. In Table 3 showing domestic buildings in London, the figures in bold give totals for V and W and the value of V/W for the whole of each borough. In effect we are lumping all blocks together and considering them as if they were amalgamated into one giant 'building' whose depth is specified by V/W. In the residential boroughs of Hackney, Islington and Camden, V/W is close to 3.5 implying a mean plan depth of 7 m, as would be expected. In the more densely developed boroughs the value rises, to 3.76 in Tower Hamlets, 4.36 in Westminster, and 5.85 in the City. This must be due to the presence here of larger numbers of flats – typically with greater depths like Bon's examples in Figure 6 – and fewer houses. There will also be buildings in these three boroughs in which offices and flats are combined.

The breakdown by size bands is more difficult to interpret. We should re-emphasise that the statistics here relate to building blocks, not buildings: specifically, these are prisms whose bases are the polygons into which building footprints are digitised. One building may be digitised with numerous polygons corresponding to sections or wings of different heights, stair and elevator towers, porches and lean-tos, and so on. This explains the fact that many building blocks are found in the very smallest size bands, between 0 and 30 m^3. In these domestic statistics, these are not dwellings but parts of dwellings. There is no reason why these blocks should extend from the fronts to the backs of buildings, or why therefore they should obey the allometric relationships discussed by Bon.

An average terrace or semi-detached house might have a volume of around 250 m^3. We find that the values of V/W for the middle bands in Table 3 lie between 2.0 and 4.0, suggesting that these do indeed relate to entire houses digitised as single ground polygons. The higher size bands must relate for the most part to blocks of flats, or sections of such blocks. Here V/W goes up to 7 or 8, consistent with Bon's data for larger American apartment buildings and hotels. It is difficult to explain why there are values of V/W between 11 and 16 in the 30,000 m^3 plus band. These are improbably deep buildings for domestic use. They could be caused by misclassifications in the Generalised Land Use Database.

142 Built form and urban form

Table 4 gives equivalent results for non-domestic buildings. We could expect more variation in V/W here, since these will include not just office and institutional buildings such as hospitals and schools, many of which can be expected to be day-lit, but also deeper air-conditioned offices. There would also be factory sheds, warehouses and supermarkets, which could be either single storey and top-lit, or lit entirely by artificial light. The plan depths of these latter structures could be extremely large. Looking at the overall V/W values (in bold) for entire boroughs however, we find values of 7.01 and 7.28 in Tower Hamlets and Westminster respectively, suggesting a predominance of 14 m-deep office and other day-lit buildings. In the City of London the overall value for V/W goes up to 10.06, indicating the presence of a proportion of deep-plan artificially lit offices. In the three largely residential boroughs by contrast, the mean values are 4.96 (Hackney), 5.71 (Islington) and 6.52 (Camden). Here much of the non-domestic stock is made up from smaller offices and shops, many of them comparable with domestic buildings in their built forms.

Within the volumetric size bands, the bulk of the accommodation in all boroughs falls in the size ranges from 1000 m^3 upwards, implying building blocks with more than 300 m^2 of floor area. Between the $10,000 - 30,000$ m^3 and the $30,000$ m^3 plus bands, V/W jumps typically from around 7, up to a value of 12 or greater. It is in this topmost size band that both the very largest office buildings and the biggest industrial and retail building blocks are likely to be concentrated. Notice the value of 17 in this band in Tower Hamlets, associated with the major offices concentrated in Canary Wharf. The land cover categories in Ordnance Survey Address Layer 2 data (which can be used in conjunction with MasterMap) distinguish a number of types of building within the broad classification of 'non-domestic'. These include Education, Industrial, Leisure, Office, Office Mixed Use, Restaurant/Public house and Retail. In future work the statistics in Tables 3 and 4 might be broken down into these categories in order better to understand the values of V/W by size band. A preliminary analysis of such a disaggregation has been carried out by Batty *et al.*[19]

A statistical analysis of allometry in the London data

So far we have examined the relationship between wall area W and volume V in terms of the ratio V/W and found that as the building blocks become bigger in wall area and volume, the depth in plan increases significantly from an average about 3.5 m for domestic buildings in Islington to just over 10 m for non-domestic buildings in the City. This is an immediate outcome of their allometry. In this section we will generate aggregate statistics consistent with these depth ratios in the spirit pioneered by Bon, going back to the original insights of the biologist Julian Huxley.[20]

The Euclidean relationship $V \sim W^\alpha$ between area and volume is given as $W \sim V^{2/3}$ where it is assumed that there is no deformation of the surface area of the object as its volume increases. If area and volume are calculated from some length measure L, then the standard Euclidean equations hold as $W = L^2$ and $V = L^3$ from which this relationship can be derived directly. It is also clear that the ratio $V/W = L$ and from this, as the object or building gets larger, the surface (or wall) area declines in proportion to this unit linear measure. In fact as Bon first demonstrated for his sample of houses, $W \sim V^{0.77}$, that is the wall area does not decrease as fast as the linear measure which implies that the shape of the building deforms to capture more natural light from its surface. In this case, as is implied in Figures 5 and 6, the ratio increases as $V^{0.23}$. To demonstrate this effect, if we take a cubic block with $V = 6 \times 6 \times 6 = 216$ then

$V/W = V^{0.23} = 3.443$ in contrast to the Euclidean case where there is no deformation of wall area which gives a ratio of 3. If we double the size of the unit length to a block with $V = 12 \times 12 \times 12 = 1728$, this gives a Bon ratio of 5.554, compared to the Euclidean ratio of 6 where there is no deformation of the wall area. These values are consistent in terms of magnitude with the results presented in the last section, and with the depth calculations for the terraced block in Table 1.

In fact previous work with respect to deriving allometric relationships between surface area and volume for entire cities is sketchy and nowhere comprehensive. Nordbeck was among the first to examine the relationship between ground area A and population P of cities in Sweden.[21] He found that populations were not distorted, filling their space according to the standard Euclidean relationship; that is for the largest 1800 towns in 1960, he found that $A \sim P^{0.664}$ where about 90 per cent of the variance was explained. This coefficient only changed marginally to 0.650 when he did the same analysis for data for the same towns in 1965. Batty and Longley in their work on relating allometry and fractals found however that there was considerably more distortion (of the area) when they compared the 70 largest towns in the county of Norfolk with their areas using 1981 population data.[22] Here they found that $A \sim P^{0.959}$, implying that population does not scale as a volumetric measure but simply directly with area. In small towns, of course, where there are few high buildings and relatively uniform densities, this finding makes sense and is consistent with other work by Woldenberg and Dutton.[23]

Until the wall areas were extracted from the London database, we could only previously relate the footprint area of building blocks to their volumes and although we computed allometric relationships between these areas and volumes, these results did not relate to detached buildings and simply worked with the blocks as defined in the original Ordnance Survey MasterMap building footprints from which the databases are constructed. Nevertheless, we have computed equivalent allometric relationships between volume and footprint for all buildings in the residential and commercial classes as defined from land uses in the MasterMap data. The relationships derived for residential (domestic) are $A \sim V^{0.755}$, for commercial (non-domestic) $A \sim V^{0.834}$, and for all buildings $A \sim V^{0.772}$. These show more distortion than might be expected but this is not for wall area, and the points contain a very large number of building blocks that might be considered to be parts of buildings.[24]

What we have done here is to fit the general allometric relationship $W \sim V^{\alpha}$ for the ten size classes that were defined to examine the volume-wall ratios in the last section. We have regressed $\log W$ on $\log V$ to determine the allometric coefficients for the domestic and non-domestic size bands for each of the six boroughs. Then we have summed the data for the domestic and non-domestic stock, finally summing domestic and non-domestic for all boroughs. The size bands in each case are normalised by taking an average of the building block size in terms of wall area and volume; that is, each band which consists of all wall area and volume of all the blocks in the band has been divided by the number of blocks. In essence, the allometric relationships that are derived in this way are thus based on an 'average building block' for each band in terms of wall area and volume.

The results are shown in Table 5 where we have excluded the first category – buildings between 0 and 3 cubic metres in volume – from the analysis, thus reducing the number of bands to nine. We have done this because it is quite clear that this category picks up tiny building blocks that do not consist of 'true' buildings in any real sense, due primarily to the

144 Built form and urban form

TABLE 5 Allometric coefficients between wall area and building volume

Borough	*Domestic*		*Non-domestic*
Westminster	0.609		0.640
City	0.610		0.578
Hackney	0.689		0.675
Islington	0.616		0.657
Tower Hamlets	0.682		0.648
Camden	0.634		0.644
All London domestic & non-domestic	0.646		0.651
All London		0.642	

way the data set is formed. It might even be argued that the next two categories should be excluded for the same reasons. But because so many blocks are included in these groups, we have retained them, working all the analysis through for the nine remaining bands in the first instance.

This table shows that all the results for both the domestic and non-domestic categories cluster around the standard allometric relation in which the coefficient is 2/3, implying that wall area increases in the manner implicit in Euclidean scaling of building volume. This in turn suggests that wall area does not increase faster than the linear measure of increase in the size of a block, and thus no apparent deformation of shape occurs. There is no real difference between the domestic and non-domestic building stock in this respect, for the biggest differences in the allometric coefficients α are between boroughs, with the largest value being 0.682 for the domestic stock in Tower Hamlets and the lowest being 0.578 for the non-domestic in the City. The coefficient for all the domestic is 0.646 compared with 0.651 for the non-domestic and for all buildings the coefficient is 0.642. In every case in Table 5, the proportion of the variances explained r^2 are greater than 0.985; for all domestic, it is 0.991, for non-domestic it is 0.995 and for all buildings it is 0.993. The values of these coefficients are all significantly different from zero but in most cases they are *not* significantly different from 0.66.

All this might seem quite surprising in the light of Bon's and our own results on building footprint areas for the same data set.[25] We know these results must be biased from our earlier analysis, however there is still a very small probability that a lack of deformation of the geometry of buildings to produce the positive allometry required to increase surface area faster than the Euclidean norm, exists because of complications due to construction and lighting. To an extent, this is also borne out by the lower coefficients for the non-domestic stock in the City, which imply that as buildings get bigger, their surface area increases less rapidly than their linear measure; proportionately the wall area is less than might be expected from geometric considerations.

Nevertheless, analysis of the data set presented here is a first pass at an extremely complicated process of extracting building volumes and surface areas from polygonal data integrated from two different sources which in no way are coordinated, and which contain many – perhaps up to a million or more – volumetric structures that are not 'true buildings'. The next step would be to rework the regression analysis on individual building volumes, building footprints and wall areas; although there are especially difficult issues in associating

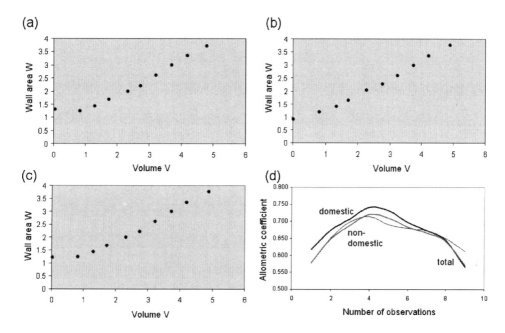

FIGURE 12 Allometric relations for (a) domestic, (b) non-domestic and (c) all building blocks

wall area with volume exactly and unambiguously from the polygonal data set. Either small blocks should be excluded altogether or the algorithms should be further developed, in order to identify how these blocks are part of their parent buildings. This will involve a serious extension of this analysis to deal with polygonal pattern recognition in the building stock.

Figure 12 shows graphs of the allometric relations for a) all domestic, b) all non-domestic and c) all buildings by the ten classes. Here is easy to see that the first class introduces bias, in that it obviously departs from the inherent linearity of these relations. In fact although all the statistical tests indicate that these relations are strongly linear, there is a slight detection of non-linearity, in that as the number of observations is systematically reduced by taking out the first, second, third and so on classes, the regression lines become slightly steeper; that is the allometric coefficients become larger. When just the top five observations are retained, the coefficients for the domestic, non-domestic and all stock change from 0.646, 0.651 and 0.642 to 0.741, 0.715, and 0.720, somewhat turning the overall results on their head in that the larger classes seem to imply much greater distortion in building shape than the overall analysis. This clearly needs further investigation. These changing coefficients are plotted for the reduced data sets in Figure 12(d).

We can get some sense of what this data set might yield with respect to the true allometric coefficients by assuming that the relation $W \sim V^\alpha$ can be fitted exactly to each value of wall area and volume that has been computed for each size band. This assumes that the relation is exact, that is, that $W = V^\alpha$ and that there is no scaling constant, or rather we assume a constant of proportionality of unity. If this is the case, then the allometric coefficient for each band can be calculated directly as $\alpha = \log W / \log V$. This can be done for each band in the entire data set, for the ten size classes in each of the six boroughs for the domestic and

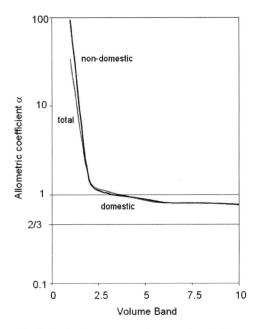

FIGURE 13 Distribution of individual allometric coefficients for all size bands across all boroughs

non-domestic stock, for the total domestic and non-domestic and then for the total stock. What we find is that for the domestic stock, the allometric coefficients progressively fall as the size associated with each band increases. When we reach the fifth band, the coefficients all fall below 1 and in the highest bands they vary from 0.766 to 0.815, very close to Bon's value of 0.77. For the non-domestic data, the range for the largest band is 0.764 to 0.776, remarkably close to Bon's figure.

If all the domestic and all the non-domestic in the largest band are added, the coefficients are 0.767 and 0.778. For the entire stock the coefficient rises to 0.857 in the largest band, which is clearly an artefact of the way these two distributions are added together. To illustrate the power of this analysis in detecting that the data does display allometry consistent with Bon's earlier analysis and considerable deformation in building shape as has been argued by Brown and Steadman[26] many times elsewhere, the distributions of these coefficients are plotted in Figure 13. It is extremely clear that consistent coefficients only begin to appear once the smallest size bands are excluded, which is tantamount to excluding the smallest blocks which are disconnected from their parent buildings referred to earlier.

Conclusions

We have shown that when very large numbers of buildings – either domestic or non-domestic – are considered in the aggregate, then their mean plan depths as measured by the ratio V/W are consistent with previous measurements on smaller samples of such buildings. We have also demonstrated that when the building blocks that make up the London sample are analysed within their separate size bands, they show allometric relationships between volume and surface of the kind demonstrated by Bon, but only in the larger bands. This is because we are examining in London a dense urban fabric in which many blocks are contiguous. By comparison, Bon measured just detached dwellings. Furthermore, what might on architectural or constructional grounds be termed single 'buildings' can, in the present data, be broken up in a haphazard way – through the process of digitising their footprints – into many small component parts, for which Bon-type allometry would not be expected to occur. It is only in the larger size bands that the blocks more closely equate to 'buildings', and become partly or wholly detached.

In future work it would be desirable to amalgamate all the smaller blocks into 'buildings'; but this is technically not straightforward, and in any case the definition of what should constitute *one* building can be elusive. We have attempted to join the footprint polygons of blocks automatically into something more like building footprints, on the basis of contiguity and data about occupants and addresses, but this has only served to show the difficulties. Another approach, which would certainly be feasible, would be to define detached 'built islands', by taking one block and adding to it progressively all blocks with contiguous footprints until the boundary of the island is reached. But in dense city centres these islands can be large.

Some anomalies in the results here could well be produced by the misclassification of buildings as 'domestic' rather than 'non-domestic' and vice versa; and of course there are many large buildings that contain both types of use. Cleaning the data of such problems might fine-tune the results. Certainly the disaggregation of non-domestic into use classes such as office, retail, industrial etc should clarify and extend some of the findings.

As for applications, the work has relevance to several areas of building science at a scale larger than that of single structures. The ratio V/W has implications for the capital costs of construction, since it expresses the area of building envelope per unit of accommodation. Building depths are important for energy use, since a distance of 6 m or 7 m from exposed walls is, as we have seen, the approximate limit of the passive zone beyond which artificial ventilation and permanent artificial lighting generally become necessary – as formalised in the LT model. The measurements for non-domestic buildings presented here have shown, in effect, the extent of non-passive core space beyond this depth limit. Recent research by Salat and Adhitya has revealed substantial variations in overall surface-to-volume ratios between different cities, and has shown the impact of the passive-to-non-passive volume ratio on total energy use for heating.[27]

Acknowledgements

The measurements on which this analysis is based were made by Stephen Evans for the EPSRC LUCID Project (the development of a Local Urban Climate model and its application to the Intelligent Development of cities: Grant Number EP/Eo16375/1) led by Professor Michael Davies at University College London.

Notes

1 M Batty and A Hudson-Smith, 'Urban simulacra', *Architectural Design*, Volume 75, 2005 pp. 42–47.
2 These measurements are made from overflying aircraft, using lasers.
3 G Dutton ed., 'Size and shape in the growth of human communities', special issue of *Ekistics*, Volume 36, No. 215, October 1973.
4 P Steadman, *The Evolution of Designs: Biological Analogy in Architecture and the Applied Arts*: revised edn, Routledge, London and New York 2008.

5 R Bon, *An Introduction to Morphometric Analysis of Spatial Phenomena on a Micro-Environmental Scale*, unpublished Master's Thesis, Department of City and Regional Planning, Harvard University, Cambridge MA 1972; R Bon, 'Allometry in micro-environmental morphology', Special Papers Series, Paper E, *Harvard Papers in Theoretical Geography*, Laboratory for Computer Graphics and Spatial Analysis, Graduate School of Design, Harvard University, Cambridge MA 1972; R Bon, 'Allometry in the topologic structure of architectural spatial systems', *Ekistics*, Volume 36, No. 215, October 1973 pp. 270–276.

6 R M Helick, *Varieties of Human Habitation*, Regent Graphic Services, Pittsburgh PA 1970.

7 Bon, 'Allometry in micro-environmental morphology' p. 10.

8 P Steadman, 'Allometry and built form: revisiting Ranko Bon's work with the Harvard Philomorphs', *Construction Management and Economics*, Volume 24, 2006 pp. 755–765.

9 This argument relates to multi-storey buildings. A single-storey block can be made deeper and the centre can be day-lit via roof lights – although these are not completely equivalent to windows in functional terms of course, since they provide views only of the sky.

10 F E Brown and P Steadman, 'The morphology of British housing: an empirical basis for policy and research. Part 1: functional and dimensional characteristics', *Environment and Planning B: Planning and Design*, Volume 18, 1991 pp. 385–415.

11 R North, *Of Building: Roger North's Writings on Architecture*, eds H Colvin and J Newman, Clarendon Press, Oxford 1981 p. 9.

12 Ibid., p. 69.

13 This argument applies to buildings like apartment blocks with continuous longitudinal circulation routes, but not to blocks broken up for example into terrace houses.

14 Brown and Steadman, 'Morphology of British housing'.

15 P Steadman, F E Brown, H R Bruhns, P A Rickaby and S Holtier, *An Approach to the Classification of Building Forms and Building Types*, Report to the Global Atmosphere Division of the Department of the Environment, Centre for Configurational Studies, Design Discipline, Open University, Milton Keynes 1993 p. 84.

16 The shallow buildings may also be air-conditioned – although they do not absolutely have to be – for reasons such as acoustic insulation from traffic noise.

17 C Willis, *Form Follows Finance: Skyscrapers and Skylines in New York and Chicago*, Princeton Architectural Press, New York 1995 pp. 24–30.

18 N V Baker and K Steemers, *The LT Method 2.0: An Energy Design Tool for Non-Domestic Buildings*, Cambridge Architectural Research Ltd, Cambridge, n.d.

19 M Batty, R Carvalho, A Hudson-Smith, R Milton, D Smith and P Steadman, 'Scaling and allometry in the building geometries of Greater London', *European Physical Journal B*, Volume 63, 2008 pp. 303–318.

20 J S Huxley, 'Constant differential growth-ratios and their significance', *Nature*, Volume 114, 1924 pp. 895–896.

21 S Nordbeck, 'Urban allometric growth', *Geografiska Annaler*, Volume 53B, 1971 pp. 54–67.

22 M Batty and P A Longley, *Fractal Cities: A Geometry of Form and Function*, Academic Press, London and San Diego, CA 1994.

23 M J Woldenberg, 'An allometric analysis of urban land use in the United States', *Ekistics*, Volume 36, 1973 pp. 282–290; G Dutton, 'Criteria of growth in urban systems', *Ekistics*, Volume 36, 1973 pp. 298–306.

24 Batty *et al.*, 'Scaling and allometry'.

25 Ibid.

26 Brown and Steadman, 'Morphology of British housing'.

27 S Salat and S Danita, 'Energy loads, CO_2 emissions and building stocks: morphologies, typologies, energy systems and behavior', *Building Research and Information* Volume 37, 2009 pp. 598–609.

8

ENERGY AND URBAN BUILT FORM

An empirical and statistical approach

(with Ian Hamilton and Stephen Evans)

(Building Research and Information, Volume 42, 2014, pp. 17–31)

The geometrical forms of buildings have important effects on their use of energy. This paper looks for such relationships at the scale of the entire non-domestic building stock of London. The Virtual London model introduced in the previous paper is used to make a series of geometrical measurements, of building volume, exposed surface area (walls plus roof) and plan depth. These are compared with figures for the consumption of gas and electricity published by the UK Department of Energy and Climate Change. The comparisons are made for different geographical areas, from boroughs to census districts.

We would expect to find a significant relationship between energy consumption and the surface area of buildings in the UK climate, because of heat loss from walls and roofs: strong correlations are indeed found with both gas and electricity use. The analysis also provides some evidence of a sharp increase in electricity use in districts with buildings whose depth in plan exceeds 14 m, and in which air conditioning and permanent artificial lighting are therefore required. A statistical model is used to measure the contribution of these effects to total energy use, as compared with floor area, activities and number of employees.

Introduction

This paper tests two hypotheses about the relationship of 3D urban morphology to the use of energy in buildings. The focus is on non-domestic buildings in Greater London. The first hypothesis is that energy use for space heating is correlated with the total exposed surface area of buildings. The second hypothesis is that there is an effective threshold value for the depth of multi-storey buildings in plan, above which energy use for air conditioning and artificial lighting rises sharply. Similar hypotheses have been proposed and investigated by other authors, as we will describe. The present study breaks new ground by taking an empirical and statistical approach, applied to all buildings in the non-domestic stock across the whole of London.

Exposed surface area and energy use for heating: previous work

We would expect the first hypothesis to be true in a temperate climate like that of the UK on the strength of the basic physics of heat loss. Ratti, Baker and Steemers studied a range

150 Built form and urban form

of geometrical measures of urban built form in relation to energy use, including the ratio of exposed surface area-to-volume.[1] They took 400 × 400 m sample areas in three cities – London, Berlin and Toulouse – and represented their three-dimensional forms with digital elevation models (DEMs). (The London sample was in the Borough of Camden, centred on the Tottenham Court Road.) They modelled energy use with the LT simulation package, using default values for everything other than geometrical parameters, with the intention of making comparisons on an equal basis rather than estimates of actual consumption.

Salat studied the relationship of surface/volume with energy use for space heating in the residential stock of Paris, again using DEMs to represent three 500 × 500 m zones with distinctive building 'typologies' of different dates, specifically two types of courtyard pattern, historic and modern, and a development of freestanding Modernist blocks.[2] The energy use was modelled, and the estimates compared with actual consumption levels for Parisian residential buildings generally.

More recently, members of the LSE Cities centre at the London School of Economics have also studied residential heating energy use and urban morphology.[3] This research took 500 × 500 m sample areas in four cities – London, Paris, Berlin and Istanbul – and represented not the actual geometry of the buildings in question, but an idealisation of the characteristic forms of the most frequently occurring types. The study area for London consisted mostly of terraced buildings. Energy use for heating was then modelled, and compared with several parameters including density, building height, and the ratio of surface to volume. We will come back to the results of all these studies.

The Virtual London model

The research reported here relates as mentioned to the entirety of London. We make use of Virtual London, a 3D digital model of the metropolis covering all buildings out to the M25 orbital motorway.[4]

[*The 'Virtual London' model was described in the previous paper: see Paper 7, Figure 1. Some repetition has been removed here.*]

In both digital elevation models and Virtual London, roofs are taken to be flat, but in Virtual London the heights for buildings with pitched roofs are averaged from all LiDAR values falling within the given footprint polygon.[5] Virtual London comprises some 3.2 million blocks, many of which are fragmentary parts of buildings. A small block for example might correspond to a lift tower, an entrance porch, or a back extension. The MasterMap data were combined with the Generalised Land Use Database,[6] making it possible to distinguish domestic from non-domestic buildings, and to categorise the non-domestic buildings as office, retail, warehouse etc. (There are weaknesses in the data in the categorisation of buildings that contain both domestic and non-domestic premises.)

Volumes of blocks are given simply by multiplying footprint polygon areas by heights. For analysis the volumes were grouped into a series of approximately logarithmic size bands: $0 - 3$ m³, $3 - 10$ m³, $10 - 30$ m³, $30 - 100$ m³, etc. Virtual London has no information on numbers of storeys. In order to obtain estimates of floor areas, volumes have therefore been divided by a standard assumed value for storey height of 3.5 m. This is somewhat greater than the typical value of 3 m for modern offices, to allow for taller ceilings in factories, warehouses and large shops. We have been guided by an analysis of storey heights in a sample

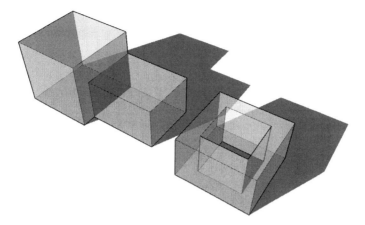

FIGURE 1 Three extruded polygon buildings are shown in 3D view with the buildings having semi-transparent walls (and casting shadows). The building at the left is adjacent to the middle building, and part of their shared wall (darker tone) is not exposed to the elements. Since these two buildings differ in height and depth, there are other sections of this wall that *are* exposed. All other walls (including the inner courtyard walls of the building at the right) contribute to the exposed surface area of the building

of some 3500 buildings in British towns made in the 1990s;[7] however the assumption of a single default value clearly means that the floor area estimates will be approximate only.

For calculating exposed surface, roof areas are taken to be equal to footprint areas. Measuring the areas of exposed walls is more complicated, since these need to be distinguished automatically from internal walls between adjoining blocks, some of which will be actual party walls between properties. Such topological relationships can be dealt with in GIS software by categorising the walls belonging to building footprints as 'children' of their 'parent' polygons. The walls can then be assigned heights; and by analysing the spatial relationships of the polygon in question to adjoining polygons it is possible to determine whether the walls face courtyards or face outwards – and so are exposed in both cases – or are internal.

Where a wall divides buildings or blocks of different heights it may be an internal wall on the lower floors but an exposed wall on the upper floors (Figure 1). The section of wall in the darker tone where the two blocks at the left of the figure meet for example is not exposed, but the parts above and to the left of this are exposed. The analysis takes care of such situations. All these exposed wall areas need to be summed and added to the roof areas to obtain total exposed surface area. (It is possible that some small light wells might be omitted from the Virtual London model, in which case the exposed areas could be underestimated. If so, we expect such effects to be minor.)

To measure the depths of buildings in plan we have used a method developed for and explained in a previous paper [*Paper 7 in this volume*]. We take the total exposed wall area W of each block and divide by its volume V. [*Some repetition is omitted here.*] The advantage of this method is that it can be applied to all shapes of plan, rectangular or otherwise, for which in many cases it is impossible to define a simple linear measurement of depth. Where groups of blocks are joined together to form 'buildings', the calculation takes account of their total volume in relation to their total exposed wall area.

152 Built form and urban form

It is worth emphasising that our hypothesis about energy use and plan depth is only relevant to multi-storey buildings, since single-storey buildings can be lit and ventilated from the roof. There are several activities that can occupy single-storey buildings with very deep plans, including factories, warehouses and 'big shed' superstores. Much work on energy use in the non-domestic building stock is predicated on the belief that a substantial fraction of that stock is made up of office buildings. However in England and Wales, the total floor areas of shops, factories and warehouses are each of them greater than the total area of offices. We will see this phenomenon of the deep-plan single-storey shed in the results presented below.

The measurements on Virtual London were aggregated geographically to lower level super output areas (LSOAs) and medium level super output areas (MSOAs) in order to make comparisons with energy data. These are spatial units designed by the UK Office of National Statistics for Census purposes. To give an idea of their size: in residential areas an LSOA would comprise between 400 and 1200 households, and an MSOA between 2000 and 6000 households. On occasion the building polygons straddled several Output Areas and in these cases, rather than split buildings, they were assigned completely to the area in which the greater part fell.

Electricity and gas consumption data

For energy data we rely on statistics for electricity and gas consumption from a national database compiled by the UK Government's Department for Energy and Climate Change (DECC).[8] These are aggregated from individual gas and electricity meter point data for all meters in London, and published at two geographical scales: local authority and MSOA.

The meters fall into different groups: daily and non-daily for gas, and half-hourly and non-half-hourly for electricity. For all electricity meters, annualised figures are derived from meter readings and are classified into eight user groups, which are defined by the type of user (domestic or non-domestic), the tariff type (standard or economy) and for non-domestic meters, the amount of electricity used. For all gas meters, annualised figures are also derived from meter readings but unlike electricity no further classification is made. Instead gas meters are generally assumed to be 'domestic' if consumption is less than 73.2 MWh/year – although for official statistics DECC goes through a process of allocating as many meters as possible to their proper classes using address details.[9]

Due to issues of privacy, half-hourly electricity and some non-daily gas meters are not allocated to geographical units below local authorities. In 2007 this meant that only 28 per cent of total non-domestic electricity use was allocated at the MSOA level. Most of these meters are non half-hourly and are generally characterised as smaller users.[10] By contrast, for non-domestic gas demand, 97 per cent was allocated at the MSOA level.

It is possible therefore to separate non-domestic from domestic energy demand from these figures, but not to break them down any further by end uses. The levels of geographical aggregation create difficulties for any spatial analysis, and it would be very desirable to have complete figures at LSOA level. Given the limitations of the data, we have carried out some broad-brush studies for both gas and electricity at the local authority scale. At the finer scale, we have worked with non-domestic gas data allocated to MSOAs, since this excludes only 3 per cent of meters. And we have used non-domestic electricity data allocated to MSOAs for exploratory and indicative purposes, even though these account for less than one-third of total consumption.

Results

Table 1 gives summary statistics for the morphological measures on non-domestic blocks across London. Remember that these blocks are in many cases parts of buildings: thus the average values will be smaller than those for complete buildings. See how the mean value for the ratio of exposed wall to volume is 3.1, implying a plan depth of 6.2 m. Figure 2 maps total volume, Figure 3 maps exposed surface area, and Figure 4 maps building depth, obtained by dividing exposed wall area by volume. The data in the figures are for LSOAs in all cases.

TABLE 1 Summary statistics for morphological parameters of non-domestic buildings in London; data derived from Virtual London

Variable	Mean	Std dev.	Median	Lower quartile	Upper quartile
Footprint area per block (m^2)	295.03	936.15	52.25	14.46	215.19
Volume per block (m^3)	2885.34	12043.6	310.67	47.33	1641.34
Wall area per block (m^2)	449.5	1023.55	136.04	35.78	420.93
Volume-to-wall ratio per block (m)	3.1	2.99	2.37	1.36	3.92
Plan depth per block (m)	6.2	5.98	4.75	2.72	7.83
Height per block (m)	6.53	5.18	5.68	3.08	8.21
Floor space per block (m^2)	901.67	3763.63	97.09	14.79	512.92

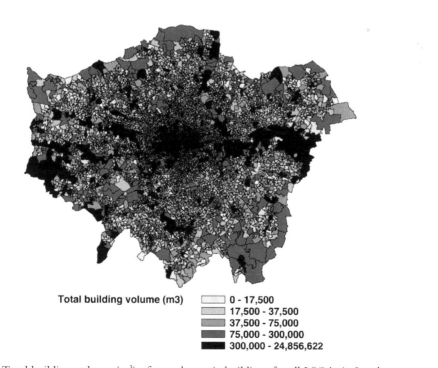

FIGURE 2 Total building volume (m^3) of non-domestic buildings for all LSOAs in London

154 Built form and urban form

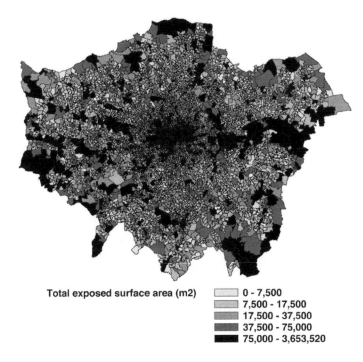

FIGURE 3 Total exposed surface area (m²) of non-domestic buildings for all LSOAs in London

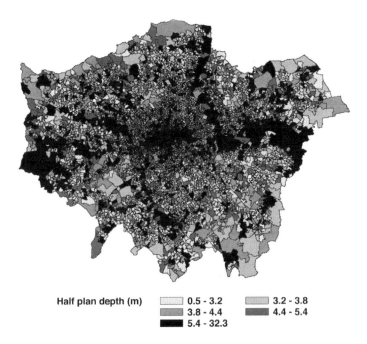

FIGURE 4 Average wall to volume ratio (m), or half-plan depth, of non-domestic buildings for all LSOAs in London

A picture emerges of several small concentrations of very large, tall and deep buildings, with the remainder characterised by low-rise, shallower plan buildings. Building volume (Figure 2) is concentrated in the office areas of the City of London and along the Thames, and in the industrial areas up the Lea River valley to the north and in Hounslow around Heathrow Airport to the west. Figure 3 shows that exposed area (walls plus roofs) follows a similar pattern to volume, but with an increase around the outer edges of the metropolis. The mean value for surface to volume in LSOAs for the whole of London is 0.35. For the Borough of Camden, the value is 0.28, indicating taller deeper buildings than in the metropolis generally. (This compares with a value of 0.216 obtained by Ratti *et al.* for their sample area in Camden, in which the buildings are large compared with much of the rest of the borough.) Figure 4 shows that deeper blocks – i.e. those with depths greater than 10 m, shown in the darkest tone – are found in central London and in the same industrial areas that have high building volume.

Figure 5 gives the distribution for the volumes of blocks, by size bands (m³), for each of London's local authorities. This shows that boroughs such as Camden, Islington, Kensington and Chelsea, Southwark, Tower Hamlets and Westminster have higher concentrations of

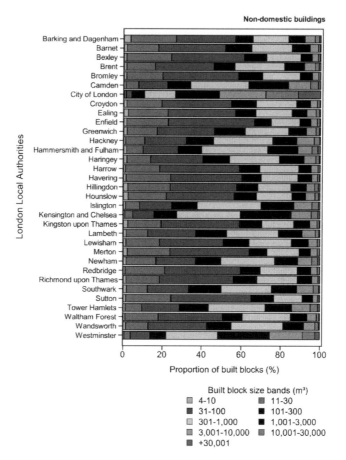

FIGURE 5 Proportion of non-domestic built blocks by volume size bands for London local authorities

TABLE 2 Summary statistics for non-domestic energy in 2007 for London at Local Authority level

Variable	Mean	Std dev.	Median	Lower quartile	Upper quartile
Mean electricity use (kWh/meter/yr)	73,275	58,472	54,527	45,061	77,574
Mean electricity intensity[a] (kWh/m²/yr)	127.0	46.9	110.7	97.4	144.0
Mean gas use (kWh/meter/yr)	571,352	292,119	496,590	358,078	616,865
Mean gas intensity[a] (kWh/m²/yr)	118.8	40.3	111.8	98.5	134.4

Note: a) gfa= gross floor area estimate

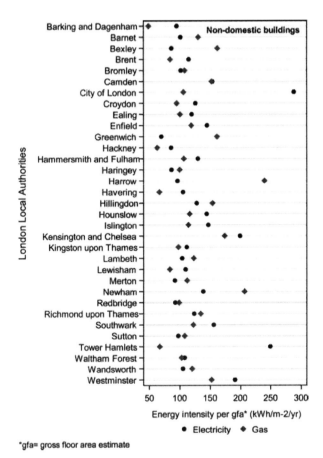

*gfa= gross floor area estimate

FIGURE 6 Non-domestic electricity and gas intensity per m² of gross floor area for London's local authorities

larger blocks with volumes above 1000 m³. More than half of the built blocks in the City of London are above 3000 m³.

Table 2 gives means for non-domestic gas and electricity use in 2007 using local authority-level data, including consumption by meter and consumption per square metre of floor area. (The floor area estimates are gross external figures, so these intensities would be somewhat lower than those measured by net internal or gross internal area.) Figure 6 breaks down the energy intensity values per square metre into separate local authorities.

Notice the particularly high values for electricity use in several boroughs with high concentrations of office activity: the City of London, Kensington and Chelsea, Tower Hamlets (location of the major Docklands office zone, including Canary Wharf) and Westminster. The City has the highest electricity intensity of all, at 287 kWh/m², compared with a gas demand of 101 kWh/m². Tower Hamlets has a comparatively low level of gas use (66 kWh/m²) suggesting that electricity may be being used extensively for space heating and cooling in Docklands. Harrow has the highest gas demand at 239 kWh/m², compared with an electricity intensity of 95 kWh/m²: the borough has a number of industrial parks with large sheds along the A40 motorway.

As mentioned, the consumption data are not broken down by end uses. Large-scale data on the construction characteristics for non-domestic buildings in the UK are severely limited. Although it is well understood that a number of non-morphological factors will directly affect the amount of energy consumed in a building (e.g. facade materials, proportion of glazing, heating and core services, IT equipment, air conditioning, and activity type) no such database exists that offers comprehensive or even indicative details on these for London.

One would of course expect that a significant fraction of the electricity use in the boroughs that are dominated by office activity would be accounted for by IT and computing equipment. This, along with lighting, would be contributing to the internal gains, and would further increase the cooling demand. All this obviously complicates the relationship between energy use and plan depth in the office stock. As a result, while we examine the morphological factors that relate to energy demand, we are not able to control for all of these other unknown factors. Analysis of such issues at the urban or borough scale would require end-use data that do not currently exist. Thus, as we present and discuss the results, we should be cautious of assigning too much significance to relationships: nonetheless they are indicative of expected patterns.

Exposed surface area

Figure 7 shows the correlations of total exposed surface area with mean annual gas and electricity demand per meter respectively, for all non-domestic buildings in London. The Pearson correlation coefficients are given in Table 3. We have opted to take surface area rather than the ratio of surface to volume, since we are looking for effects relating to space heating demand, which would tend to be proportional to volume; and to compare surface/volume with energy use/volume would mean having the same denominator in both variables. As we would expect, the correlation of surface area to both gas and electricity use is significant ($p < 0.001$ at the 95 per cent level), with coefficients of 0.82 and 0.76 respectively, showing that energy use does indeed increase with exposed surface area.

This goes some way to confirming our first hypothesis, although we cannot attribute all of the energy demand to the explanatory power of surface area since we lack information on

158 Built form and urban form

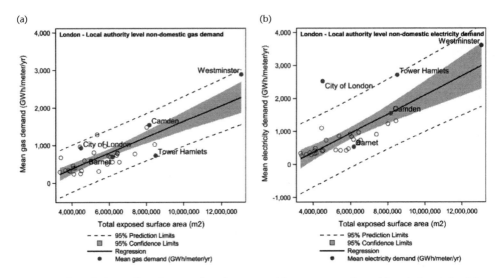

FIGURE 7 Correlations of total exposed surface area with mean annual gas (a) and electricity (b) demand per meter (GWh/meter/yr), for all non-domestic buildings in London at the local authority level

TABLE 3 Pearson correlation between local authority level energy use and morphological parameters in London

Pearson correlation coefficients, N = 33 Prob > |r| under H0: rho=0						
	Volume (m³)	Plan depth (m)	Exposed surface area (m²)	Height (m)	Electricity (kWh/yr)	Gas (kWh/yr)
Electricity (kWh/yr)	0.92003 <.0001★★★	0.50219 0.0029★★★	0.75935 <.0001★★★	0.43374 0.0117★★	1	0.76066 <.0001★★★
Gas (kWh/yr)	0.88739 <.0001★★★	0.38221 0.0282★★	0.81731 <.0001★★★	0.5148 0.0022★★★	0.76066 <.0001★★★	1

Note: ★p<0.1; ★★p<0.05; ★★★p<0.01

other building features. Gas is the dominant heating fuel in Britain: however there is a large but unknown extent of electricity use for space heating in the non-domestic stock. We would also expect electricity consumption to be associated with cooling and fans in larger prestige buildings. Notice in this context that electricity use in three of the 'office boroughs' lies well above the regression line.

It is possible that some further complications are masked in the overall correlation. For instance it may well be that thermal properties of their envelopes vary in systematic ways with the ages and geometrical properties of buildings, specifically their ratios of exposed surface to volume. Such effects could potentially be examined in further studies.

Meanwhile we can compare the basic result with the findings of previous work. Rode et al. looked at the exposed surface areas of residential buildings.[11] They compared this with (modelled) energy use for heating, and found a positive correlation for their London building typologies with a coefficient of 0.63. The LSE team also found negative correlations of heat energy demand with density, ground coverage and building height. This last result is somewhat perplexing since energy use for heating can hardly be affected by height as such. It might perhaps be a result of tall buildings being predicted by the modelling to have increased solar exposure, hence greater solar gains?[12]

Ratti et al. found different values for the ratio of surface to volume for their three sample areas in London, Toulouse and Berlin of 0.216, 0.248 and 0.169 respectively. They did not quantify the relationship with energy use, but remarked on these large differences and their implications for heat loss. Salat also made comparisons of surface to volume for different parts of Paris and showed that values have increased from the eighteenth to the twentieth centuries with the transition from courtyard developments to freestanding Modernist slabs. These changes were associated with a difference in modelled heat energy use of 58 kWh/m^2/yr for the eighteenth-century fabric, compared with 100 kWh/m^2/yr for the twentieth century. As mentioned earlier, Salat's results (and those of Rode et al.) are however for residential buildings and are therefore not directly comparable with the present work. It should be said that the types of morphology studied by all these authors tended towards the upper end of the scale of building size and density. We have revealed a rather different picture by plotting values for exposed surface across the entire city.

Plan depth

Figure 8 shows the correlation of mean plan depth with gas and electricity demand respectively, again for all non-domestic buildings in London. The correlation coefficients are again given in Table 3. Here the correlations are weaker, with coefficients of 0.50 (electricity) and 0.38 (gas). As in Figure 7, the 'office boroughs' depart from the regression line.

Our hypothesis about plan depth however relates to multi-storey buildings whose depth effectively requires air conditioning and permanent artificial lighting. The LT Method

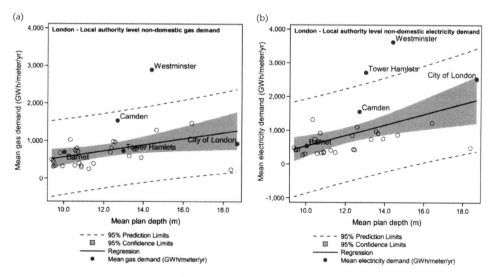

FIGURE 8 Correlations of plan depth with mean annual gas (a) and electricity (b) demand per meter (GWh/meter/yr), for all non-domestic buildings in London at the local authority level

160 Built form and urban form

generally assumes that this dimension is $2 \times 6 = 12$ m, with perhaps an additional 2 m for a central corridor, giving 14 m. In the nineteenth- and early twentieth-century literature on office design, a figure of 25 ft (7.6 m) was repeatedly quoted as the extreme limit of depth for rooms to be lit acceptably from windows. This would imply a total depth, with corridor, of up to 17 m. Empirical measurements of a sample of 19 large office buildings in Swindon (Berkshire) reported by Steadman et al. [*Paper 7 in this volume*] show two peaks in the distribution of their plan depths, around 14 m and 20 m.[13] This would suggest a first group that (potentially) has natural lighting and natural ventilation, and a second group that is certainly air-conditioned.

Calculations made using simulation models would indicate significant implications of plan depth for energy demand. Steemers for example reported an experiment with the LT Method to investigate the consequences of increasing the depth of a notional office building from 12 to 24 m.[14] A doubling of energy use was predicted. This assumed that the non-passive areas were mechanically ventilated. For efficient air conditioning the difference was less marked, but energy use was still 20 per cent greater in the deep building.

Returning to Figure 8, we see that the mean plan depths for almost all boroughs are below 14 m, and only in the City of London, Barking and Dagenham do they rise above 18 m. Because these are means taken across relatively large geographical areas they may of course conceal large local variations in plan depth. Nevertheless the evidence of this high-level analysis does suggest that very deep buildings tend to be concentrated in just a few boroughs. The City of London in particular is at the same time relatively small in land area, and consists predominantly of high-rise office buildings. (The deep-plan buildings in Barking and Dagenham are likely to be warehouses and factories.) We therefore turn our attention to this and a small number of other 'office boroughs'.

We referred earlier to previous work in which mean plan depths were computed for building blocks in selected London boroughs, in a series of size bands defined by volume. This showed that only in the topmost band, >30,000 m^3, did mean depths rise above 14 m. One might expect this result on simple geometrical grounds. Only blocks with this kind of volume would have plans this deep. Imagine a building block with a footprint 20×60 m and a storey height of 3.5 m. This gives a volume of 4200 m^3 per floor. In a block with total volume 30,000 m^3 this would mean seven floors. Many major office buildings would have larger footprints than this.

Figure 9 shows the distribution of plan depth by LSOA within the City of London and the boroughs of Camden, Tower Hamlets and Westminster. The mean for the City is around 18 m. We can compare this with Figure 10, which gives values for annual electricity use per meter at the MSOA level for the same boroughs. The City has the highest value. We can break down the analysis in a different way by selecting MSOAs that have high concentrations of particular activities: retail, office, retail plus office, or industrial. Figure 11 shows correlations of mean plan depth for these areas with annual electricity and gas use per meter. We see that in MSOAs where more than 60 per cent of total floor space is office use, both electricity and gas consumption are positively correlated with plan depth; and that with electricity consumption the slope of the regression line is particularly steep.

We could not claim that this analysis is conclusive: but it is at least a suggestive indication of the truth of our second hypothesis, that electricity use rises sharply above a threshold of plan depth around 14 m. (There might be additional causes at work here, including the possibility that tall buildings at very high densities – as in the City – are cutting off daylight from the lower storeys, so further raising the demand for artificial lighting. Baker and Ratti have modelled some effects of this kind.[15]) Recall that these figures only include 28 per cent of electricity meters, many of which are non-half-hourly; as such they should be treated with caution. It would be desirable to pursue these questions at a finer spatial scale: unfortunately the limitations of the available electricity data make this difficult. Again, as with surface area,

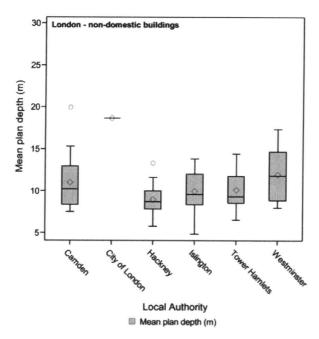

FIGURE 9 Mean plan depth at the MSOA level for selected London local authorities

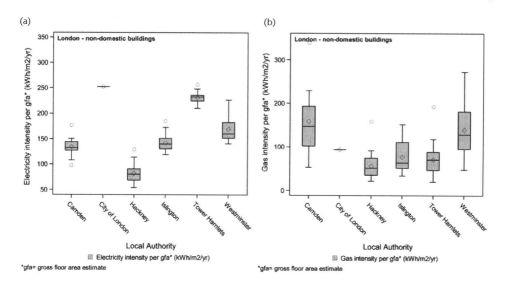

FIGURE 10 Mean a) electricity intensity (kWh/m²/yr) and b) gas intensity (kWh/m²/yr) at the MSOA level for selected London local authorities

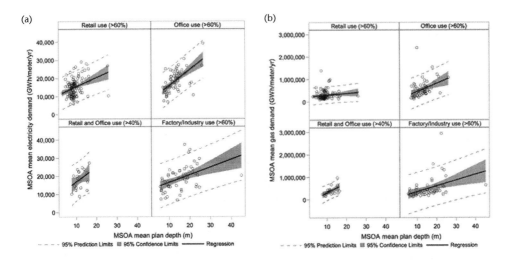

FIGURE 11 Relationship between MSOA level a) mean electricity demand and b) mean gas demand and mean MSOA plan depth for areas with a high proportion of a single non-domestic floor space use

there could be confounding effects related to the age and fabric characteristics of buildings. Certainly we would not find deep-plan air-conditioned offices dating from earlier than the 1940s.

The authors cited earlier who have also looked at plan depth have taken a different approach, and it is not so easy to compare their findings with ours. Ratti *et al.* and Salat both used GIS tools to draw boundary lines in the plans of buildings modelled in DEMs, set back from the exposed perimeter by some specified distance. These define outer 'passive' zones, which can be lit and ventilated naturally. Any remaining space deeper in the building is designated as 'non-passive', and would have to be artificially lit and air-conditioned. In the two studies in question, the passive depth was taken as 6 m, which is the standard assumption in the LT Method used to predict energy use. The volumes of buildings that are respectively passive and non-passive could then be calculated. All this work was applied to multi-storey buildings where the passive:non-passive distinction may be expected to be significant for energy use.

Ratti *et al.* found that the percentage of total building volume made up by passive zones was for Toulouse 84 per cent, London 77 per cent and Berlin 61 per cent. Modelling energy consumption for the non-passive zones showed that this did not differ greatly between the three cities. However consumption in passive and non-passive zones combined was somewhat higher in Berlin at 73 kWh/m^2/yr, compared with values of 67 and 68 for the other two cities.[16] This does indeed suggest an effect on energy consumption of depth above 12 m. Whether the results can be compared with our own is another matter. We use actual energy consumption data, while Ratti *et al.*'s figures are modelled. The LT Method assumes *a priori* that the boundary between passive and non-passive zones is 6 m away from the exposed walls, and consumption is modelled on that assumption. Our analysis by contrast suggests an effect on electricity use at a somewhat higher value for plan depth, around 18 or 20 m.

The contribution of morphological factors to total energy use

We have demonstrated a correlation of energy use with the exposed surface areas of buildings, although we cannot assign the full significance of the correlation to this parameter. We have also produced some evidence of an effect of plan depth on electricity use above about 14 m. The question remains as to what degree these factors explain energy consumption, and their significance by comparison with other known drivers. To address this question we used the MSOA level gas and electricity demand, and have developed two multiple regression models that measure the explanatory power of a series of variables besides the basic morphological measures.

These variables include numbers of employees, areas of floor space, and the proportions of that floor space that are represented by retail, offices and warehouses.[17] Details are given in Table 4. As mentioned earlier, we are not able to account for a number of construction features of the non-domestic building stock at the analysis level and thus our results provide only initial indications of the relationships between these variables and energy use. We intend to explore this further in future studies using data that may become available from a number of sources including Valuation Office Agency data on non-domestic buildings.

Initially, we used a stepwise selection approach to determine the predictive strength of variables; we then used this information along with the addition of variables of interest to develop a model with a reasonable statistical fit and significance. To ensure that possible collinearity of variables did not overly affect the model, we assessed the variance inflation factors (VIF) and condition indices (CI).[18] In most cases the VIF was larger than 5 with most tolerances not larger than 0.25 and all less than 0.5. In checking the model we ensured that condition indices were less than 35, a general rule of thumb.

Table 5 gives the results of the regression models for total MSOA gas demand (kWh/yr) and total MSOA electricity demand (kWh/yr). We find that the model for gas demand has a moderately good fit (adj. R^2 of 0.64) using number of employees, total exposed surface area, total building floor space, total plan depth, number of gas meters, the number of built blocks, and the proportion of warehouse and factory floor space. We see that an increase in the number of employees reduces demand. There is also a negative relationship between the proportion of warehouse floor space and a positive relation with factory space. In terms of morphology, we see that exposed surface area and floor space increase gas demand, while plan depth decreases it.

For electricity demand, we find a very good model fit (adj. R^2 of 0.96) using number of employees, total exposed surface area, total building floor space, total plan depth, number of electricity meters, number of built blocks, total built block height, proportion of retail and office floor space and the rateable value of office and warehouse floor space. We see that a greater proportion of retail and office floor space increases electricity demand, as does the rateable value of the office floor space. We also find that a greater number of employees increases electricity demand, the opposite of gas demand. This might be explained by areas of high electricity demand being predominantly in the service sector with more employees, while warehousing and manufacturing use more gas with fewer employees. In terms of morphology, we find that exposed surface area and total plan depth increase demand, while floor space reduces it.

Taking the results overall, the regression models show that average plan depth per MSOA is significant in explaining both gas and electricity use. We find that every additional metre

164 Built form and urban form

TABLE 4 Multiple regression model results for annual gas and electricity in London at the MSOA level

Predictors	Est.	Std. Error (P-value)	
MSOA (N= 983)	Total MSOA gas demand (kWh/yr)		
Intercept	8174278	3642731	(0.0251)
Number of employees 2008 (N)	−14.474	2.79	(<.0001)
Total exposed surface area (m²)	162.414	36.468	(<.0001)
Total building floor space (m²)	57.98	18.404	(0.0017)
Total MSOA plan depth (m)	−48823	13326	(0.0003)
Number of non-domestic gas meters (N)	165115	32649	(<.0001)
Count of buildings (N)	−12411	6204.459	(0.0458)
Total building height (m)	2274.477	7983.093	(0.7758)
Proportion of warehouse floor space (%)	−29231839	6806387	(<.0001)
Proportion of factory floor space (%)	16415659	8003783	(0.0405)
Maximum VIF (mean VIF)	51.97	(12.89)	
Condition Indices (CI)	30.97		
Adj. R²	0.6392		
MSOA (N= 983)	Total MSOA electricity demand (kWh/yr)		
Intercept	−4513232	744652	(<.0001)
Number of employees 2008 (N)	1.836	0.246	(<.0001)
Total exposed surface area (m²)	19.385	3.266	(<.0001)
Total building floor space (m²)	−5.17	1.634	(0.0017)
Total MSOA plan depth (m)	4832.04	1302.48	(0.0002)
Number of allocated non-domestic electricity meters (N)	15596	537.001	(<.0001)
Count of buildings (N)	208.945	701.176	(0.7659)
Total building height (m)	−4863.912	830.07	(<.0001)
Proportion of retail floor space (%)	2923156	760024	(0.0001)
Proportion of office floor space (%)	1688160	981963	(0.0865)
Rateable value of office floor space 2007 (000's £)	11685	4964.628	(0.0191)
Rateable value of warehouse floor space 2007) (000's £)	−18536	7320.305	(0.0118)
Maximum VIF (mean VIF)	59.21	(12.69)	
Condition Indices (CI)	25.37		
Adj. R²	0.9687		

of total MSOA plan depth adds a further 4832 kWh/yr of electricity use and reduces gas by 44,956 kWh/yr. These findings go some way to confirming that MSOAs characterised by deeper built blocks use more electricity and less gas.

There may be some broad implications for policy in the findings reported here. Geometrical parameters might be incorporated into energy benchmarking for non-domestic buildings, a possibility that is explored for schools in a paper by Hong et al.[19] Controls on energy demand will naturally tend to focus on different features and systems, depending on building geometry: lighting and core services in deeper buildings, façade treatment and ventilation control in shallower buildings. The results presented here may help in framing such policies based on stock-level considerations, not just the design and management of individual buildings.

TABLE 5 Energy, morphology and economic measures: summary statistics for London at MSOA level

London	MSOA level			
Label	Sum	Mean	Std. dev.	Median
Total building external wall area (m²)	115,684,534	117,566	159,640	85,386
Total building volume (m³)	706,897,957	718,392	1,466,341	396,801
Total building footprint area (m²)	72,939,332	74,125	87,399	50,137
Total exposed surface area (m²)	188,623,866	191,691	238,296	139,492
Count of built blocks (n)	496,951	505	295	445
Total built block height (m)	570,642	580	339	493
Total built block floor space★ (m²)	220,905,612	224,498	458,231	124,000
Mean MSOA plan depth (m)	.	10	4	9
MSOA gas demand in 2007 (Gwh/yr)	224,561	230	637	96
Number of allocated non-domestic gas meters (N)	44,756	46	70	30
Mean gas demand in 2007 (kWh/meter/yr)	.	473,158	972,309	304,075
Per capita employee gas use 2007 (kWh/person)	.	135	189	95
Gas intensity (kWh/m²)	.	101	85	80
MSOA electricity demand in 2007 (Gwh/yr)	279,285	284	931	131
Number of allocated non-domestic electricity meters (N)	494,565	503	694	378
Mean electricity demand in 2007 (kWh/meter/yr)	.	48,178	42,667	35,545
Electricity use per employee 2007 (kWh/person)	.	163	118	133
Electricity intensity (kWh/m²)	.	119	48	114
Proportion of retail floor space	.	31%	24%	28%
Proportion of office floor space	.	21%	23%	13%
Proportion of warehouse floor space	.	15%	22%	1%
Number of employees 2008 (N)	245,404,000	249,394	1,150,805	95,000
Retail floor space 2007 (000's m²)	15,507	16	36	7
Office floor space 2007 (000's m²)	27,591	28	186	4
Rateable value of retail floor space 2007 (000's £)	103,914	127	64	111
Rateable value of office floor space 2007 (000's £)	75,503	116	42	106

★gross floor area estimate

Notes

1 C Ratti, N Baker, K Steemers, 'Energy consumption and urban texture', *Energy and Buildings* Volume 37, 2005 pp. 762–776.
2 S Salat, 'Energy loads, CO_2 emissions and building stocks: morphologies, typologies, energy systems and behaviour', *Building Research and Information* Volume 37, 2009 pp. 598–609.
3 P Rode, C Keim, G Robazza, P Viejo, J Schofield, 'Cities and energy: urban morphology and residential heat energy demand', *Environment and Planning B: Planning and Design*, Volume 41, 2014 pp. 138–162.
4 M Batty and A Hudson-Smith, 'Urban simulacra', *Architectural Design*, Volume 75, 2005 pp. 42–47.

166 Built form and urban form

5 Note added 2016: problems with buildings whose forms are not simple prisms are likely to be more serious than indicated here. Ordnance Survey footprint polygons are often drawn in such a way as take in parts of buildings of very different heights. Thus multiplying footprint area by average height may give inaccurate estimates of floor area and volume. The issue could in principle be resolved by using the high resolution LiDAR data to build more accurate 3D representations.

6 data.gov.uk *Land Use Statistics (Generalised Land Use Database)* http://data.gov.uk/dataset/land_use_statistics_generalised_land_use_database: accessed January 2013.

7 F E Brown, P A Rickaby, H Bruhns, P Steadman, 'Surveys of nondomestic buildings in four English towns', *Environment and Planning B: Planning and Design* Volume 27, 2000, pp. 11–24.

8 DECC Guidance note for the DECC MLSOA/IGZ and LLSOA electricity and gas consumption data, www.decc.gov.uk/media/viewfile.ashx?filepath=statistics/regional/mlsoa2008/1_20100325 121429_e_@@_mlsoallsoaguidance.pdf: London 2009.

9 Ibid.

10 Ibid.

11 Rode *et al.*, 'Cities and energy'.

12 An alternative explanation [added 2016] would be that the LSE group are plotting energy use in dwellings of a series of different built forms, from detached through semi-detached and terrace to flats; and that this is both a transition from a higher to a lower ratio of surface to volume, and an increase in average number of storeys.

13 P Steadman, S Evans, M Batty, 'Wall area, volume and plan depth in the building stock', *Building Research and Information* Volume 37, 2009, pp. 455–467.

14 K Steemers, 'Energy and the city: density, buildings and transport', *Energy and Buildings* Volume 35, 2003 pp. 3–14.

15 N Baker and C Ratti C 'Simplified urban climate models from medium-scale morphological parameters', in *Proceedings of the International Conference on Urban Climatology*, ICUC99, Sydney, Australia, November 1999.

16 The units for these figures in Ratti *et al.*'s paper (Fig.21 p. 773) are incorrect. They are given as kWh/m^2/yr, but are in fact MWh/m^2/yr.

17 Employment data (see Table 4) are from Office of National Statistics (2009) *Business Register and Employment Survey (BRES) 2008*, London.

18 SAS Institute Inc. *SAS 9.2 User's Guide, Second Edition*. Cary, NC, USA 2013.

19 S-M Hong, G Paterson, D Mumovic, P Steadman, 'Improving comparability in benchmarking energy consumption of primary and secondary schools in England', *Building Research and Information*, Volume 42, 2014 pp. 47–61.

9

DENSITY AND BUILT FORM

Integrating 'Spacemate' with the work of Martin and March

(*Environment and Planning B: Planning and Design*, Volume 41, 2014, pp. 341–358)

In the early 1970s Leslie Martin and Lionel March carried out pioneering research on the relationships between urban density and the forms of buildings. Martin set up the Centre for Land Use and Built Form Studies at the Cambridge University School of Architecture, and March became its first Director; the centre's name referred to this density work. March and Martin took three simple generic forms: freestanding 'pavilions', parallel 'streets' and inward-looking 'courts'. They showed how – all other things being equal – the 'courts' achieved higher densities than the 'streets', which in turn achieved higher densities than the 'pavilions'. Counter-intuitively, land was not always saved by building high-rise towers.

These findings were appreciated and acted on at the time, but in the decades that followed they arguably did not receive the attention they deserved. More recently however the topic of density has risen back up the research and political agendas. Meta Berghauser Pont and Per Haupt at TU Delft have carried out the most interesting work. They have collected data on the densities of large numbers of residential estates in Holland and elsewhere, and have plotted these data in an ingenious graphical tool called 'Spacemate'. Their results show Martin and March's mathematical results confirmed in practice.

This paper brings the two pieces of work together and shows how Martin and March's analysis can provide further theoretical explanation for Berghauser Pont and Haupt's empirical findings. Two additional variables are introduced: depth of buildings in plan, and 'cut-off angles' describing the distances by which buildings are separated in relation to their height. This allows a more precise morphological categorisation of forms of development with different densities.

Prologue: Raymond Hood's 'City of Towers'

In the 1920s the American architect Raymond Hood, designer of splendid art deco office buildings, published a series of propositions for a 'City of Towers'.[1] Figure 1 shows a standard Manhattan block with the existing development replaced by three slender skyscrapers of roughly fifty storeys. Several schemes were published by other architects around this time, intended to solve the growing problems of traffic congestion with multi-level plans for New York, separating pedestrians from automobiles and trucks. Hood was also concerned about traffic growth. His proposal by contrast was for circulation on a single level: the plan involved creating incentives for developers to release ground area to public ownership in return for permission to build higher. As he wrote,

> Whole blocks would soon develop of their own accord, where two or three towers would provide more floor space than there is in the average block of today, and there would be ten times as much street area round about to take care of the traffic.[2]

Figure 1 shows the results: 'Three operations have completed one block'. Once most of the ground has been freed up, traffic can then flow in straight lines in all directions.

Setting aside the nightmarish implications of these transport aspects, it is instructive to compare the densities of Hood's towers with what they are intended to replace. Since Manhattan blocks have a standard width of 60 m, it is possible to make rough measurements of Hood's buildings, which seem to have plans some 25 m square. Three such 50-storey towers on a 60 × 180 m block give a floor space index (FSI) of around 5.7. The floor space index is given by dividing the total floor area on all levels by the ground area. It is convenient to include half the widths of the streets surrounding a block, to give a gross ground area figure. The ground coverage, measured by dividing the total footprint of the buildings by the gross ground area, is 0.11. (Expressed in a different way: 11 per cent of the ground is covered by buildings.)

FIGURE 1 Illustration by Raymond Hood of a Manhattan block with three towers of approximately 40, 50 and 60 storeys and 'average blocks of today' at left and right; from H Robertson 'A City of Towers', *Architect and Building News*, 1927

Density and built form **169**

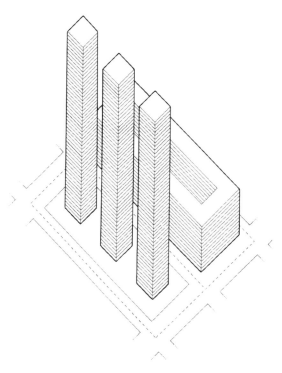

FIGURE 2 Three 50-storey towers on a Manhattan block measuring 60 × 180 m, similar to Hood's scheme in Figure 1, compared with a 13-storey court building on the same size block. Density as measured by floor space index (FSI) is 5.7 in both cases. Ground coverage is 11 per cent and 44 per cent respectively

Compare this now with a development on a block of the same size, in which buildings are set along all four street fronts to create an enclosed court (Figure 2). Their depth in plan is 17.5 m, typical for day-lit offices, and they are on 13 storeys. The FSI for this development is 5.7, the same as Hood's towers, but in buildings less than one-third of their height. Ground coverage is 0.44.[3]

The general public and large parts of the architectural and planning professions still believe, with Hood, that in order to raise densities it is necessary to build higher. The comparison of Figure 2 shows that this belief needs to be seriously questioned and carefully qualified. Leslie Martin and Lionel March first drew attention to the issue in the 1960s in their pioneering research on 'land use and built forms'.[4] Specifically they compared the performance in terms of density and ground coverage of three generic forms of building: freestanding 'pavilions' (or towers), parallel 'streets' and inward-looking 'courts' (Figure 3). This is explained in more detail below. Their findings had some influence in practice – in particular on the work of the architect Richard MacCormac[5] – and a 1972 essay by Martin has been republished;[6] but it is arguable that the lessons have still to be widely understood.

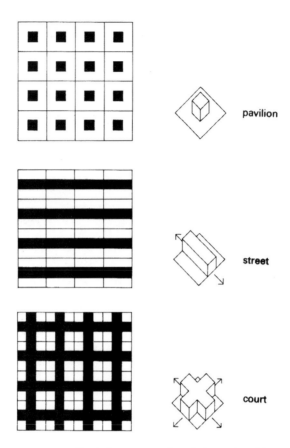

FIGURE 3 Three different arrays of built forms – 'pavilions', 'streets' and 'courts' – considered by Leslie Martin and Lionel March in their work on the use of land by buildings. From Martin and March eds, *Urban Space and Structures*, Cambridge 1972

The 'Spacemate' diagram of Berghauser Pont and Haupt

Meanwhile there has recently been a revival of interest in issues of residential density in Holland, a country where land is in short supply, and architects are still much involved in the design of public housing. Two researchers at the Technical University Delft, Meta Berghauser Pont and Per Haupt, have recently published an ingenious and useful graphical tool called 'Spacemate'.[7] This allows floor space index and ground coverage for buildings of different forms to be compared in a two-dimensional coordinate system (Figure 4). FSI is plotted on the *y*-axis, and ground coverage, or what the authors call 'ground space index' GSI, on the *x*-axis. (One further variable plotted on the diagram is the Open Space Ratio (OSR), which is ignored here since it is in effect just another way of expressing the same data. It takes the ground area, subtracts the area of the building footprint(s), and divides by total floor area.)

The result is for buildings with the same numbers of floors to lie along straight lines radiating from the origin. This is because of the intrinsic relationship between FSI and ground coverage. For a single-storey building the two variables take the same value; they describe

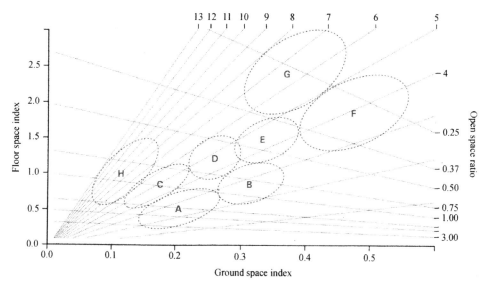

FIGURE 4 The 'Spacemate' diagram of Meta Berghauser Pont and Per Haupt. The *y*-axis plots Floor Space Index (FSI) and the *x*-axis plots Ground Space Index (GSI) or ground coverage. The diagonal lines passing through the origin correspond to different numbers of storeys. The ellipses enclose groups of Dutch housing developments with distinct morphological characteristics: the letter key is given in the text. (Spacemate also plots a fourth variable, the Open Space Ratio (OSR), which is ignored here.) From Berghauser Pont and Haupt, *Spacemate*, Delft 2004 with kind permission of Meta Berghauser Pont

the same thing. In a multi-storey building, FSI is equal to ground coverage times number of storeys. See for example on the 10-storey line that where ground coverage equals 0.1, FSI equals 1. (It is assumed that buildings have the same floor area on every storey.)

One of the first points made by Berghauser Pont and Haupt is the same as that made about Hood's plan by Figures 1 and 2. Developments which have what are clearly very different morphologies – different heights, different spacing of the buildings – can share similar FSI values. They illustrate four examples of very diverse housing developments which all have FSIs of around 0.7 (Figure 5).

Berghauser Pont and Haupt have measured a large number of residential estates in Amsterdam and Rotterdam, and have plotted values for the relevant variables in Spacemate.[8] The ground areas are gross values throughout, and include associated open spaces, gardens, and the appropriate fractions of road areas. The result is that what to the eye seem to be similar morphologies become clustered within separate regions of Spacemate, as indicated by the zones enclosed by ellipses and marked with letters in Figure 4. Berghauser Pont and Haupt name these groups as:

A   Low-rise spacious strip developments
B   Low-rise compact strip developments
C   Mid-rise open building blocks
D   Mid-rise spacious building blocks

172 Built form and urban form

FIGURE 5 Four Dutch housing developments of very different heights and morphological character but the same FSI (around 0.7). From Berghauser Pont and Haupt 'The Spacemate', *Nordisk Arkitekturforskning*, No. 4, 2005, with kind permission of Meta Berghauser Pont

E   Mid-rise closed building blocks
F   Mid-rise compact building blocks
G   Mid-rise super blocks
H   High-rise developments

By 'low-rise' the authors mean two or three storeys, and by 'mid-rise' four to seven storeys. The 'high-rise' buildings (H) are typically on ten storeys: notice how these achieve FSIs of around 1, comparable with the 'low-rise' group B, and lower than most of the 'mid-rise' groups. There is a noticeable gap in these housing data above and to the right of the high-rise group H. This is presumably because most if not all of the 'mid-rise' groups are comprised of walk-up buildings; and once lifts are introduced in the 'high-rise' buildings it makes economic sense to jump up to nine or ten storeys. So the position between these respective groups is empty.

Berghauser Pont and Haupt arrived at these intriguing findings empirically. But why should their buildings become grouped in these particular patterns? We can provide some theoretical interpretation by examining them in the light of Martin and March's work.

The 'land use and built form studies' of Martin and March

Martin and March imagined continuous regular arrays of their three generic forms: 'pavilions', 'streets' and 'courts' (Figure 3). They compared FSI values under controlled conditions. They kept three variables constant: the depth of the forms in plan d, the storey height h, and the cut-off angle α between opposing facades. The cut-off angle is the angle between the ground and a line joining the base of one facade to the roofline of the facade opposite (Figure 6). As the cut-off angle is made smaller, the built forms are pushed further apart. The implication

Density and built form   **173**

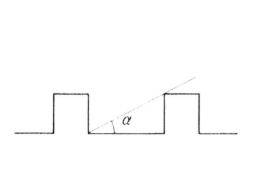

FIGURE 6 A 'cut-off angle' α between the ground and a line joining the base of one building facade to the top of the facade opposite

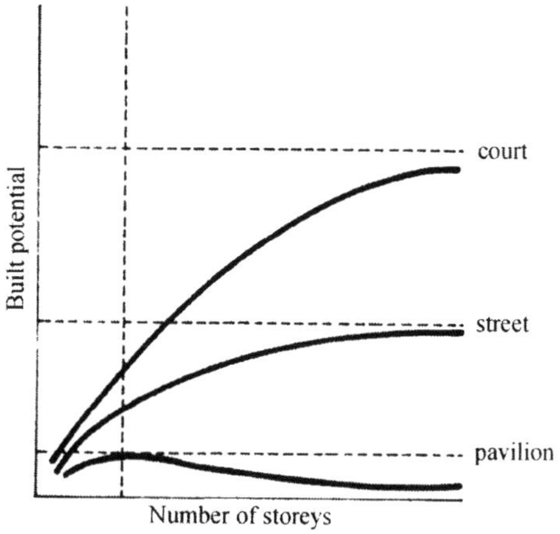

FIGURE 7 Floor space index FSI (here referred to as 'built potential') on the y-axis plotted against number of storeys on the x-axis, for the three arrays of built forms in Figure 3. Building depth d, storey height h and cut-off angle α are kept constant throughout. For 'streets' and 'courts' FSI reaches a maximum, beyond which the density does not rise further despite the increase in number of storeys. In the case of 'pavilions' FSI reaches a maximum and then *declines* as more storeys are added. From Martin and March eds, *Urban Space and Structures*, Cambridge 1972

is that equal values of α can assure equivalent levels of day lighting in the three forms (a questionable assumption, to be discussed later). March and Martin then varied the number of storeys n. Figure 7 shows the general results: FSI is plotted against n for the three forms. For the 'street' and 'court' forms, FSI increases with n and approaches a limit asymptotically in both cases. A law of diminishing returns applies: above a certain number of storeys, density cannot be further increased by building higher. In the case of 'pavilions' FSI reaches a maximum at some particular height and thereafter *declines*.

This means that when the numbers of storeys are the same, 'court' forms always provide much more floor area on a given land area than 'streets', which in turn provide much more floor area than 'pavilions'. At the number of storeys for which the FSI for 'pavilion' forms reaches its maximum, the 'streets' fit twice as much floor area on the given area of land as the 'pavilions', and the 'courts' fit three times as much floor area as the 'pavilions'. There are serious implications here for urban design, which Martin and March emphasised and explored.

What is the explanation for these theoretical results? Let us consider Martin and March's built form units in a slightly different way. Figure 8 shows square sites on which sit a) a 'pavilion' form at the corner, b) a 'street' form along one edge, and c) an L-shaped form along two edges. If these respective units are repeated they recreate Martin and March's arrays, as

174 Built form and urban form

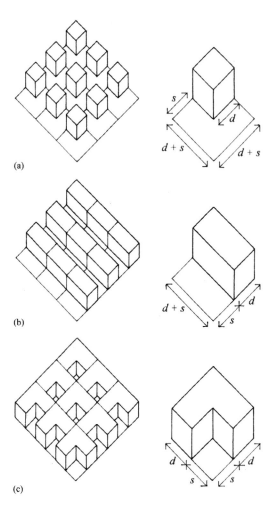

FIGURE 8 Martin and March's 'pavilions', 'streets' and 'courts' represented in a slightly different way, as repeating units. The 'courts' are created with repeating L-shapes. All are drawn such that plan depth *d* equals the spacing apart *s* of the forms. The areas of the sites of the three units are the same. The L-shaped 'court' unit occupies 75 per cent of the site, the 'street' occupies 50 per cent, and the 'pavilion' occupies 25 per cent. Their FSI values are therefore in the ratio 3: 2: 1

shown. The adjacent Ls join together to enclose courts. Let us denote the distance by which adjacent forms are spaced apart by *s*. Figure 9 gives a worked example for all three forms, where *d* = 17.5 m, *h* = 4 m and α is 45°. Forms on one, four and ten storeys are illustrated. The graph of Figure 10 shows what happens to FSI as more storeys are added and the site is made larger as *s* increases in conformity with the fixed cut-off angle. For 'pavilions' the value of FSI rises to reach a maximum of 1.1 in this example, and then falls again as further storeys are added. For 'streets' and 'courts', FSI rises continuously towards values above 3 and 5 respectively. Notice that, at the point of greatest density for 'pavilions', between four and five storeys, the spacing of the forms *s* is equal to 17.5 m, the same value as *d*.

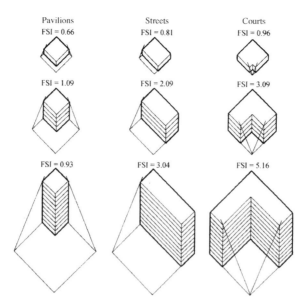

FIGURE 9 A worked example for the three built form types of Figure 8, where $d = 17.5$ m, $h = 4$ m and $\alpha = 45°$ throughout. Forms on one, four and ten storeys are illustrated. FSI = floor space index

Now look again at the three different forms as they appear in Figure 8. These have been drawn such that $d = s$; that is at the specific point for the 'pavilions' where density (FSI) is at its maximum. It is clear that they occupy varying fractions of the area of the site: they have different values for ground coverage. Specifically the (L-shaped) 'court' occupies three-quarters of the site, the 'street' occupies half of the site, and the 'pavilion' occupies a quarter of the site. For one-storey buildings, the FSIs would take the same values: 0.75, 0.5 and 0.25. If the three types of form have greater numbers of storeys but are still equal in height, then their FSI values must always (at this point where $d = s$) be in the ratios 3: 2: 1. For the examples in Figure 9 this situation is reached at something just over four storeys, as illustrated.

When s is not equal to d the ratios differ, as we can see in the graphs of Figures 7 and 10. But the rank ordering of the three forms in terms of their FSIs does not change. To think about this result in somewhat qualitative (if slightly misleading) terms we can imagine how, in a continuous array, each facade of a form obtains its light and air from the area of open space onto which it fronts. For both the 'pavilions' and the 'streets' the same piece of space between opposite facades is 'used twice'; however in the array of 'pavilions' there are spaces diagonally between buildings that are not 'used' at all in this way. For 'court' forms, all four facades share the same piece of space, which is 'used four times'.

Since Martin and March published their original research, building scientists have challenged certain aspects of the argument. (It should be appreciated that the work predated the general introduction of computers, and Martin and March made all their calculations by hand. They were conscious that their model was "a gross simplification in practical terms" and that "more elaborate models can be designed".[9]) One point the authors themselves acknowledged was that there are losses of day-lit floor space at the internal corners of courtyards

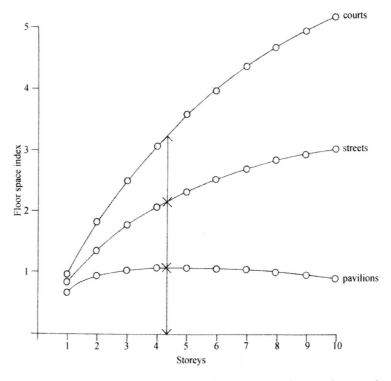

FIGURE 10 Graph of the worked example in Figure 9, with arrows showing how, at this position, the floor space index (FSI) values for pavilion, street and court are in the precise ratio 1: 2: 3. At the point of greatest density for 'pavilions', between 4 and 5 storeys, both d and the spacing of the forms s are equal to 17.5 m

(often used in practice for vertical circulation or service rooms), which do not occur in 'street' or 'pavilion' forms. Indeed an external corner on a 'pavilion' obtains light from two facades.

More serious is the question of whether setting a specific value for the cut-off angle α between opposing facades can assure an equal standard of day lighting in the three forms (all other things being equal, such as the sizes of windows, the reflective properties of the walls etc). The effective assumption behind the use of the simple 2D cut-off angle to determine this spacing is that daylight only arrives perpendicularly to the facades of buildings, but clearly this is not true. In reality light is received from the whole of the visible part of the sky. More of the sky can be seen from a given position and floor level in 'pavilions' — other things being equal — than from equivalent positions in 'street' or 'court' forms, since in the latter the respective solid angles are obstructed to a greater extent by adjacent forms or parts of forms. March and Trace discussed this issue when carrying out the original work.[10]

Carlo Ratti studied such lighting effects using simulation software to estimate levels of illumination at the bases of the facades of equivalent arrays of 'pavilions', 'streets' and 'courts'.[11] The reflective properties of surfaces, as well as the relevant dimensions, were all standardised throughout. Ratti found as one might expect that light levels at these positions are highest for pavilions, lower for streets, lowest for courts. He demonstrated nevertheless that for *equal* lighting levels, the rank ordering of 'courts'/'streets'/'pavilions' in terms of FSI remains the same, although the differences are not so great as Martin and March calculated. With these reservations, it is worth emphasising that cut-off angles remain a simple and useful geometrical way of expressing the distances by which building facades are spaced apart in relation to their height; distances that can bear on other aspects of performance besides lighting, such as privacy and natural ventilation.

Bringing Spacemate and Martin and March's work together

Let us return now to Spacemate. Berghauser Pont and Haupt arrived at their intriguing findings empirically: but why should these Dutch developments be grouped in these particular patterns? We can provide some further theoretical interpretation, by examining them in the light of Martin and March's work, and introducing two more variables, discussed in the last section. These are plan depth d, and cut-off angle α. The Dutch buildings in Figure 4 are all residential, mostly terraced houses or blocks of flats. We might expect on the basis for example of data collected by Ranko Bon that their plan depths d would range between about 7 and 14 m.[12] Let us take a central value of 10 m just for the sake of illustration. Let us assume a standard storey height h of 3 m. As for cut-off angles, these could obviously vary very widely, between patterns of detached houses with extensive gardens at one extreme, and central city apartments at the other. To begin with, let us take a value of 27° throughout, corresponding to the spacing of buildings by a distance equal to twice their heights. We will consider other values for these variables shortly.

Of course few real buildings conform exactly to Martin and March's schematic types. Depth may vary even in different parts of the same plan, and the actual cut-off angles on different sides of a building may vary greatly depending on its exact relationship to neighbouring buildings. The Martin and March forms and their associated measures can nevertheless capture some important generalised features of real developments, and can serve to characterise broad tendencies and average values.

Once d, h and α are fixed for the three types of form, these determine the relationship between number of storeys, ground coverage and FSI, as we saw in Figure 9. We can vary numbers of storeys n and plot the results in Spacemate (Figure 11). They describe three curves, for 'pavilion' forms, 'street' forms, and 'court' forms. The positions of Berghauser Pont and Haupt's groups are again shown by ellipses with key letters. Consider the curve for 'pavilions', following it from right to left. As height increases, FSI reaches a maximum of about 0.4 and then declines again, in the way we would expect from Martin and March's analysis. No built forms of this type with cut-off angles equal to or less than 27° can occur above this line: all must fall in the band below the curve. The same applies for the lines for 'street' and 'court' forms. If 27° is a reasonable cut-off angle to assume throughout for residential buildings (and this is certainly debatable) then we would expect to find the 'pavilion' forms in the lowest band, the 'street' forms in the middle band, and the 'court' forms in the upper band.

Let us see how the real Dutch buildings fall relative to these bands. It is clear from the photographs accompanying Berghauser Pont and Haupt's data (as well as examination on Google Maps and StreetView) that groups A, B and C are terraces of varying lengths. Groups B and C do indeed fall within the band for 'street' forms. The 'low-rise spacious strips' of group A however have lower densities and fall partly in the 'pavilions' band. This is because although they are also terraces they have values for α lower than 27°. Group H consists mostly

178 Built form and urban form

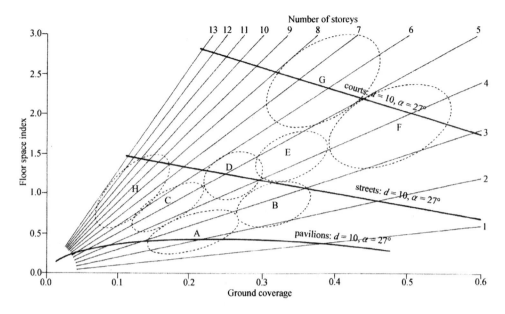

FIGURE 11 Curves plotted in Spacemate for 'pavilions', 'streets' and 'courts', where $d = 10$ m, $h = 3$ m and $\alpha = 27°$. The lines create three bands in which we might expect to find forms of the three types. The lines are superimposed on the sample of Dutch buildings from Figure 4. The real buildings fall broadly into the appropriate bands

of elongated high-rise *slabs*, which therefore also qualify as examples of 'street' forms, in whose band they lie.

The photographs show that groups D, E, F and G are courtyard developments of various types: Berghauser Pont and Haupt's word 'block' means either a perimeter development around a central open space or a single-court building, in both cases surrounded by streets. The adjectives 'open' or 'closed' mean respectively several buildings separated by gaps, or completely continuous courts. They are all therefore broadly comparable with Martin and March's 'courts' (but see below). Large parts of all four groups lie indeed within the 'courts' band. The actual Dutch developments, that is to say, are found for the most part in the bands for the Martin and March built forms to which they approximate. Of course the lines and bands would move up or down for different plan depths and cut-off angles. The specific values taken in Figure 11 are just for illustration and comparison on a common basis.

Consider groups F and G for example, and how they overlap the 'courts' line. There are two possible explanations as to why these buildings should fall above the line here. The first is that they are deeper in plan than 10 m. Figure 12 shows lines plotted for 'court' forms where again $\alpha = 27°$ and $h = 3$, but d is varied between 7, 10 and 14 m. Greater plan depths give higher densities, and the 'courts' line is shifted progressively higher in Spacemate, as the figure shows. The whole of groups F and G now fall below the line for $d = 14$ m.

A second possibility for the higher density Dutch courts F and G is that the cut-off angle is steeper than 27°. Figure 13 plots results for court forms where $d = 10$ and $h = 3$, but α is varied between 11°, 13°, 18°, 27° and 45°. These angles mean that the spacing of the forms s is equal to 5, 4, 3, 2 and 1 times the overall building height respectively. It is unlikely that

Density and built form 179

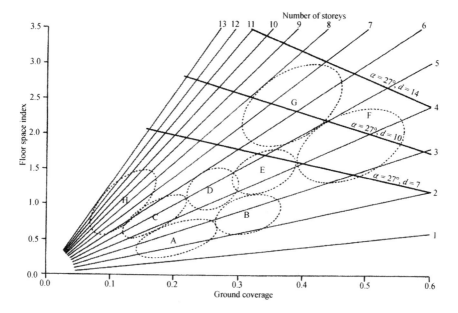

FIGURE 12 Curves plotted in Spacemate for 'courts' where $\alpha = 27°$, $h = 3$, and d is varied between 7, 10 and 14 m

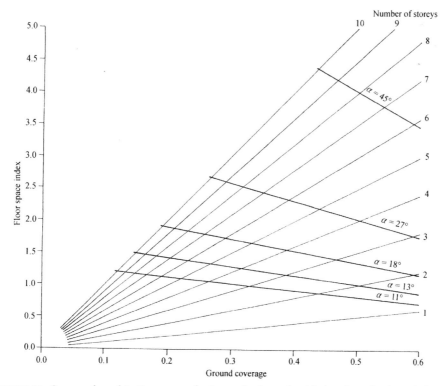

FIGURE 13 Curves plotted in Spacemate for 'courts' where $d = 10$, $h = 3$, and α is varied between 11°, 13°, 18°, 27° and 45°

180 Built form and urban form

α would go higher than 45° in modern residential buildings. Figures 14 and 15 plot equivalent results for 'street' forms and 'pavilion' forms. In practice it might be expected that the steepest angles in this range would be associated with 'courts', and the lowest angles with 'pavilions'. Of course both α and d are in reality continuous variables, and so specific combinations of values for a given built form type will define precise point locations in Spacemate. It would be possible in principle to make measurements of plan depth in the actual Dutch sample. This could be done by dividing plan area by plan perimeter: the ratio gives an approximate value for $d/2$ that becomes more accurate as the plan becomes more elongated. Mean values for α could then be inferred. This would allow morphological types to be yet more precisely distinguished.

It should be said that the Dutch (and most other) courtyard buildings differ in a significant way from Martin and March's 'courts', in that the former are surrounded by roads, while the

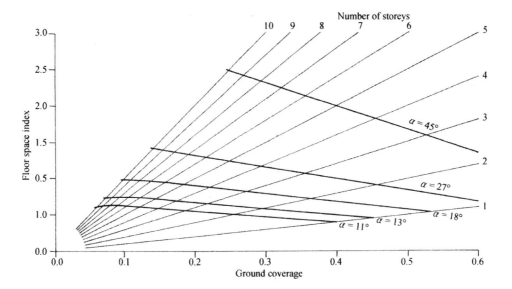

FIGURE 14 Curves plotted in Spacemate for 'streets' where $d = 10$, $h = 3$, and α is varied between 11°, 13°, 18°, 27° and 45°

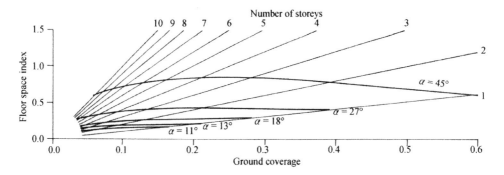

FIGURE 15 Curves plotted in Spacemate for 'pavilions' where $d = 10$, $h = 3$, and α is varied between 11°, 13°, 18°, 27° and 45°

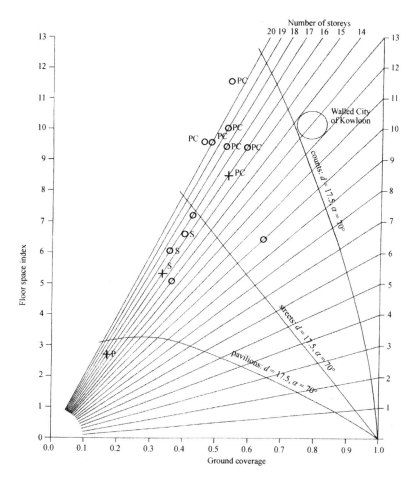

FIGURE 16 Curves plotted in Spacemate for 'pavilions', 'streets' and 'courts', where $d = 17.5$ m, $h = 4$ m and $\alpha = 70°$. The positions of three notional 16-storey buildings of 'pavilion', 'street' and 'pavilion/court' form are marked by crosses. The positions of a sample of real high-rise Chicago buildings are also shown, by circles. Those labelled PC are 'pavilion/court' forms like the building in Figure 17. Those labelled S are 'street' forms like the building in Figure 18. The remaining buildings have hybrid or partial forms in these terms

latter create a continuous grid (and it is unclear where any roads might run). Loosely speaking, one might describe the real buildings as being like 'pavilions' on the outside, and 'courts' on the inside: they might be called 'pavilion/courts'. As a consequence the FSIs of the real buildings are lower than those for equivalent true 'courts'. March himself illustrated and discussed built forms of the 'pavilion/court' type.[13]

For a final comparison let us consider central city office buildings, where values for both d and α take higher values still. For example nineteenth-century day-lit office skyscrapers in Chicago had plan depths typically around 17.5 m, and cut-off angles around 70°. These steep angles were a consequence of the fact that the heights of the buildings were generally in the range 15 to 20 storeys, and they faced on to Chicago streets whose standard width is 25 m. (There were of course exceptions, and some facades faced onto alleys with widths of just

182 Built form and urban form

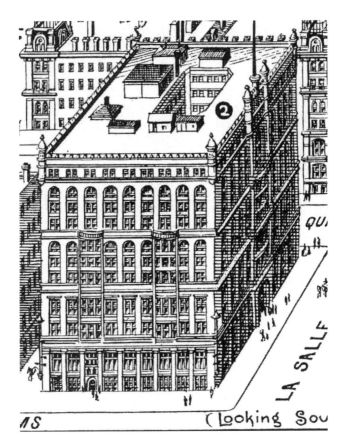

FIGURE 17 Rookery Building, Chicago 1884, architects Burnham and Root. An example of a high-rise office building with a 'pavilion/court' form. From Rand, McNally, *Bird's Eye Views and Guide to Chicago*, Chicago and New York, 1893

5 m.) The lines for the three built form types now rise yet higher in Spacemate, as we can see in Figure 16.

The positions of a sample of actual Chicago buildings are shown. The sample is drawn from a number of historical books on skyscrapers.[14] Most fill near-square quarter blocks in the city and are of the 'pavilion/court' type. Figure 17 illustrates an example, the Rookery Building of 1884, designed by Burnham and Root. In Spacemate these buildings are clustered tightly together. (All ground-floor atria or halls at the bases of the courts are ignored, so that the built forms are prismatic.) Two buildings, the Old Colony and the Monadnock, are sited by contrast on long narrow blocks around 20 m deep to the south of the Chicago Loop. As a result they have elongated slab forms, and appear in the relevant 'street' band in Spacemate. Figure 18 shows the Monadnock Building of 1891, again by Burnham and Root, together with its 1893 extension whose architects were Holabird and Roche. (There were few if any 'pavilion' type office skyscrapers – like Hood's towers – in Chicago at this date, for reasons that Figure 2 perhaps makes clear.)

One might ask, in conclusion, what happens at the extreme edges of the 'Spacemate' diagram, at lower left and at upper right? Are buildings to be found here, and if so, what is

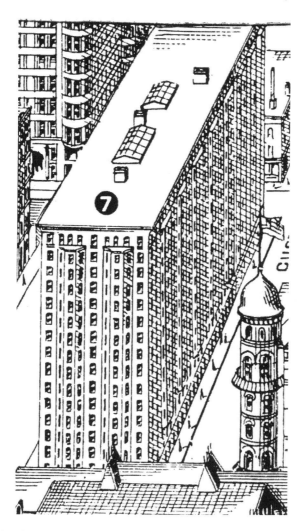

FIGURE 18 Monadnock Building, Chicago 1891, architects Burnham and Root; with its 1893 extension, architects Holabird and Roche. An example of a high-rise office building with a 'street' form. From Rand, McNally, *Bird's Eye Views and Guide to Chicago*, Chicago and New York, 1893

their character? At bottom left are 'pavilion' buildings on one or two storeys with very low ground coverage: typically semi-detached or detached houses with large gardens. In the opposite direction, upwards and to the right, are buildings whose plans are extremely deep, and/or where cut-off angles go even higher than 70°. Among residential buildings these would only be those pathological cases where special pressures have raised densities to extraordinary levels. There were tenements built on the Lower East Side of Manhattan in the late nineteenth century for example whose depths in plan exceeded 20 m (Riis, 1971).[15] However the supposedly 'habitable' rooms in the interior lacked both natural light and ventilation. On six storeys these had ground coverage values of around 0.7 and FSIs above 4. Ground coverage for multi-storey buildings would very rarely go higher than this: but there is one strange exception.

184 Built form and urban form

Epilogue: the Walled City of Kowloon

Probably the highest mean FSI ever achieved over an extended urban area was in the Walled City of Kowloon, a territory of some 2.6 hectares within the boundaries of Hong Kong but outside its jurisdiction.[16] During the 1970s and '80s the Walled City attracted large numbers of migrants from China, especially criminal elements, and a high-rise informal settlement was built piecemeal without the benefit of building controls. It consisted of buildings up to 12 or 14 storeys (only two of them with lifts) set within metres of each other (Figure 19). The population reached an estimated 35,000. One way to travel about the City was to go up to the roof and jump from building to building. There was one large courtyard but otherwise the composite structure was nearly solid, and the FSI must have approached 10. In terms of Spacemate it would be located at the upper right, beyond the line for 70° courts in Figure 16. From the authorities' point of view it was of course intolerable, and was demolished in 1993.

FIGURE 19 The Walled City of Kowloon in Hong Kong; photo by Ian Lambot with kind permission, from Girard and Lambot, *City of Darkness*, Watermark, Haslemere 1993. The approximate location of the Walled City in Spacemate is marked by a circle (upper right) in Figure 16: the values for FSI and ground coverage are guesses based on this and other illustrations in Girard and Lambot

Notes

1 H Robertson, 'A City of Towers (Proposals made by the well-known American Architect, Raymond Hood, for the solution of New York's problem of overcrowding)', *Architect and Building News*, 21 October 1927, pp. 639–643; this article quotes at length from Hood himself, but without any reference to the original source.

2 Ibid., p. 639.

3 The comparison is not entirely fair in Martin and March's terms: the 'cut-off angles' between the forms in the two cases should be the same (see later in text). These angles are in fact *steeper* for Hood's towers: that is to say the towers are actually *closer* together in relation to their height than are the court forms (if they were repeated on adjacent blocks). For Hood's towers the cut-off angles are 80° between the buildings themselves, and 76° and 80° between the buildings and adjacent blocks. For repeated courts, the corresponding angles are 64° inside the courtyards, and 58° and 70° with adjacent blocks. What is more, Hood's towers are *deeper in plan* than the court form.

4 L Martin and L March eds, *Urban Space and Structures*, Cambridge University Press, Cambridge 1972; L Martin, 'The Grid as Generator', in Martin and March 1972, pp. 6–27; L March, 'Elementary models of built forms' in Martin and March 1972, pp. 55–96.

5 I Latham ed., *Building Ideas – MJP Architects*, Right Angle Publishing, London 2010.

6 Martin 'The Grid as Generator' in *Architectural Research Quarterly (arq)* Volume 4, 2000, pp. 309–322.

7 M Berghauser Pont and P Haupt, *Spacemate: The Spatial Logic of Urban Density*, Delft University Press, Delft, Holland 2004; originally published as *Spacemate: FSI-GSI-OSR als instrument voor verdichting en verdunning*, PERMETA architecten, Amsterdam 2002; M Berghauser Pont and P Haupt, 'The Spacemate: density and the typomorphology of the urban fabric', *Nordisk Arkitekturforskning* Number 4, 2005, pp. 55–68; M Berghauser Pont and P Haupt, 'The relation between urban form and density', *Journal of Urban Morphology*, Volume 11, Number 1, 2007 pp. 62–64; M Berghauser Pont and P Haupt, *Space Matrix: Space, Density and Urban Form*, NAi Publishers, Rotterdam 2010.

8 These data are set out in Berghauser Pont and Haupt, *Spacemate: The Spatial Logic* Section 2.1 pp. 37–53. Many more measurements including data for estates in Berlin and Barcelona are included in Berghauser Pont and Haupt, *Space Matrix* pp. 126–166.

9 Martin and March, *Urban Space and Structures* p. 95.

10 L March and M Trace, *The Land Use Performances of Selected Arrays of Built Forms*, Land Use and Built Form Studies Working Paper No. 2, Cambridge University School of Architecture 1968.

11 C Ratti, *Urban Analysis for Environmental Prediction*, PhD thesis, Cambridge University School of Architecture 2001.

12 R Bon, *Allometry in Micro-Environmental Morphology*, Special Papers Series, Paper E, Harvard Papers in Theoretical Geography, Laboratory for Computer Graphics and Spatial Analysis, Graduate School of Design, Harvard University 1972; R Bon, 'Allometry in the topologic structure of architectural spatial systems', *Ekistics* Volume 36, 1973 pp. 270–276.

13 March, 'Elementary models' pp. 90–91.

14 D Bluestone, *Constructing Chicago*, Yale University Press, New Haven, 1991; C Condit, *The Rise of the Skyscraper*, University of Chicago Press, Chicago IL, 1952; C Willis, *Form Follows Finance: Skyscrapers and Skylines in New York and Chicago*, Princeton Architectural Press, New York, 1995; J Zukowsky ed., *Chicago Architecture 1872–1922: Birth of a Metropolis*, The Art Institute of Chicago and Prestel, Munich, 1987.

15 J A Riis, *How the Other Half Lives: Studies among the Tenements of New York*, Dover, New York, 1971.

16 G Girard and I Lambot, *City of Darkness: Life in Kowloon Walled City*, Watermark, Haslemere, UK, 1993; B Shelton, J Karakiewicz and T Kvan, *The Making of Hong Kong: From Vertical to Volumetric*, Routledge, London and New York, 2011 pp. 26–30.

PART IV

Theoretical approaches to possibility in built form

10

THE ANALYSIS AND INTERPRETATION OF SMALL HOUSE PLANS

Some contemporary examples

Frank Brown and Philip Steadman

(*Environment and Planning B: Planning and Design*, Volume 14, 1987, pp. 407–438)

This paper is the odd one out in the collection. It is much older than all the others – published in 1987 – and I was not the first author. Frank Brown wrote it, reporting work on which we collaborated. I have included it not just as a contribution to the morphological history of housing, but because it establishes a philosophical and methodological approach to architectural research that is developed in the two papers that follow. Specifically, this paper makes use of a method for generating all plans of a certain class exhaustively. It then uses this enumeration to investigate issues in the design of small British houses. The actual plans of houses found at different dates are compared against the 'worlds of theoretically possible plans'. Why did architects and builders fail to exploit some apparently feasible plans? Why did they employ other plans so frequently?

The work relies on computer methods developed previously by several authors for enumerating plan layouts exhaustively. These produced plans consisting of rectangular rooms packed within plan boundaries of simple rectangular shape – what mathematicians call 'rectangular dissections'. Several such methods were devised in the 1970s, as described in my book Architectural Morphology *(1983) and in paper 1 in this volume (pp. 12–13). The present paper uses the DIS [dissection] software written by Ulrich Flemming.*

This is not the place to go into detail. The key point in this enumeration of possible plans is that the basic configurations are considered independently from their dimensions. When dimensions are ignored, the numbers of possible arrangements are small – at least for small numbers of rectangles – and can be counted. For two rectangular rooms, if they are to pack together inside a rectangular boundary, there is only one option (see Figure 0). The arrangement might be placed on the page in different orientations; but we can treat these by convention as the same arrangement. For three rectangles there are two possibilities, for four rectangles there are seven, and so on. In some cases a configuration can exist in two differently handed versions, like a pair of gloves. Again these are treated as the same configuration.

The 'undimensioned' arrangements can then be given dimensions as required. In the DIS program one can specify a set of rooms and can put constraints on their sizes, including maximum and minimum dimensions and limits on proportions. It is also possible to specify contiguities between rooms to allow access: that the hall be next to the living room for example, the dining room next to the kitchen, and

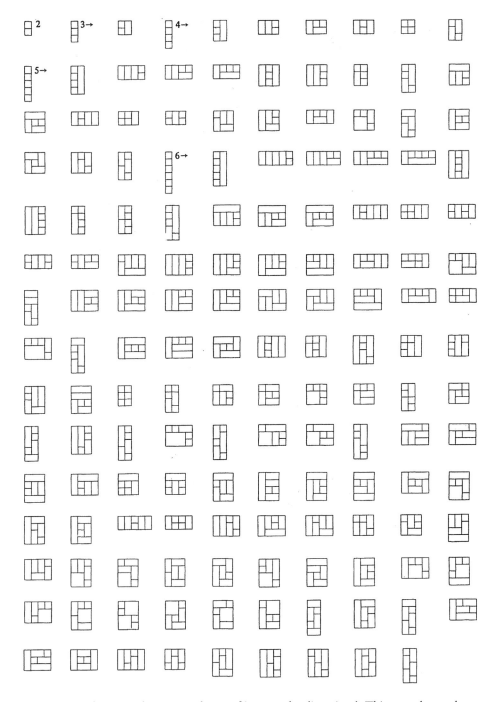

FIGURE 0 Part of a comprehensive catalogue of 'rectangular dissections'. This page shows plans with up to six rooms. From Mitchell, Steadman and Liggett, 'Synthesis and optimisation of small rectangular house plans', *Environment and Planning B*, Volume 3, 1976 p. 70

so on. Required orientations to the north, south, east or west sides of the plan can be set for individual rooms. The program then produces dimensioned instances of all plans that are geometrically and topologically feasible under the given constraints. There may be large numbers, small numbers, or no feasible plans at all, depending on the severity of the constraints. By designating some rectangles as dummies standing for exterior spaces such as yards, it is possible to represent plans whose outer boundaries are not simple rectangles but have L, U, T or court shapes.

These results have never to my knowledge been exploited by architects or policy makers. One reason, at least at the outset, was that practitioners simply did not believe that such a thing could be done. William Mitchell, Robin Liggett and I developed the first program of this kind. Mitchell described our work to an architect acquaintance in Los Angeles, who told him "That's impossible". Mitchell and I submitted a paper on the work to the British Architects' Journal, *which was turned down in no uncertain terms. "This work is strictly non-architectural . . . it has nothing to do with architecture."*

Nothing daunted, Frank Brown and I used the DIS software in a different way: not to produce individual designs, but to study at a more strategic level the interactions between sets of dimensional and topological constraints, and the resulting variety of plans that are possible within those constraints. We had previously made a major field survey of the housing stock in Cambridge. The material gathered in that survey formed the basis for these investigations. The paper was published in a special issue of Environment and Planning B *on 'The analysis of building plans in history and prehistory'.*

There is an intrinsic and unavoidable limitation on the application of this kind of work, to do with the numbers of rectangles in dissections. As Figure 0 indicates, the number of distinct dimensional configurations grows at an accelerating rate as the number of component rectangles is increased. By the time we reach ten rectangles, the number of options is more than half a million (depending exactly on how they are counted). This is just manageable by computer, but adding only a few more rectangles results in astronomical numbers of arrangements that not even computers can count and catalogue. We are up against a 'combinatorial explosion'.

The implication of course is that the method can be applied only to architectural plans up to a certain size. However if the representation of plans is moved to a higher level of abstraction and is made not at the level of single rooms but at the level of zones within layouts, then it becomes possible to enumerate much larger and more complex building plans. That is the subject of the two papers that follow.

Introduction

Of three house types to be discussed, the nineteenth-century terrace house and the semi-detached of the interwar period will perhaps be the most familiar. Both the terrace and the semi-detached were built in great numbers and together they constitute about two-thirds of the British housing stock. The second type – the local authority 'cottage' – is less numerous but is of crucial importance in the evolution of housing design over the last century. Though largely superseded as a type, the new working-class cottage embodied principles of planning and layout that set the standard for all subsequent housing. The private semi-detached house is as much part of its legacy as later municipal housing.

The three house types are each marked by distinctive forms of plan arrangement. The aim here was, through morphological analysis, to understand better the relationship between the different plan configurations and the forces – social, technical and functional – that shaped them.

Much can be learnt about each kind of dwelling from historical research. In the case of both the terrace and the semi-detached house, however, the information relating specifically to plan

192 Theoretical approaches to built form

arrangement is sparse and incomplete. In neither case did design ideas form part of polite architectural discourse. Both house types were produced to a large extent, not by architects, but by speculative builders, who seldom bothered to expound their methods of working.[1]

The local authority cottage, by contrast, is one of the best documented of modern house types. Designed by professional architects, it had its roots in a school of architectural and social thought, which sought a radical change in the standard of housing produced for the working classes. This entailed not simply an improvement in the quality of design and construction, but a change in the very form of the house itself. The aims of the movement were set forth in numerous papers and polemical articles, and found their way ultimately into the explicit recommendations and requirements of the design guides produced after World War 1.

This makes for an interesting difference in the character of the studies. For the local authority cottage, we can hope to produce a very exact design grammar, corresponding to actual historical constraints. From this, we can generate, with some confidence, the range of plans that in reality could and should have occurred.

For the other two examples, however, our grammar will be much looser and more conjectural. The status of the generated plans will, in consequence, be less certain. The grammar thus becomes more of an exploratory tool, allowing us to speculate on the feasibility of different solutions in the historical context.

The approach taken in the study has been to treat all dwelling plans as close packings of rectangles within a single larger rectangle, that is, as *rectangular dissections*.[2] This system of representation, as will be seen, is well adapted to the different sorts of house plan we shall be examining. The great advantage of the approach is that it permits a complete and exhaustive enumeration of the possibilities of plan arrangement for different numbers of rooms. Any particular set of architectural plans (provided they are based on a rectangular geometry) must lie within the appropriate class of geometrical solutions, its scope being determined by the range of additional constraints that are imposed on the dimensions of spaces and on the relationship between them. The closer, therefore, we can define these latter constraints, the more exactly should we be able to describe the range of feasible solutions for any given situation.

Flemming's 'DIS' program is an automated system for generating rectangular dissections under specified constraints of adjacency and dimension.[3] This system greatly facilitates the testing of different sets of hypothesised constraints, and was the principal tool used in the study. The discussion and conclusions below are based on the dialogue that was conducted between DIS and the empirical evidence for each of our house types.

Plan material was drawn from various sources. The largest single source was our own survey of contemporary housing in Cambridge.[4] The recorded sample comprises just over 300 dwellings, and has been shown to reflect fairly closely the composition of the British housing stock in terms of dwelling type, age, and ownership. Terrace and semi-detached houses are both therefore well represented. Since the range of plan types is limited, however, and not free from local peculiarities, this information has been supplemented by other examples taken from the architectural and historical literature.

For the second type of house – the 'cottage' of the municipal housing schemes – our main source will be the recommendations and type plans given in official publications of the period. These were clearly enormously influential. But incidental reference will also be made to some of the designs that appeared in contemporary projects and competitions, as well as to some later buildings taken from the Cambridge sample.

The house types will be examined in chronological order, beginning with the nineteenth-century terrace. We shall then look at the new public-authority housing of 1918/1919, and finally discuss the archetypal semi-detached house of the interwar period.

Examination of house types: the 'byelaw' terrace, about 1880–1900

Background and general characteristics

Terrace housing has a long history, and was one of the most widespread and successful of house types in England during the eighteenth and nineteenth century.[5] In this analysis, however, we shall be concerned specifically with terraced dwellings that were built in the latter part of the nineteenth century. These for the most part come under the category of 'byelaw' housing.

Model Byelaws were introduced in 1877 under the aegis of the Public Health Act, with the aim of improving the sanitation of dwellings.[6] New standards were set with respect to drainage and the provision of sanitary accommodation, and to the construction of dwellings. Beyond these measures, there were also controls aimed at maintaining a 'sufficiency of space' about buildings: new streets were to be built to a standard width, a minimum amount of space was demanded in front of dwellings, and at the rear, the yard or garden was also required to be of a minimum area, and of a depth which related to the height of the building. A further clause governed the size of windows in the dwelling.[7]

The new recommendations were by no means universally observed; they were permissive, not mandatory. Moreover, many local authorities had by this time already framed their own, less stringent byelaws through private acts of parliament, and these continued to apply in their own areas. Nonetheless, local byelaws were progressively brought into line with the model series, and the housing developments that were produced are sufficiently alike to be virtually unmistakable in any part of the country (see Figure 1). Streets were normally laid out on a rectilinear grid, and houses were set out along the street edge in rows, broken at regular intervals by passages at ground level which gave access to the back yards.

Though the new controls did effect a very real improvement in the quality of housing, the inflexible application of rules, together with a tendency to build down to the lowest possible standard, gave rise to a uniformity in outward aspect that has made the byelaw street notorious for its monotony and repetitiveness.

Whatever the controls exercised on external space, however, it is clear that local byelaws did not dictate the internal planning of the house. The regularities that arose in the dwelling plan (and these were considerable) seem to stem from other influences, most of which remain quite obscure. In general, our knowledge of terrace house design, and of the people responsible for it, is poor. This is partly because of the nature of the historical evidence, which is dispersed and often not easily accessible. It also reflects the general lack of interest in the subject by architectural historians until very recently.[8] For this reason, inferences were drawn mainly from the analysis of the plans themselves, and the various regularities of plan form were taken as the starting point for the DIS experiments, without further explanation.

To many, the salient features of the terrace-house plan will be familiar enough. It was characteristically a narrow-frontage type, the width ranging typically from 3 to 5 m, although it might on occasion be greater. Most terraces were basically two rooms deep, giving a long dimension of 7 m to 7.5 m.[9] A staircase, which might be located against one of the party

194 Theoretical approaches to built form

FIGURE 1 An example of nineteenth-century byelaw housing in Cambridge, by kind permission of the Ordnance Survey

walls or at the centre of the plan, gave access to the first floor, which contained two bedrooms, positioned over the two ground-floor spaces. This was the basic 'two-up, two-down' terrace house (see Figure 2). A great many terraced dwellings were constructed to this minimal specification, especially in the northern industrial cities, during the latter part of the nineteenth century.

More commonly, however, in the houses with which we are concerned, there was also a back projection on the ground floor, which provided extra space, while still admitting direct daylight to the main back room. The back projection normally housed the scullery, leaving the main back room as a general living or cooking space. The front room would then be used as a second living space or, preferably, set aside as a parlour (Figure 3).

FIGURE 2 'Two-up, two-down' terrace house built in Willis Street, Salford, apparently in the second half of the nineteenth century. From Burnett, *A Social History of Housing* 1978: drawing by C G Powell

FIGURE 3 Terrace house with back projection on ground floor; little Albert Street, Bristol. From Burnett, *A Social History of Housing* 1978: drawing by C G Powell

The annexe at the back also provided the opportunity for an additional bedroom on the first floor, and the better quality terrace house usually had three main rooms on each floor. This type of house, with a full-height projection at the back, was termed a 'tunnel-back' in northern cities.[10] With the increasing extension of piped water to homes, the outside privy, located at the end of the yard, gave way to the WC, which was attached to the back of the scullery on the ground floor. The house normally had a slightly wider frontage than the two-up, two-down, and an entrance passage or hallway was frequently inserted at the front, giving onto the staircase. This ensured greater privacy for most rooms, and allowed the front room to become a fully-fledged parlour. This house (see Figure 4), a common type by the end of the century, ranked as a 'respectable' dwelling in the south of England, and represents the top end of the spectrum of working-class housing.[11]

The plans of terraced houses were extremely stereotyped. The types of layout described appear with little variation throughout the country. And, in general, no attention was paid to the orientation of rooms, the same plan arrangement being repeated on both sides of the street.

196 Theoretical approaches to built form

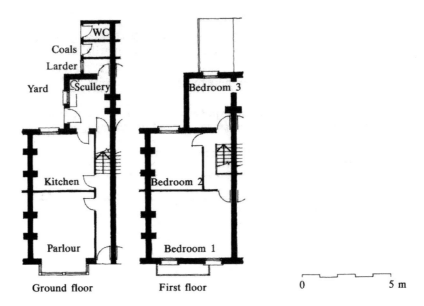

FIGURE 4 Standard terrace house with back projection on both floors; Longford, Coventry. From Burnett, *A Social History of Housing* 1978: drawing by C G Powell

Plan generation

In the DIS experiments, attention was focused on the ground-floor plan of the larger type of terrace house, that is, that with three main rooms – the scullery, the kitchen or living room, and the parlour. The plan was represented as five spaces in all (see Table 1). These included, in addition to the main rooms, the staircase, and a dummy space, which was used to denote the backyard. This dummy space was necessary to make up the full width of the house at the back, and so accommodate the back projection within a single rectangular envelope.

A hallway was not defined. This was left out in part to reduce the total number of spaces, and hence make the experiments more manageable. More importantly, however, the hall was not universal in terrace housing, and its inclusion would have placed artificial limits on the range of possible solutions. Indeed, it seemed from the Cambridge sample that the presence or not of a hall was largely a function of the frontage width of the house, and the experiments were used, among other things, to test this relationship. Broadly speaking, there were two ways of approaching the problem: to include a hall in all the experiments, and eliminate it from the results where it seemed unacceptable; or to omit it from the specification, but add it in later to those generated plans that appeared generous enough to accommodate it. In this case, the second course was taken.

Various constraints were then introduced, as shown in Table 1. *Adjacency constraints* were specified according to the normal room positions (the parlour at the front, the scullery and the dummy space at the back), basic access requirements (the scullery was to be adjacent to the living room), and requirements for daylighting (the living room and scullery were both to be adjacent to the dummy space, that is, the backyard). The staircase was also required to be adjacent to the living room.

TABLE 1 Set of constraints used in the terrace house experiments (Figures 5, 7 and 10). A hallway was not included among the spaces in this instance. A void or dummy space was introduced to define the backyard

Space		Adjacency constraints*	Dimensions (m) Min.	Max.	Area (m²) Min.	Max.	Aspect ratio
1	Parlour	f	3.0	4.5	7.5	20.25	2.0
2	Living room	3, 4, 5	3.0	4.5	7.5	20.25	2.0
3	Scullery	2, 4, b	1.5	6.0	4.0	20.0	3.0
4	Void	2, 3, b	1.0	6.0	2.5	15.0	6.0
5	Stairs	2	0.9	4.5	2.0	4.5	5.0
0	Overall plan	–	–	–	30.0	80.0	

Note: * f front, b back

Dimensional constraints were then set for each space, and for the plan as a whole. The minimum and maximum dimensions for each space were derived from analysis of the Cambridge sample, and were made sufficiently 'loose' to encompass all the plans recorded in the survey. The minimum and maximum areas, and the aspect ratio for each space were similarly taken from the recorded evidence. (Aspect ratio, AR, is the maximum permissible ratio of length to width for a particular space, that is, ratio ≤ AR and ratio ≥ 1/AR.) For the overall plan (0), it will be noted, only the frontage width was specified, together with a maximum and minimum floor area, and the depth was left to be determined by these constraints.

Plans were generated for a range of frontage widths from 3 to 5 m at 0.5 m intervals. At the narrowest frontage (3 m), the physical constraints were such that only one plan type was produced: the central-staircase plan (Figure 5). This does indeed seem to be the characteristic type for the narrowest houses (compare the plan in Figure 6). The possibility of running the staircase longitudinally against one of the wide walls was precluded in this first DIS experiment by the minimum dimension – 2.5 m – adopted for the living room and the parlour: there was not space for the room and staircase to be placed side-by-side. This dimension would seem, therefore, to be a realistic one.

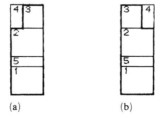

FIGURE 5 Plans generated by DIS for a house of 3 m frontage, when subject to the constraints set out in Table 1. Plan (a) is a reflection of plan (b)

198 Theoretical approaches to built form

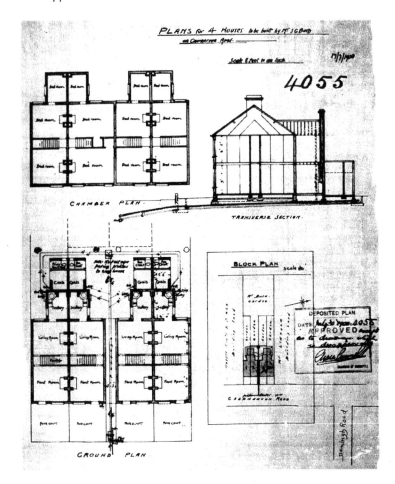

FIGURE 6 Houses of the central-staircase type, Norwich, 1900; from S Muthesius, *The English Terraced House*, 1982, with kind permission of Stefan Muthesius. Compare Figure 5

Houses of such a narrow frontage are unusual, however, and do not occur at all in the Cambridge sample, where the lowest class of terrace normally measures about 3.5 m across the front. When plans were generated for this slightly wider frontage, many other solutions emerged, including those with a side-staircase (Figure 7). The plan outlined in the figure, with the staircase set to one side of the back room, is by far the most common arrangement found in Cambridge (see Figure 8), though central-staircase plans were also recorded in the survey. The predominance of the side-staircase plan may reflect local preference, for elsewhere in the country the central-staircase pattern was evidently much more frequent in these small houses.

There were clearly also local variations in the attitude towards the hallway. In the south of England, an entrance hall seems to have been usual in all classes of home, and plans such as that in Figure 9, with a hall running fully from the front to the back of the house, were repeated in even the smallest dwellings. Muthesius records one example in Bristol where an

FIGURE 7 Solutions generated by DIS for a 3.5 m frontage (twenty six in all). The constraints otherwise were as in Table 1. Outlined are the two most common plans: the central-staircase plan, as in Figure 5, and that with a side-staircase in the back room

entrance hall was included in a house measuring only 2.9 m across the front.[12] Our minimum room dimension of 2.5 m obviously did not apply here. It was an exceptional case, however, and one wonders, in fact, how workable the resulting spaces actually were.

Among the solutions generated by DIS were some interesting plan configurations that do not seem to have occurred in practice. These include, for example, arrangements in which the backyard extends forward into the main body of the house (for example, solution 23 in Figure 7). Most of these are quite feasible as buildings – the staircase, living room, and scullery become in this instance an extended back projection, which would receive side lighting from the long narrow 'yard'. However, it is easy to see why they were not adopted. For one thing, the arrangement is wasteful of space. In a plot where space is at a premium, the back living room and stairwell are both narrower than they need be, and gain little except perhaps improved daylighting. And if the yard is not to be built over at first-floor level – thus making it ineffectual – the main roof of the house would have to shrink to one-room depth, and a much more

200 Theoretical approaches to built form

FIGURE 8 Example of the 'side-staircase' plan, from the Cambridge survey

FIGURE 9 House in Little Albert Street, Bristol, with central staircase and hallway running from front to back. From Burnett, *A Social History of Housing* 1978: drawing by C G Powell

extensive roof would be required to cover the enlarged back projection. From the builder's point of view, it would have been both more straightforward and more economical to make the main body of the house two rooms deep than to break up the plan, and the roofing, in this way.

Another interesting and suggestive group of plans consists of those with the staircase positioned at the very back of the house (for example, solution 14 in Figure 7). This, again, is an arrangement that seems never to have been used in building practice. The explanation for this would appear to lie in the inconvenience of the back stair with respect to the first-floor layout. It is important to remember that the plans that DIS generates are based solely on the constraints specified at the outset of each experiment, and take no account of the effects that the arrangements might have on upper or lower floor levels. Each floor plan has to be dealt with independently: DIS does not 'think' in three dimensions. Consequently, plans might be produced which fully meet the constraints at ground-floor level, but which are wholly impracticable from the point of view of the accommodation above or below.

These limitations are evident to some extent in the previous example. They appear to be decisive here. If the back stair is to work, it is essential in the first place that the back projection is on two floors. In the smaller type of house, like that in Figure 3, a staircase in the scullery would obviously be pointless since it would simply lead up into the open air! But even in a true 'tunnel-back' house, a rear stair would still present problems: at ground-floor level it would involve a long circulation route from the front to the back of the house, and, on the first floor, unless a corridor were formed alongside each of the back bedrooms, one would need to pass through both of these in order to reach the main bedroom at the front. For practical purposes, the best policy is to keep the stairs towards the centre of the house, as this allows easy access to all bedrooms with a minimum of through circulation.

One may also speculate on whether it was ever socially acceptable to have the staircase placed in the scullery. Few special guests were likely, of course, to be shown to any room other than the front parlour, which was set aside especially to accommodate them.[13] But there were presumably occasions when a visitor – the family doctor, for example – would require access to the bedrooms. For this purpose, a staircase that could be reached directly from the front of the house was the ideal. To have to lead any visitor through to the scullery – the messiest part of the house – was the last thing that any respectable, or aspiring, working-class family would want.

As the frontage width of the house was increased in the experiments to 4.5 m and 5 m, a cluster of new plans appeared, in which the scullery was brought into the main body of the house and set alongside the living room (see Figure 10). This is made possible, however, only by reducing the scullery to the minimum width (approximately 1.5 m). Though plans of this kind are found at a later date, most notably in local authority housing between the wars, they were obviously considered to be cramped, and in Cambridge, the semi-detached version frequently incorporated a single-storey projection at the side to give the scullery extra space (see Figure 11). With the byelaw terrace, the preference was clearly to retain a wide back projection to house the scullery and to use the additional width of the plan to introduce an entrance hall or passageway at the front of the house. The hall layout seems, from the Cambridge evidence, to have been the rule in plans of 4.5 m or more across the front (that is, where the parlour could still be at least 3.5 m wide). In the somewhat grander terraces, the hall would extend through the whole depth of the house, and so give separate access to each of the ground-floor rooms. In Cambridge, this arrangement appears to have been restricted to houses of at least 5 m frontage width. (The example shown in Figure 12 has a frontage of about 5.25 m.)

One feature of the experiments is the fact that the central-staircase solution continued to be generated by DIS even for the wider frontages of 4.5 m and 5 m. Given that the dimensional constraints were reasonably accurate (as seems to be the case), it is curious, therefore, that

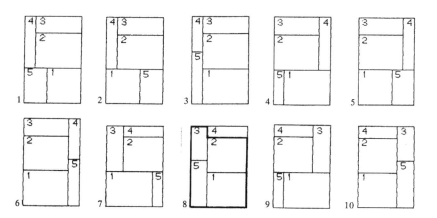

FIGURE 10 Plans generated by DIS for a 5 m frontage. Constraints are otherwise as in Table 1

202 Theoretical approaches to built form

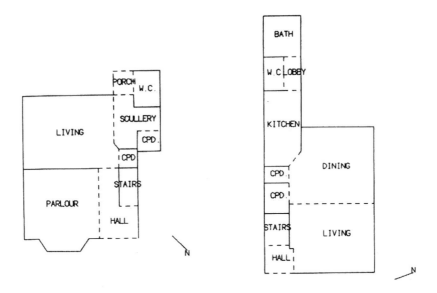

FIGURE 11 Two interwar local authority houses from the Cambridge sample. Extra space for the kitchen or scullery was provided in each case by a projection – at back or side. Both are standard plan types, but the right-hand plan has been extended to provide a bath and WC: the basic plan is that shown in Figure 10. Continuous lines in the plan represent walls without doors. Broken lines represent walls with doors

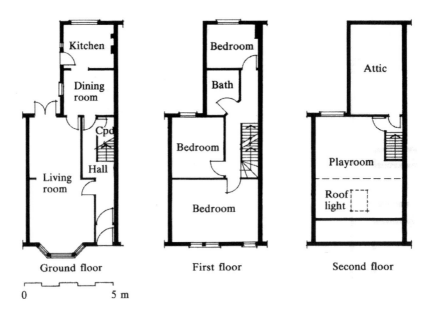

FIGURE 12 Terrace house with hallway through to back projection; Cambridge, about 1900. Here the attic space has been converted to provide an extra floor

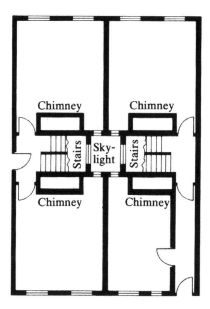

FIGURE 13 Seventeenth-century houses at Newington Green, with central staircases, lit by a light well at half-landing level; based on a drawing in Kelsall, 'The London house plan', 1974

this plan arrangement should, on existing evidence, have been so rare. Examples do occur, like that shown in Figure 9. But in terraces of wider frontage (4.5 m or more), the side-staircase appears to have been almost universal.

This was not always so. In the latter part of the seventeenth century, in the years following the Great Fire, the central-staircase plan emerged as a common – perhaps the most common – pattern in London for terraces of this frontage. But its popularity was short-lived, and the type appears to have been superseded by the familiar side-staircase plan at some time during the 1680s.[14] The reasons for its demise are unclear, but these may have had something to do with the problem of daylighting. In the seventeenth-century examples, the staircase was lit in one of two ways – by roof lights, which were prone to leak, or by light wells (see Figure 13).[15] Both would have involved extra expense for the builder. In addition, as Kelsall has pointed out, the layout often required the provision of a heavy cross-wall to give additional structural support to the staircase.[16]

It seems, in any event, that the central-staircase type proved unattractive in large-scale speculative development for terraces of all but the narrowest of frontages, and when the type does occur in byelaw housing, the staircase is most often without any source of daylight. The greater convenience of the side-staircase – the fact that it could, in most circumstances give access to all bedrooms without through circulation – and the ease and economy with which daylight could be admitted through the back wall, may together explain its success.

In a final exercise, the above series of experiments was repeated, but with the adjacency constraints on the dummy space (the backyard) relaxed. Only dimensional constraints were applied. In this particular series of experiments, a hallway was also included. The exact set of constraints is given in Table 2. As might be expected, the number of solutions was greatly increased for all the wider frontages: at 4.5 m width, the program generated 215 dimensionally

204 Theoretical approaches to built form

TABLE 2 Set of constraints used in second terrace house experiment (Figure 14). Note the absence of adjacency constraints for the void, and the inclusion of an entrance hall

Space		Adjacency constraints*	Dimensions (m)		Area (m²)		Aspect ratio
			Min.	Max.	Min.	Max.	
1	Hall	f, 2, 3, 4	0.9	6.0	0.8	5.4	7.0
2	Stairs	1	0.9	4.0	2.0	4.0	5.0
3	Living room	1, 5	2.4	8.0	11.0	30.0	2.0
4	Parlour	1, f	2.0	6.0	8.0	20.0	2.0
5	Scullery	3, b	1.5	6.0	5.0	15.0	3.0
6	Void	–	1.0	6.0	2.5	15.0	6.0
0	Overall plan	–	–	–	32.5	75.0	–

Note: * f front, b back

feasible possibilities. A great many of these were quite different from anything that had appeared before, in that the void was now located at the heart of the plan, separating the front room from the back of the house. It was no longer a back yard but a courtyard, albeit a very small one. The same kinds of solution appear at the narrower frontages, though the total number of solutions is reduced. Figure 14 shows the results obtained for a 3.5 m frontage.

Courtyard planning did not apparently figure at all among the late nineteenth-century house types, though it is interesting to see how close certain of the solutions are to the seventeenth-century terraces discussed above (compare Figures 13 and 14). True courtyard plans were not uncommon in medieval urban houses, in London and elsewhere, owing to the custom of siting the kitchen at some distance from the living quarters to avert the danger of fire. This kind of layout largely disappeared during the sixteenth century, however, as the kitchen was absorbed into the main body of the house.[17] The most obvious advantage of the various courtyard configurations is that they permit a greater depth of development in a narrow plot, while still ensuring that daylight reaches all rooms in the house. The most obvious disadvantage is the increased cost of construction where a house is under two roofs instead of one. Though there has been a revival of courtyard planning in the work of some contemporary architects[18], it is understandable that it offered no real challenge to the standard byelaw plans.

The 'byelaw' terrace: conclusions

From the DIS experiments, various additional plans have emerged for the byelaw terrace, some of which can be classed as feasible, and may, through further historical research, be shown to have been built. On the whole, however, there were rather few distinct solutions to the problem of terrace housing when convenience and economy of construction are also taken into account. This is especially true for houses of narrow frontage, owing to the physical constraints.

Terrace houses were clearly ranked in quality according to their size and width of frontage. Increase in frontage width was accompanied by an increase not only in the number of rooms (through the inclusion of a back projection), but also in the size of those rooms. It also made possible the insertion of an entrance hall at the front, thereby increasing the privacy of the ground-floor rooms.

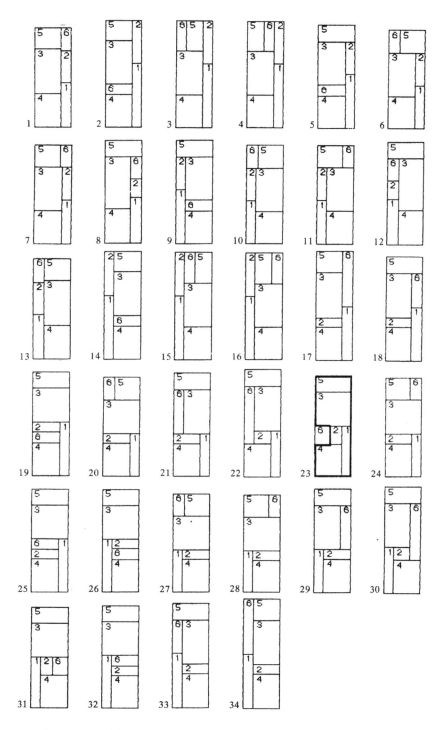

FIGURE 14 Plans generated by DIS from the constraints in Table 2. The frontage is 3.5 m. In many cases the dummy space is located within the body of the plan. The plan in heavy outline is essentially the 'light well' arrangement in Figure 13, but with an additional room at the back

206 Theoretical approaches to built form

The principal restriction on internal arrangement was that of room location. Traditionally, the main ground-floor rooms were noninterchangeable: the parlour was located at the front, the living room or kitchen lay behind, and the scullery was at the back. The experiments point up the important, but largely tacit, social distinction between the front and the back of the house.

The working-class cottage, about 1919

Background and general characteristics

Public housing scarcely existed to any significant extent before World War 1. The great bulk of Victorian housing, as already pointed out, had been provided by private developers on a speculative basis, the terrace house being the characteristic product of the period. Such attempts as there were to provide housing for the poorer sections of society centred on the independent efforts of philanthropic housing associations, societies, and trusts, which have been well documented.[19] Steady pressure for housing reform during the latter half of the century produced a sequence of legislation (the Torrens Act, 1868; the Cross Act, 1875), culminating in the Housing of the Working Classes Act of 1890, which, for the first time, gave local authorities the powers needed to purchase land and build houses on their own account. But the scope of their work remained limited. It was the Housing and Town Planning Act of 1919 which finally transformed the situation, by turning the optional powers of the municipal bodies to build houses into a duty. This opened a new era of state involvement in housing provision.

The conditions for this radical development had been created by the Great War. With the diversion of resources to the war effort, and a dramatic increase in construction costs, housebuilding was brought effectively to a halt. The impact of the housing shortage seems first to have been felt in the munitions industry, and between 1915 and 1918 the Government undertook a unique programme of state-subsidised housebuilding to provide homes for munitions workers in various parts of the country.[20] The problem did not abate, however, and, as the end of the War approached, the whole question of housing provision assumed a new urgency. Faced with the imminent demobilisation of millions of military personnel, and the prospect of social unrest, perhaps even of revolution, Lloyd George's coalition government saw the housing shortage as a grave danger.

As Swenarton has shown, a vigorous housebuilding programme was viewed as a political necessity – both to absorb the unemployed work force and to demonstrate the government's commitment to improving social conditions. In the months following the Armistice, Lloyd George pledged himself to secure "habitations fit for the heroes who have won the war".[21] Half a million homes were promised in this great 'homes fit for heroes' campaign, and, though the actual figures were to fall far short of this, in the period 1919 to 1921 there was an unprecedented housing drive, implemented by means of the 1919 Housing Act.

The expressed aims of the government, however, were not simply to build houses, but to build houses on quite different lines from those of the past.[22] The inspiration for the new housing came above all from the Garden City movement, which offered a comprehensive approach to residential design, exemplified in the pre-War schemes for New Earswick (1902), Letchworth (1903), and Hampstead Garden Suburb (1906). In origin the idea and ideal of the garden city, as propounded by Ebenezer Howard, was a social rather than an architectural vision.[23] It was conceived as an alternative environment, distinct from both town and country, but combining the best features of the life of both. The physical form of the garden city was never precisely specified by him, and was left open to interpretation.[24] But subsequent projects and publications quickly established a particular model for garden city development, the main features of which were a low residential density (eight houses to the acre in the rural areas, 12 to the acre in urban areas), and an emphasis on low-rise houses with extensive gardens set around the perimeter of large blocks, or along comparatively narrow closes or culs-de-sac.

This model was largely the creation of the architect Raymond Unwin, who was one of the central professional figures in the movement, and of key importance in the propagation and implementation of the garden city ideal. It was he, together with his partner in practice, Barry Parker, who planned New Earswick, Letchworth, and Hampstead Garden Suburb. In 1914, when their architectural practice was officially dissolved, he joined the civil service as Chief Town Planning Inspector at the Local Government Board. As a member of the committee chaired by Sir John Tudor Walters from 1917 to 1918, Unwin clearly exercised a decisive influence on what was the first comprehensive examination of the political, technical, and practical issues involved in the design of the small house. The *Tudor Walters Report* of 1918 established the yardstick for the post-war debate on housing design.[25]

The *Tudor Walters Report* paved the way for an improved standard of accommodation and equipment in working-class housing. More importantly, for this analysis, it established a new *type* of housing. Instead of narrow-frontage houses with back projections, the *Report* proposed dwellings of wide frontage – where possible greater in width than in depth – in which all the accommodation was brought under the one roof. And as against the standardised plan of the terrace, reproduced regardless of aspect or prospect, it advocated a range of plans to suit different site conditions, and ensure that sunlight would enter the living room in each dwelling (compare the 1919 *Manual* discussed below, and Figure 15).

These changes reflect the preoccupations of the garden city movement, and, above all, of Unwin himself. Both he and Barry Parker regarded the penetration of sunlight into the home as of overriding importance. In *The Art of Building a Home* they remarked: "It is now pretty generally realised that no sacrifice is too great which is necessary to enable us to bring plenty of sunshine into all the main living rooms."[26] The traditional terrace plan was seen by them as particularly objectionable because its back projection prevented light and fresh air from reaching the main rooms at the rear of the house. In a Fabian Tract entitled 'Cottage plans and common sense' Unwin declared: "Every house in a row should contain all its rooms and offices under the main roof, and present an open and fair surface to sun and air on both its free sides."[27] The self-contained house, without extensions or projections, was, he argued, not only better but more economical, as a "given cubic space can be built more cheaply when it is all within the main walls and under the main roof". Although the frontage width of the house would need to be increased, the depth of the plan would be correspondingly reduced.

For Parker and Unwin, then, the main objective was, not to build on the example of contemporary housing, but to replace this by a completely new, and better model. This they did rigorously and systematically. Hawkes has observed:

> More than most of their contemporaries Parker and Unwin were concerned with developing an *approach* to design founded on a set of explicit principles, embracing both the goals of the design and the means by which the designer might systematically achieve them.[28]

208 Theoretical approaches to built form

The approach expressed itself, most markedly, in the consideration of the functional requirements of the home as a set of *topological relations* – relations of proximity and separation, conditioned by the needs of daylighting, view, privacy, and accessibility – which had to be resolved in the spatial configuration of the dwelling. It is a philosophy and method that strongly underpinned the work of the Tudor Walters group.

In April 1919, the detailed recommendations of the *Tudor Walters Report* were taken up, virtually unaltered, in the Local Government Board's *Manual on the Preparation of State-aided Housing Schemes*, and thus became the official basis for local authority schemes under the 1919 Housing Act. The 1919 *Manual* was used here as the framework for the DIS experiments.

Plan generation

The 1919 *Manual* laid down a series of precise recommendations and requirements to be observed by local authorities in the design of new housing schemes. These were accompanied by 12 type plans, which were intended to give a general idea of the kinds of layout that would meet with the Local Government Board's approval. Eight of the plans were for self-contained, two-storey cottages (see Figure 15). This was the principal type of house to be adopted. All of the cottages are semi-detached. The remaining four plans were for special circumstances (flats, bungalows, and agricultural cottages).

Cottages were divided into two classes: class A, in which the accommodation consisted of living room, scullery, and three bedrooms; and class B, which contained, in addition, a parlour on the ground floor. The type plans showed appropriate layouts for each of these, taking account of different aspects. Thus, plans 1 and 2 are for class A cottages with a southerly aspect, plans 3 and 8 for class A cottages with a northerly aspect, plans 4 and 7 for class B cottages with a northerly aspect, and plans 5 and 6 for class B cottages with a southerly aspect (Figure 15).

In our experiments we concentrated on the larger of the two kinds of cottage – the parlour cottage (type B) – and examined possible configurations for the ground-floor plan under various conditions. The plans all refer to the left-hand cottage in a semi-detached pair (that is, the right-hand wall was assumed to be a party wall). In every case, we confined ourselves to the physical constraints that were actually given in the *Manual*, either explicitly in the recommendations, or by example in the set of suggested plans. Table 3 gives the full list of constraints that was drawn up for the south-facing parlour house with front access.

It will be seen that six spaces were designated altogether, all of them internal. (Since the back projection of the terrace house was now resolutely banished, it was unnecessary to introduce any dummy external spaces as in the previous experiment.) The first three spaces – the living room, the parlour, and the scullery – represent the major ground-floor rooms. The larder (space 6), though considerably smaller, was also treated as a separate space, with specific requirements, in accordance with the policy of the *Manual*. The hall and stairs were amalgamated in space 4, since a requirement that "the stairs should usually start from the entrance lobby" effectively made the two into a single unit. Space 5 similarly denotes a grouping of spaces – the WC, the coal store, and other ancillary functions. Although the *Manual* was less specific in its stipulations for these spaces, both the WC and coal store were required to be accessible under cover, and, as the type plans show, they were generally brought together, so that they could be reached from a common lobby.

Analysis and interpretation of house plans **209**

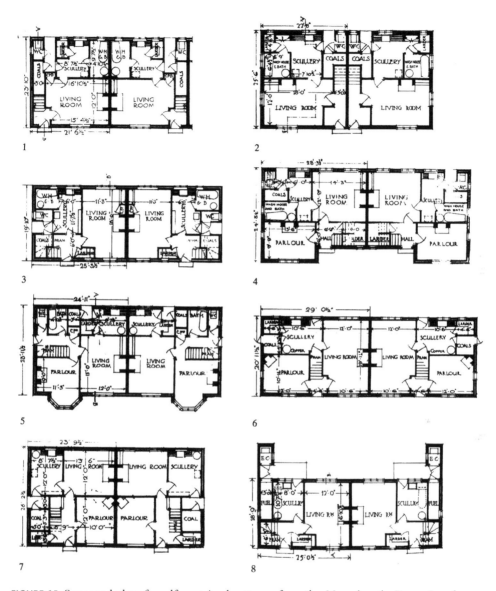

FIGURE 15 Suggested plans for self-contained cottages, from the *Manual on the Preparation of State-aided Housing Schemes*, Local Government Board, 1919

The *adjacency constraints* specified in the table stem from requirements relating to access (internal and external) and orientation, most of which are quite unambiguous. Hence, for the living room: "The best aspect is south-east, and it must never have a northerly aspect except when sunlight can be admitted at the other end of the room" (p. 9). Internally, the room was to "be arranged with as few doors as practicable". In the *Tudor Walters Report*, it was considered that "any doors in the living-room beyond the one from the lobby and the one from the scullery are best avoided if a comfortable room is to be secured" (p. 30).

210 Theoretical approaches to built form

TABLE 3 Set of constraints derived from the *Manual on the Preparation of State-aided Housing Schemes* (Local Government Board, 1919)

Space		Adjacency constraints★	Dimensions (m)		Area (m²)		Aspect ratio
			Min.	Max.	Min.	Max.	
1	Living room	s, 3, 4	3.0	8.0	16.7	30.0	2.0
2	Parlour	s, 4	2.4	6.0	11.2	20.0	2.0
3	Scullery	n, 1, 5	1.8	6.0	7.5	15.0	2.5
4	Hall and stairs	s, 1, 2	1.5	4.0	5.25	8.0	4.0
5	WC and coal store	w, 3	1.5	4.5	5.0	10.0	4.0
6	Larder	n	0.9	1.8	1.1	1.5	2.5
0	Overall plan width	–	6.0	9.0	53.0	65.0	2.0
	depth	–	4.5	9.0	–	–	–

Note: ★ s south wall, n north wall, w west wall

This judgment was observed in all of the *Manual*'s plans (see Figure 15). Together, then, these topological requirements give the specification shown in Table 3: space 1 (the living room) is placed at the front of the house, that is, against the south wall, and is to be adjacent to spaces 3 (the scullery) and 4 (the hallway).

On the parlour, the *Manual* is less explicit, and apparently more flexible. Although a westerly aspect was considered preferable for the room, this was not insisted upon, and it was added: "Preference should . . . be given to the living-room in this matter of aspect" (p. 9).

In the type plans, the aspect of the parlour does indeed vary, but the plans are consistent to the extent that the room is always at the front of the house. This appears to follow primarily from the demand for access from the hallway. The *Tudor Walters Report* was specific on this point: "The advantage of the parlour is very greatly diminished if direct access to it from the front entrance is not obtainable" (p. 29). In all of the model plans, in both Tudor Walters and the *Manual*, the door from the hallway constituted the sole means of access to the room. For space 2, therefore, two adjacencies were specified: one to the front of the house, the other to space 4 (the hallway).

In the case of the scullery, discussion centred on the internal organisation of the space – the placing of the sink, the cupboards, and so on. The principal adjacency requirements, however, are evident from the plans. The connection with the living room has already been noted. In addition, the scullery normally provided access, directly or indirectly, to the various ancillary spaces we have grouped together in space 5. This, again, follows from Tudor Walters, where it was noted, clearly with regret, that the scullery

> will generally have to be encumbered by several doors; one to the outer lobby, one to the living-room and one to the larder will be usual, occasionally another is required to give access to the coal store, although it is desirable that access to the latter should not be obtained directly from the scullery but from an outer yard or lobby (p. 31).

Since space 5 represents all the ancillary spaces, with or without a lobby, an adjacency between 2 and 5 was specified to cover these various possibilities. No adjacency, however, was specified between the scullery and the larder, as this was not always observed (for example, see plan 4). A northern adjacency was added, because the scullery was invariably placed at the back of the house. The main criterion here was outlook. The *Tudor Walters Report* took its cue from the testimony of women witnesses, who "emphasised the importance of the housewife when working in the scullery being able to obtain a full view of the garden in which the children were at play" (p. 31). Although the comments in the *Manual* are considerably less emphatic, requiring simply that the sink "should be placed under or near the window, which should preferably overlook the garden" (p. 9), a further reference to the fact that "a suitable area outside the back door should generally be paved with cement or other impervious material" reveals the assumption that the scullery was to be at the *back* of the house.

It should be noted, incidentally, that in none of the type plans was direct access provided from the front entrance to the scullery, as it was considered wasteful to run a passage alongside the stairs.[29] In later public housing, this was superseded by the more familiar arrangement, shown below (Figure 18(a)), in which the hallway gave onto all of the ground-floor rooms.

The remaining adjacencies in the experiment were all external. For the larder, a cool, fresh, and airy position was regarded as essential, and the *Manual* required that it "should be on the northerly side of the house" (p. 9). A north adjacency was therefore specified. The *Tudor Walters Report* also considered it "best that the larder should be entered from the back lobby or scullery" (p. 33), but, as already mentioned, the *Manual* did not insist on any fixed position for the larder, giving priority instead to the matter of orientation. Hence, no internal adjacencies were specified.

The front access to the house was, by definition, along the south wall. The secondary access (that is, the 'back' lobby included in space 5) was, for the purposes of this experiment, set against the side wall.

The *dimensional constraints* assigned to each of the spaces were derived, in most cases, from measurement of the type plans. Minimum room areas, however, were taken, where possible, from figures actually specified in the Appendix (page 29). These figures – 180 ft^2 (16.7 m^2) for the living room, 120 ft^2 (11.2 m^2) for the parlour, 80 ft^2 (7.4 m^2) for the scullery – were identical with those given in Tudor Walters. This was not true of the larder, for which Tudor Walters proposed the generous minimum of 24 ft^2 (2.2 m^2) in recognition of the special needs of rural tenants who required extra space in which to salt their pig (page 33). The lower figure of 12 ft^2 (1.1 m^2) given in the *Manual* was the one adopted here.

Where dimensions were based on the plans alone, these were set somewhat above and below the observed maxima and minima, respectively, to give reasonable scope for other realistic solutions to be generated.

The overall plan area, that is, the gross area of the ground floor, as measured from the drawings, is generally larger than in Tudor Walters, ranging from 595 to 650 ft^2 (55.3–60.4 m^2). The minimum was again set slightly below this figure, and the upper limit was increased to 700 ft^2 (65 m^2), in agreement with the new figure given by the Ministry of Health in June, 1919.[30] The minimum plan width of 6.0 m followed from the *Manual*'s recommendation that "adequate frontage, generally of not less than 20 ft., should be given to the buildings . . .".

The *results* of this particular experiment are shown in Figure 16. They were unexpected. With the constraints described, DIS generated only one solution and this was precisely the one shown in the *Manual* (see Figure 15, plan 6). Given the generous space standards, the wide frontage of the house (more than twice that of many terrace houses), and the move to

212 Theoretical approaches to built form

FIGURE 16 Single solution generated by DIS for south-facing parlour house with front access (compare Figure 15, plan 6)

loosen the old constraints on room position, this is surprising, and might be considered a freak effect. Further experiments, however, produced results that were scarcely less dramatic.

For the complementary plan to the one described – a south-facing cottage, but with the main access at the side, and the secondary access at the back – three feasible plans were produced, one of which was the plan shown (plan 5 in Figure 15), the other two, slight variations on the same plan. And for a north-facing cottage with front access, once again three solutions were given, one of these – the first – being the suggested plan, that is, plan 7 (see Figure 15). As Figure 17 shows, the third solution is a variant of the first plan, incorporating a wider scullery. The second represents an interesting alternative, although access to the larder by way of the parlour would undoubtedly have been seen as unacceptable.

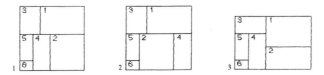

FIGURE 17 Three solutions generated by DIS for north-facing parlour house with front access (compare Figure 15, plan 7)

Clearly, then, whatever the original intentions of Unwin and other members of the Tudor Walters Committee regarding the planning of the parlour cottage, the requirements that were eventually formulated were highly restrictive. In one case, at least, the recommendations were necessary and sufficient to account for the type plan given in the 1919 *Manual*.

The working-class cottage: conclusions

The results of this experiment have shown that the framework of constraints imposed on local authority cottage design after World War 1 were highly deterministic. From a historical point of view, this is of interest since it appears that the authors of the 1919 *Manual* were unaware of the full effects of their recommendations. In the section on house accommodation, they were at pains to point out that the typical plans included at the end of the *Manual* were

Analysis and interpretation of house plans **213**

"only for general guidance" and were "not intended to hamper initiative or to prevent full expression being given to local customs and traditions . . ." These sentiments were repeated in the Ministry journal, *Housing*, where it was noted:

> The plans in the Manual were offered only as suggestions to meet conditions laid down in respect of the dimensions and aspects of rooms, their accessories in proper relation to each other, their suitability to the requirements of different kinds of workers, and the disposal of the accommodation in a compact manner.[31]

Yet, clearly, in the case of the parlour house examined above, the architect would have searched in vain to find an alternative solution to the plan shown.

How did they come to overlook the limited range of real possibilities? Perhaps the main reason was the preoccupation with aspect that, *prima facie*, introduced a new freedom into the planning of the house. Parker and Unwin had inveighed from the first against the "superstitions of front and back", and the absurdity of repeating a cottage plan "unaltered in street after street, heedless of whether it faces north, south, east or west".[32] Their own schemes demonstrated the variety that could be achieved when each house was designed to suit its site and its aspect. In their plans, the parlour might just as easily be at the back as the front, if conditions so dictated.[33] Likewise, the scullery and even the toilet might be placed at the front of the house, as in some cottages at New Earswick.[34] By the time of the Tudor Walters recommendations, however, many of these innovations had been quashed (in many cases understandably), and, as shown above, the parlour and the scullery, as well as the WC, had reverted to their customary positions. These constraints on *position* could conspire with those of aspect to place considerable restrictions on the plan of the house.

Nonetheless, if the adjacencies alone are considered, there remain a very large number of theoretically possible plans for most of the house types. For the south-facing parlour house discussed above, there are no less than 103 topologically feasible solutions. Paradoxically, therefore, it would seem to have been not so much the topological constraints, as the additional constraints of dimension, that were decisive in reducing the options – in this case to one only.

As a final point, it should be added that the solutions generated by DIS, though exhaustive, are still open to variation and adjustment at a detailed level, for example, in the cranking or displacement of walls, the insertion of cupboards, etc, and the positioning of doors. Much of the discussion by Ministry architects was concerned with such questions of detailed design, rather than strategic planning. Interestingly, type plan 6 was singled out in *Housing* as one in which "many variations can be made",[35] a fact which is to some extent borne out by subsequent designs and projects (see the examples from the Cambridge survey in Figure 18). Without a change in the constraints, however, the basic plan form remained fixed and inescapable.

The private semi-detached house, 1918–1939

Background and general characteristics

Through its adoption in the 1919 *Manual* and subsequent official guidance, the *Tudor Walters Report* set the pattern for municipal housing between the wars. But it also exercised a profound influence on private housing, chiefly by way of town planning legislation. Crucial here

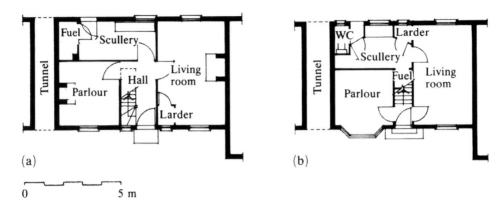

FIGURE 18 Ground-floor plans of two interwar parlour houses from the Cambridge sample. Both date from the 1920s, and both are based on plan 6 in the *Manual on the Preparation of State-aided Housing Schemes*, Local Government Board, 1919. Plan (a), a local authority house, is still built to generous space standards (ground floor area is 52 m^2 = 560 ft^2), and now provides direct access to the scullery from the entrance hall. Because the same plan was used on both sides of the street, which runs east-west, the larder might be moved, as here, to the front of the living room to maintain the correct northerly aspect. Plan (b), a standard type used by a local housing association, is much meaner, but otherwise closer to the 1919 plan. Note, however, that the larder is now adjacent to the living room, and the coal store has been inserted beneath the stairs

were the limitations imposed on density, Unwin's recommendation of 12 houses per acre (eight houses per acre in rural areas) being taken up as the general standard. Although the development controls were frequently flouted by private builders – in a not untypical speculative estate in Bexley, Kent, for example, houses were laid out on farmland at 15 to the acre[36] – the ground coverage on interwar private estates was always well below that associated with Victorian byelaw developments. Thus, the character of housing was changed across the whole spectrum. If the low-density council estate became "one of the standard visual symbols of twentieth-century Britain",[37] the low-density private estate established an image which is every bit as potent and pervasive (see Figures 19 and 20).

Indeed, in terms of sheer numbers, the contribution of the speculative developer to the housing stock was to exceed that of the local authorities. The output of houses in the interwar period was impressive. Altogether, some 4 million new houses were constructed. About two-thirds of these were put up by private builders. Much of the development took place in the suburbs, particularly in the Midlands and the South, and was stimulated in part by the system of state subsidy, which, in 1923, was directed away from local authorities and towards the encouragement of private enterprise.[38] But, more fundamentally, the expansion of suburbia reflected the growth of the middle classes in these years. The new private estates were built overwhelmingly for owner-occupation, and the building societies, by providing the money for mortgages, played a major part in the building boom.[39]

In its physical form, private housing had certain features in common with that produced by local authorities. But there were also profound differences between the two. Whereas municipal dwellings were increasingly grouped in short terraces of four, six, or even eight houses, with tunnel access to the back gardens, the houses on private estates were almost

Analysis and interpretation of house plans **215**

FIGURE 19 Private semi-detached houses in Cambridge: a typical speculative development of the 1930s. By kind permission of the Ordnance Survey

FIGURE 20 View of a typical pair of 1930s semi-detached houses, Radegund Road, Cambridge

216 Theoretical approaches to built form

invariably laid out in pairs. The 'semi-detached' was the classic dwelling type of interwar speculative development. Estates were typically composed of repeated pairs of dwellings, set out along meandering roads, or along culs-de-sac, which were multiplied in the effort to cover every available piece of land. There was little concern for the 'street picture', as advocated by Unwin,[40] the houses being set out to regular building-lines.

The semi-detached house was, of course, the type illustrated in the 1919 *Manual*. And, though built for middle-class, not working-class occupation, the speculative 'semi' followed many of the other basic precepts of the *Manual*: it was on two floors, it was of wide frontage, and it contained all the main accommodation under one roof. Although the back projection did make a reappearance in some of the later houses, as it did also in council designs (Figure 11 above), it was never the dominant and integral part of the plan that it had been in the terrace house. For reasons of economy, however, frontage widths were reduced as much as possible. A plot width of 25–30 ft (7.6–9.1 m) became the norm on many estates.[41] The frontage of the house itself was normally around 20 ft (6.1 m), sometimes a little less, rarely very much more. This gave sufficient width for two medium-sized rooms (or one ample room and one small room) to be placed side-by-side.

The internal planning of the house was extremely standardised – far more so than public housing, which usually offered a range of type plans for each estate. The typical layout is illustrated in Figure 21. On the ground floor, there were three rooms. At the back was the kitchen and, beside this, the living or dining room, which frequently had French doors opening on the garden. At the front was a second living room or parlour. In some cases, the two main living rooms were connected by folding doors, and so could be thrown into one space when necessary. Each of the rooms, however, had separate access by way of the entrance hall.

On the first floor, there were three bedrooms, two of which were large enough to contain a double bed. The third was considerably smaller, and was usually referred to as the 'box room'. There was also a bath and a WC, which might be combined or in separate, but adjacent rooms. In some plans, the box room at the front of the house and the bathroom at the back, in others vice versa. This was the 'universal plan', which was repeated in vast numbers of houses all over the country.[42] Like the terrace plan before it, the same layout was used for all sites, regardless of aspect.

Stylistically, features such as bows, bays, and oriel windows were very popular: the two-storey bay became a regular and indispensable attachment to the front of the house. Mock Tudor was the preferred style, and the facade was commonly crowned with gables replete with imitation half-timbering. These, and a wealth of other details, were used to articulate the differences between homes, and to express their individuality.

Such stylistic affectations were anathema to progressive architects, and the basic uniformity of the semi-detached house has made it the object of widespread criticism and ridicule. Yet this very standardisation attests to the success of the type. In many ways, it is understandable. The speculative builder was concerned to meet the market, and, as others have observed, he managed to produce what most people wanted.[43] Most importantly, the semi-detached house offered three rooms on the ground floor, instead of just two, as was common in local authority schemes (that is, the type A house, see above); it provided independent access to each of these rooms, avoiding through circulation; and it gave two good-sized bedrooms and an upstairs bathroom. Moreover, the main living rooms were of such a size (normally about 12 ft or 3.7 m square) as to be very flexible in the furniture and activities they accommodated.[44]

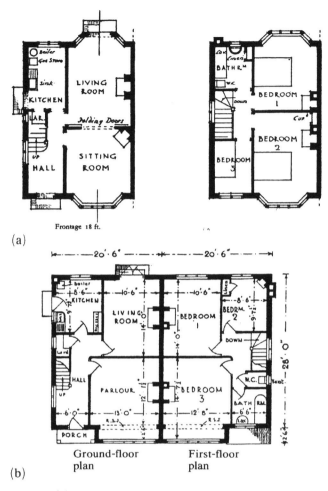

FIGURE 21 Two variants of the 'universal' plan for semi-detached houses; from Allen, 'Building to sell', 1934

The question this raises, however, is whether these requirements could have been adequately met in any other plan forms. If so, why did these alternatives not occur in practice? Although it may be that the conservatism of the speculative builder was sufficient to ensure the repetition of a well-tried formula, the extreme standardisation of the house plan suggests that there might have been constraints at work, other than those that are immediately evident.

Plan generation

As with the previous experiments, attention was focused, initially at least, on the ground-floor arrangement. For the internal accommodation, three living rooms and a hallway were taken as the basic requirement. Thus, four spaces were specified: 1, representing the front living or sitting room, 2, the back living or dining room, 3, the kitchen, and 4, the hall together with the staircase (see Table 4). The topological constraints reflect both the customary

218   Theoretical approaches to built form

TABLE 4 Set of constraints used in the generation of ground floor plan arrangements for the semi-detached house

Space		Adjacency constraints*	Dimensions (m)		Area (m²)		Aspect ratio
			Min.	Max.	Min.	Max.	
1	Living room or parlour	f, 4	3.0	5.5	11.0	20.0	2.0
2	Living or dining room	b, 4	3.0	5.5	11.0	25.0	2.0
3	Kitchen	b, 4	1.7	4.0	5.0	14.0	3.0
4	Hall and stairs	f, 1, 2, 3	1.7	7.5	5.0	17.0	5.0
0	Overall plan width	–	6.0	6.0	30.0	75.0	–

Note: * f front, b back

location for each of the rooms and the access requirements as discussed above, that is, each room was to be independently accessible from the hallway. It was assumed that the plans were to refer to the left-hand house of the pair, and that the right-hand side would, therefore, denote the common party wall, and the left-hand side, the flanking or end wall. The hallway was fixed either at the front of the house, the usual position, or at the side, against the end (or 'west') wall. The dimensions given in the table were based on analysis of the Cambridge sample, and, like those for the terrace plans, were made 'loose' enough to accommodate all the recorded examples.

To begin with, only the adjacency constraints were specified. With the entrance at the front, DIS generated twenty-four topologically feasible solutions for the plan; with a side entrance, there were 12. Thus, even without dimensions assigned to the rooms or to the overall plan, the number of possibilities was very small – much smaller, in fact, than for the local authority cottage examined above. When realistic dimensions were added, the range of options was reduced further. At the standard 6 m frontage, four plans only were generated for the front-access house (see Figure 22). Plans 3 and 4 in the figure, it will be noted, are simply mirror images of plans 1 and 2, but represent distinct solutions, in that spaces 3 and 4 (the kitchen and the hall) are here against the party wall as opposed to the end wall. If we require the entrance hall to be against the outer edge of the building, only the first two solutions apply. These two plans approximate the 'universal' plan of the semi-detached house (Figure 21).

The first plan would seem to have been employed rather less frequently than the second, presumably because it results in a very narrow kitchen and/or an oversized hallway. The second plan gives a more generous kitchen, but is still likely to make the hallway wider than it need be: the layout is most suitable in narrow-frontage houses, like Figure 21(a). At the 6 m frontage, the latter plan could be simply adjusted by shifting the internal wall between the parlour and the hallway across towards the end wall, thereby giving more space to the parlour and less to the hall. This makes the hallway into an L-shape, as in Figure 21(b). From the Cambridge survey, this would appear to have been by far the most common solution for houses of standard width.

It would seem, then, that the options were not great, given the various geometrical and dimensional requirements. More importantly, it appears that the placing of the entrance hall

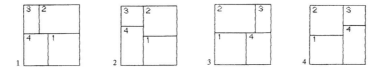

FIGURE 22 The four solutions generated by DIS for the ground-floor plan of a semi-detached house of 6 m frontage. The full list of constraints is given in Table 4

against the end wall was responsible, in the final instance, for determining the plan. This position for the main entrance was certainly realistic: from all the evidence, it seems to have been quite unusual, in the fully-fledged semi-detached house of the 1930s, for the front door to be positioned anywhere other than next to the end wall of the house. Of a total of twenty-eight private, interwar, semi-detached dwellings in the Cambridge sample, twenty-five had their front door adjacent to the end wall. (The remaining three had side access through the end wall itself.)

Since this was such a strong feature of the semi-detached house, it was clearly worth examining further its influence on the internal planning of the house. This was done with reference to the upper floor. In the universal plan, the first floor was of the same extent as the ground floor, and, as noted above, normally contained three bedrooms and a bathroom. Each space had separate access from the landing (Figure 21). Following this pattern, five spaces were specified (the stairs and landing being treated as a single space), and realistic dimensions assigned to each (see Table 5). The dimensions, once again, were derived from the recorded Cambridge data. As will be seen, the only adjacencies specified were those required to ensure acceptable internal access to each of the bedrooms and the bathroom. *No* external adjacencies were defined in this instance since it was clear that neither aspect nor room position was held to be of much importance at first-floor level.

With these constraints alone, DIS generated a vast number of possibilities: for the stock 6 m frontage, 192 dimensionally feasible solutions were produced. Many of these plans were three or more rooms deep, but they were all clearly workable as long as daylight could be admitted to the inner rooms through the side wall. Yet there was certainly nothing like this

TABLE 5 Set of constraints used in the generation of first floor plan arrangements for the semi-detached house

	Space	Adjacency constraints*	Dimensions (m) Min.	Dimensions (m) Max.	Area (m²) Min.	Area (m²) Max.	Aspect ratio
1	Bedroom 1	5	3.0	6.0	11.0	20.0	2.0
2	Bedroom 2	5	2.7	5.5	8.0	17.0	2.0
3	Bedroom 3	5	2.0	5.0	4.8	9.0	2.0
4	Bathroom	5	1.5	2.7	3.0	6.0	2.0
5	Stairs and landing	1, 2, 3, 4	0.9	5.0	2.0	4.5	5.0
0	Overall plan width	–	6.0	6.0	30.0	75.0	–

220 Theoretical approaches to built form

variety of plans in the houses as built. Why was this? The crucial factor is precisely that of daylighting. In a semi-detached house, the greatest flexibility is achieved by placing the staircase against the inner, that is, the party wall, as this ensures that most of the rooms requiring daylight are located against the end wall. When the staircase occurs against the end wall, however, conditions are much more restrictive. Since no light at all can be admitted through the party wall, the house cannot be more than two rooms deep. And this is the situation that follows almost inevitably when the ground-floor entrance is positioned at the far end of the facade.

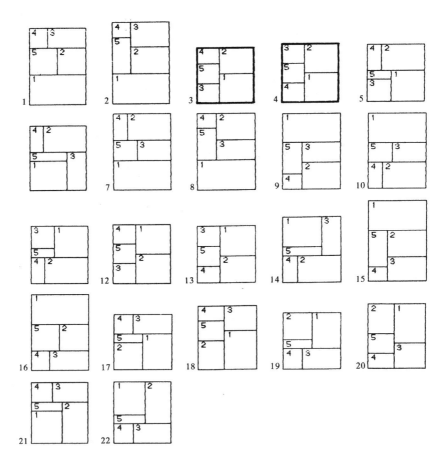

FIGURE 23 Solutions generated by DIS for the upper floor of a semi-detached house of 6 m frontage once the staircase and bathroom are fixed against the end (in this case the west) wall. Those plans with three rooms against the party (east) wall have to be discounted since the central room would be without direct daylighting. The standard solutions adopted in practice are shown in heavy outline; compare Figure 21. The remaining constraints are set out in Table 5

Hence, at first-floor level, the effects of the front door position are far more dramatic than on the ground floor. Figure 23 shows the results obtained when the stairwell and the bathroom are located against the end wall. There are twenty-two solutions. Eight of these have three rooms from front to back against the party wall, and must therefore be treated as unacceptable. If we also set aside those plans in which the staircase and landing are either oversized or too cramped to permit the required access to the bedrooms, we find that the remaining plans are essentially variations on two simple arrangements – those outlined in the figure. These, not surprisingly, are the ones repeated with such alacrity by the speculative builders.

The private semi-detached house: conclusions

We have noted the severe spatial limitations that arise when the main entrance to the house is placed at the edge of the block. But the arrangement had other drawbacks, as observed elsewhere, with regard to convenience and economy.[45] If centrally placed in the block, that is, against the party wall, the entrance halls would have afforded greater acoustic privacy for each dwelling. And with the kitchens and bathrooms grouped together, there would have been an opportunity too for savings in drainage and servicing.

Seen in this light, the wide separation of the two entrances appears a perverse and irrational gesture. Why then was it so consistently applied? The answer lay, quite clearly in its visual imagery. Individual expression was vital in the private house: it was this that set the owner-occupier apart from the council tenant. Logically, the search for uniqueness and individuality would lead to the detached house, but in practice this was too costly to be accessible to most people. The semi-detached thus offered a nice compromise, and the more this could be made to approach in appearance the ideal type – the detached dwelling – the better. The builder certainly realised this[46] and strove to create the illusion of the separate house. In sales brochures and advertisements the house would sometimes be pictured as if it were, indeed, detached (see Figure 24). The location of the entrance against the far wall greatly helped in this illusion: each house now had its own path, its own gateway, as far as possible out of view of its neighbour.

With the semi-detached house, then, we see a crucial constraint introduced, not by functional or technical requirements, but by the demands of symbolism and external expression. Here it was the social message that was all-important.

General conclusions

This series of studies has demonstrated that it is possible, through interactive use of the DIS program, to build up a very full picture of the constraints that applied in house design in different historical circumstances. All of the examples described here are, of course, comparatively modern, and this allows one to take advantage of documentary evidence as well as, to some extent, an intuitive 'feel' for the material. The reconstruction and interpretation of historical influences is clearly much less problematic when supplementary evidence is available. In the second example – that of the local authority cottage – we were able to compile an exhaustive list of constraints wholly by reference to contemporary documents.

Nonetheless, as the other two examples show, the method is still of value – and arguably of most value – where the historical evidence is incomplete. By systematically generating

FIGURE 24 Advertisement from *The Daily Telegraph*, 1935 for semi-detached Costain houses in Surrey. Notice how the left-hand house has been omitted from the illustration

plans from the constraints that are available, one can make informed guesses as to those that are missing. These can then be added to the original constraint set, and by an iterative process of hypothesis and test, one can work progressively towards a plausible *design grammar*.

It has to be recognised that there is a certain circularity of explanation here: by reference to the physical characteristics of a particular class of empirical objects, a set of constraints is inferred which is then used to account for those physical characteristics and to define the class of objects which is considered feasible. The dangers of this approach are enhanced by the fact that there may be many sets of constraints that serve to restrict the range of objects in a similar, and equally convincing, manner. In the absence of an external check, there may be no obvious way of choosing between these, and the process of plan generation is likely to reinforce the impression that our constraints are authentic when they are not. Moreover, it is easy to overstep the mark, and to build in increasing numbers of constraints, until the results approximate the actual corpus of surviving buildings or other objects. In principle, one can always devise a grammar (at least one) that will produce a given set of objects and no more. But unless the range of objects we are examining constitutes a balanced and fully representative sample, such a grammar is likely to be excessively 'tight'. Just how 'loose' our grammar should be remains a matter for conjecture.

With this cautionary note sounded, however, there is much that can be learnt through the systematic analysis of building form. The further we go into the past, and the more we are obliged to depend on archaeological evidence alone, then the more significant formal analysis must be. Regularities of planning and layout are the key to the design grammar; and though these may be masked and obscured for a whole variety of reasons, not least through taphonomy or selective survival of the evidence,[47] they are rarely obliterated 'in toto'. So our grammar need not be entirely speculative, even in the absence of contextual evidence.

The greatest leap, from an archaeological viewpoint, must remain one of interpretation of the constraints. This may be comparatively straightforward when we are dealing with strictly technical or functional matters. A given system of construction (for example, post-and-beam), or a requirement for daylighting or for a particular aspect, each impose very definite, and measurable, constraints on building form. The 'meaning' of these constraints is quite clear from the architectural record. The situation is very much more complicated, however, when we are confronted with questions of social convention and custom. Such traits may be highly specific to the culture concerned, and in the absence of general laws, the best one can hope for is calculated guesswork.

It was previously suggested that one can usefully imagine feasible architectural plans as lying within the larger world of geometrical possibility.[48] Unlike the geometrical world, this inner realm, which we have called the world of 'technical and functional possibility', is subject to change over time in response to new requirements, developments in technology, and so on. It cannot therefore be defined 'a priori', but only through empirical study. It is tempting to take the model one stage further, and to see another, still smaller world, that of 'social possibility', lying within the other two. One could then conceive of social meaning as a residue, to be sifted out by a process of elimination as we work our way inwards. Such a neat hierarchy is attractive but illusory.

One fact that became clear from the study of the semi-detached house is that matters of association and social signification can be a prime determinant of architectural form, far outweighing practical considerations. And although, in the case of the local authority cottage, it may appear that our nested series of worlds holds good, it is important to recognise that the preoccupation with technical and functional characteristics was itself conditioned by social (and political) factors. The guiding principles of design were undeniably utilitarian: the emphasis was on higher space standards, on improved facilities, and on the admission of sunlight and fresh air. But the fact that these conditions – what Unwin termed "the essential conditions of life and health"[49] – should have loomed so large is indicative of the extreme concern in this period for social health and social stability. Hence, the functional programme is, in itself, pregnant with social meaning.

All of this simply underscores the point that historical reconstruction is not easy. The process of exhaustive plan generation under constraints that has been illustrated here is not a magic wand with which to conjure up ideology. It does, however, offer a sure and reliable tool that should be as useful to archaeology as to architectural design.

224 Theoretical approaches to built form

Notes

1 Recent historical research suggests that local architects may have had a far larger role in the design of Victorian speculative housing than was believed hitherto. (See F Trowell, 'Speculative housing development in Leeds and the involvement of local architects in the design process 1866–1914', *Construction History* Volume 1 1985 pp. 13–24). There is no evidence, however, that they were any more explicit about their aims and priorities than the developers themselves.

2 F E Brown and J P Steadman, 'A computerised database of contemporary house plans', *Environment and Planning B: Planning and Design* Volume 13, 1986 pp. 405–414.

3 U Flemming, 'Wall representations of rectangular dissections and their use in automated space allocation', *Environment and Planning B* Volume 5, 1978 pp. 215–232.

4 Brown and Steadman, 'A computerised database'.

5 S Muthesius, *The English Terraced House*, Yale University Press, New Haven, CT 1982.

6 Public Health Act, *Public General Acts—Victoria* Chapter 55, HMSO, London 1875.

7 J N Tarn, *Five Per Cent Philanthropy: An Account of Housing in Urban Areas Between 1840 and 1914*, Cambridge University Press, Cambridge 1973 pp. 75–77.

8 The study of mass housing is now an expanding field, and much valuable information on the terrace house is contained in Muthesius, *The English Terraced House*. Our knowledge of ordinary building practice will no doubt be improved further as the number of detailed local studies increases. For example, see Trowell, 'Speculative housing development' on Leeds.

9 As shown elsewhere, the depth of the house is essentially governed by the need to maintain daylighting to all the main spaces in the home. In the Cambridge sample, the great majority of the houses, of *all* types, were found to have a depth of 7 to 7.5 m. See J P Steadman and F E Brown, 'Estimating the exposed surface area of the domestic stock', in *Urban Built Form and Energy Analysis*, D Hawkes, P Rickaby, J P Steadman eds, proceedings of a conference held at Darwin College, Cambridge, 26–27 June 1986; Butterworth, Sevenoaks, Kent 1987

10 J Burnett, *A Social History of Housing 1815–1970*, Methuen, Andover, UK 1978 p. 157; A Quiney, *House and Home: A History of the Small English House*, BBC Publications, London 1986 p. 118.

11 Burnett, *Social History of Housing* pp. 168–169.

12 Muthesius, *English Terraced House* p. 86.

13 Burnett, *Social History of Housing* p. 169; Quiney, *House and Home* pp. 118–119.

14 A F Kelsall, 'The London house plan in the later 17th century' *Post-Medieval Archaeology* Volume 8, 1974 pp. 80–91.

15 Also Quiney, *House and Home* p. 83.

16 Kelsall 'London house plan' p. 88.

17 F E Brown, 'Continuity and change in the urban house: developments in domestic space organisation in seventeenth-century London', *Comparative Studies in Society and History* Volume 28, 1986 pp. 558–590.

18 For example Phippen, Randall and Parkes: see *Architectural Review*, September 1972.

19 See Tarn, *Five Per Cent Philanthropy*.

20 S Pepper and M Swenarton, 'Home front: garden suburbs for munition workers', *Architectural Review* Volume 163, 1978 pp. 366–376.

21 *The Times*, 13 November 1918, quoted by M Swenarton, *Homes Fit for Heroes: The Politics and Architecture of Early State Housing in Britain*, Heinemann Educational Books, London 1981 p. 79.

22 Swenarton, *Homes Fit for Heroes* pp. 85–87.

23 Ebenezer Howard, *To-morrow: A Peaceful Path to Real Reform*, Swan Sonnenschein, London 1898.

24 S Pepper, 'The garden city legacy' *Architectural Review* Volume 163, 1978 pp. 321–324.

25 *Tudor Walters Report*, 'Report of the Committee appointed by the President of the Local Government Board and the Secretary of State for Scotland to consider questions of building construction in connection with the provision of dwellings for the working classes in England and Wales, and Scotland, and report upon methods of securing economy and despatch in the provision of such dwellings', HMSO, London 1918; see Swenarton, *Homes Fit for Heroes* pp. 92 ff.

26 B Parker and R Unwin, *The Art of Building a Home*, Longmans Green, London, 1901 p. 112.

27 R Unwin, 'Cottage plans and common sense', *Fabian Tract 109*, The Fabian Society, London, 1902 p. 6.

28 D Hawkes, 'The architectural partnership of Barry Parker and Raymond Unwin', *Architectural Review* Volume 163, 1978 pp. 327–332: see p. 327.

29 See discussion in *Housing*, Volume 1, Number 1, 19 July 1919, a fortnightly journal published 1919–1921 by Housing Department, Ministry of Health.

30 See Swenarton *Homes Fit for Heroes* pp. 156–157.

31 *Housing* Volume 1, Number 1 p. 6.

32 Unwin 'Cottage plans' p. 4 and p. 6.

33 Ibid., Plate VI.

34 Swenarton *Home Fit for Heroes* p. 21.

35 *Housing* Volume 1, Number 1.

36 M C Carr, 'The development and character of a metropolitan suburb: Bexley, Kent', in *The Rise of Suburbia*, F M L Thompson, ed., Leicester University Press, Leicester 1982; Quiney, *House and Home* p. 160.

37 W Ashworth, *The Genesis of Modern British Town Planning*, Routledge and Kegan Paul, Andover, UK, 1954 p. 196.

38 J Burnett, *A Social History of Housing 1815–1970*, Methuen, Andover, UK, 1978 p. 227.

39 A A Jackson, *Semi-detached London: Suburban Development, Life and Transport, 1900–39*, George Allen and Unwin, Hemel Hempstead, UK, 1973 pp. 190–198.

40 See Swenarton, *Homes Fit for Heroes* p. 16.

41 T A Lloyd, 'The architect, and housing by the speculative builder', in *House-building 1934–1936*, E Betham ed., Federated Employers' Press, London, 1934 pp. 119–135; see pp. 132–133.

42 G Allen, 'Building to sell', in *House-building 1934–1936*, E Betham ed., Federated Employers' Press, London, 1934 pp. 137–153; see p. 145.

43 P Oliver, I Davis and I Bentley, *Dunroamin: The Suburban Semi and Its Enemies*, Barrie and Jenkins, London, 1981; Quiney, *House and Home* p. 156.

44 Oliver *et al.*, *Dunroamin* pp. 148 ff.

45 Bentley, in Oliver *et al.*, *Dunroamin* p. 117.

46 For example see the comments of John Laing in 'Houses for sale', in *House-building 1934–1936*, E Betham ed., Federated Employers' Press, London, 1934 pp. 199–205; see p. 203.

47 C Chippindale, 'Archaeology, design theory, and the reconstruction of prehistoric design systems' *Environment and Planning B: Planning and Design* Volume 13, 1986 pp. 445–485; see p. 456.

48 Brown and Steadman, 'A computerised database'.

49 Unwin, 'Cottage plans' p. 2.

11

GENERATIVE DESIGN METHODS, AND THE EXPLORATION OF WORLDS OF FORMAL POSSIBILITY

(*AD*, special issue on *Empathic Space: The Computation of Human-Centric Architecture*, eds C Derix and A Izaki, September 2014, pp. 24–31)

This short piece was written for a special journal issue on computer systems to support architectural design. It starts with a brief account of methods for enumerating small rectangular plans, as for example the DIS system applied in the previous paper (10). As I explained, such methods are intrinsically limited by combinatorial considerations to treating plans with relatively small numbers of rooms. What is sketched here by contrast is a technique for representing rectangular plans characterised at a more abstract level, in terms of zones rather than rooms. One zone could contain many rooms, but their detailed arrangement within the zone is not specified. Complex plans with potentially large numbers of rooms can then be exhaustively enumerated and catalogued. All possibilities can be laid out in a morphospace, or space of possible forms – as with the doughnut plans of Paper 2. Actual plans characteristic of different historical building types – hospitals, schools, office buildings – can be located in this morphospace. The ground is laid for a more detailed explanation of the technique and its possible applications, in the paper that follows (12).

Fifty years of computer-aided design

A significant anniversary for computer-aided design (CAD) passed recently [2013] without much notice in the architectural world. In 1963 Ivan Sutherland, then a PhD candidate at MIT, submitted his thesis on the 'Sketchpad' system, one of the most influential doctoral dissertations ever presented.[1] With additional developments by Timothy Johnson and others, Sketchpad contained in embryo most of the features of CAD systems as they have developed over the intervening fifty years. It had the first ever graphical user interface. It allowed both 2D drafting and 3D modelling of designs – the latter displayed not just in wireframe but with hidden lines removed. It allowed simulation of the performance of designs, for example calculations of the behaviour of engineering structures, or predictions of flows of current through electrical circuits. And Sketchpad was also linked directly to MIT's numerically controlled milling machines in the world's first integrated CAD/CAM system.

Generative systems for automated plan layout

All these features of Sketchpad – drafting, 3D modelling, simulation of performance, links to component manufacture – have become mainstream in architectural computing, even if some of them took decades to filter through from engineering and product design. What Sketchpad did not try to do was to *generate* designs. It was conceived rather as a tool for supporting designers. In architectural computing by contrast there was much interest from the outset in generative design systems, and in particular methods for the automated layout of plans. Several programs were developed in the 1970s for producing layouts in which the total amount of pedestrian movement would in theory be minimised.[2]

These were conceived very much within the functionalist paradigm that pervaded the 'design methods movement' of the 1960s, and drew on techniques borrowed from operations research and mathematical programming. Typically, surveys were made of movement patterns in existing buildings of the relevant type, to give numbers of journeys between rooms of specified function. Various systematic methods were then deployed for assembling and rearranging spaces so as to minimise total travel. There were three major problems.

First was the questionable assumption that the patterns of trips observed in existing buildings would be reproduced in new buildings with different layouts. Arguably geometry and movement are interdependent, rather than independent of each other. Second, because of the goal of minimising movement, the methods tended to produce deep concentric plans clustered around the most highly connected spaces. Third and most important was the fact that a single criterion of performance was used to generate designs. Subsequent work tried to introduce constraints related to other considerations such as lighting and orientation, and such efforts continue today. But the tools have rarely if ever been taken up in practice.

Exhaustive enumeration of small rectangular plans

Other methods for producing room layouts by computer developed at this time might have appeared superficially similar, but were in truth based on a diametrically opposite philosophy of design. It came to be appreciated that, if consideration was confined to rectangular rooms in rectangular packings, and the number of rooms was not large, it was possible to enumerate *all possible arrangements* exhaustively. Bill Mitchell, Robin Liggett and I developed the first of these methods in the mid-'70s.[3] At the heart of our system was a complete listing of 'rectangular dissections' (rectangles cut into rectangles) represented as configurations without dimensions (Figure 1).

[*Methods for enumerating dissections were discussed in the previous Paper 10, along with applications to the analysis of small house plans. Some duplication has been cut.*]

The important point is that this approach did not search for some single supposedly 'optimal solution'. On the contrary, it laid out entire fields of possibility, within which architects have free rein. Should they elect to confine themselves to a rectangular geometrical discipline of this kind however, they have no other choices.

Shape grammars came from a very different intellectual tradition – Chomskian linguistics – and have generally been applied to the study of questions of architectural style and composition. It is worth noting all the same that a shape grammar is defined as the universe of all designs that can be produced from a given set of shape rules. That universe can be large, and is not generally laid out for inspection. Nevertheless in the case of the first

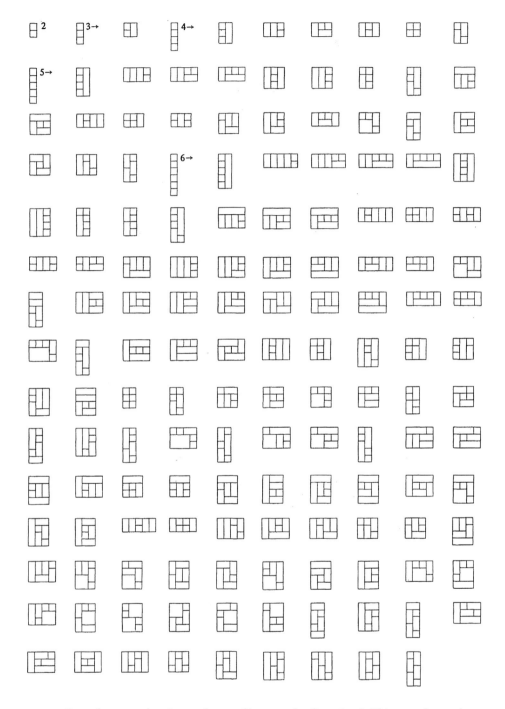

FIGURE 1 Part of a comprehensive catalogue of 'rectangular dissections'. This page shows plans with up to six rooms. These are dimensionless configurations; each room can be assigned dimensions as required. From Mitchell, Steadman and Liggett, 'Synthesis and optimisation of small rectangular house plans', *Environment and Planning B*, Volume 3, 1976 p. 70

architectural shape grammar, devised for Palladian villas by George Stiny and Bill Mitchell, all possible villa plans based on 3 × 3 and 5 × 3 grids were enumerated, by similar methods to those used for counting rectangular dissections. Again these are configurations, whose dimensions are assigned by the rules of the grammar.[4]

There is however a fundamental and insuperable limitation on the scope of these methods for enumerating possible plans. This is the 'combinatorial explosion' that causes the numbers of arrangements to grow rapidly with increasing numbers of component rooms, to the point where complete catalogues of plans with more than ten or a dozen rooms would become astronomically large. Flemming's DIS system pushed this limit somewhat by generating only those arrangements that conformed to a specified constraint set; but the basic problem remained. Practical applications of the approach were thus confined to small houses or other buildings of similar size. Bill Hillier took this to mean that architecture was not, after all, an *ars combinatoria*.[5] But his conclusion was premature.

Enumeration of built forms: an 'archetypal building'

It is certainly true that no complete enumeration can be made of arrangements of larger plans, *if these are represented at the room scale*. But this is a matter of the level of representation. If we are prepared to move to a higher level of abstraction, and consider not individual rooms but zones within buildings, then an approach by enumeration becomes feasible again. I have been experimenting over the last ten years with a method for representing built forms made up of ranges, wings and courtyards in different configurations.[6] These are all cut from a larger 'archetypal building' as shown in Figure 2.

FIGURE 2 An 'archetypal building', from which many other simpler built forms can be derived by a process of selection or cutting. More floors and courts would be possible. This is an undimensioned configuration. Day-lit space is in dark grey, artificially lit space in light grey. From Steadman *Building Types and Built Forms*, 2014 p. 105

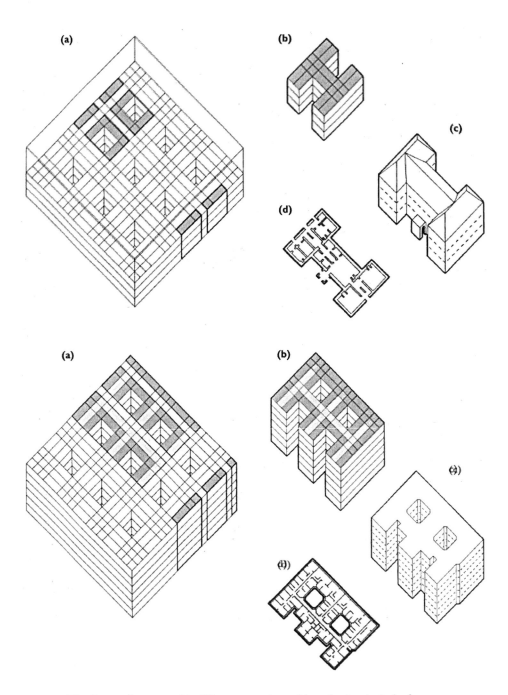

FIGURE 3 The forms of two actual buildings approximated by selecting 'strips' of accommodation, courts and floors (a) from the archetypal building. These parts are then moved together (b) and given appropriate dimensions. The actual forms and plans are given in (c) and (d). Above: an H-shaped eighteenth-century hospital designed by Edward Foster. Below: Crescent Court, New York 1905, designed by Neville and Bagge. From Steadman *Building Types* p. 108

Dimensions of the various parts are not specified at the outset. The numbers of courts and storeys are arbitrary: there could be more. The space in dark grey is day-lit from the exterior or from the courts. The space in light grey is artificially lit. The archetype thus embodies the constraints on form of some elementary 'generic functions' of architecture, in particular those of day lighting. Simpler built forms approximating to real buildings – an eighteenth-century hospital, a twentieth-century block of apartments – can be cut from the archetype by selecting 'strips' of accommodation, 'strips' containing courts, and floors, and moving these together (Figure 3). The parts can then be given appropriate dimensions.

There is no space here to go into the technicalities: but it is possible to enumerate *all* built forms that can be generated from the archetypal building by means of a method of coding, whereby every strip that is retained is coded with a 1, and every strip that is removed is coded with a 0. This produces two strings of 0s and 1s, an *x* string and a *y* string. Putting these together gives, for the nine-court archetype, a 30-digit code in each case. All these codes are binary numbers. The sequence of all binary numbers produces all possible selections and permutations of strips, hence all possible plans. The combinatorial problems are now quite manageable again: with the removal of duplicates by symmetry and some other redundant codes, the number of possible plan forms generated from the nine-court archetype is 1,708,518.

[*The representation and method of coding are explained in more detail in the following Paper 12.*]

An 'architectural morphospace'

For visualisation, it is convenient and informative to lay out all these plans across a two-dimensional space (Figure 4). Here the *x* strings of the binary codes are plotted on the *x*-axis, and the *y* strings on the *y*-axis, so that each plan is mapped to a unique location. It turns out that plans of similar shape are clustered together within rectangular or triangular zones; so for example the part of the space nearest the origin contains zones for simple rectangular plans, L-shapes, U-shapes, single courts and so on (Figure 5). Notice two points. These are generic plan shapes, each of which can occur in many variants depending on the presence of day-lit and artificially lit strips. And once again they are undimensioned shapes: each part can be assigned any desired size. This is what in biological morphology is termed a 'morphospace' or space of possible forms. In biology and architecture, we can expect to find real organisms or real buildings respectively at different locations within morphospaces.

I have plotted the plans of nineteenth-century 'pavilion' hospitals (Figure 6), English elementary schools and Chicago and New York office skyscrapers across this architectural morphospace. They turn out to lie on particular lines as a result of their characteristic cross-sections and arrangements of day-lit space, artificially lit space (corridors) and courts. The morphospace that is to say effects a formal classification. The courtyards of the archetypal building can be filled with 'halls' to represent say the central assembly halls of late nineteenth-century Board schools, or the top-lit entrance halls and atria of office blocks. Generic formal properties of plans can be mapped across morphospace, as for example bilateral and diagonal symmetries (Figure 7). The circles in the figure mark a number of nineteenth-century schools: their architects gave them all plans with bilateral symmetry.

Standard dimensions can be assigned to the various parts of all plans in morphospace, for example dimensions of depth in the day-lit strips sufficient to allow day lighting, typical corridor widths for the artificially lit strips, minimum dimensions for courts and so on. It is then possible

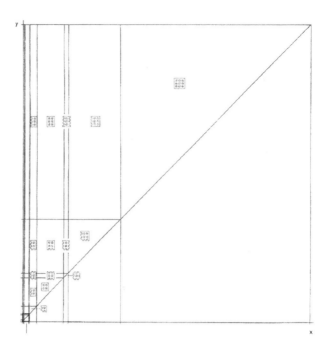

FIGURE 4 An architectural 'morphospace' or space of possible plans produced from the archetypal building. These are all encoded with strings of 0s and 1s in the x and y directions (see text). The x strings are plotted on the x-axis of morphospace, and the y strings on the y-axis. Each plan is thus mapped to a unique location. Plans with the same generic shapes are clustered within triangular or rectangular zones as shown. Many variants of each shape occur, depending on the numbers and arrangements of day-lit and artificially lit strips. From Steadman *Building Types* p. 174

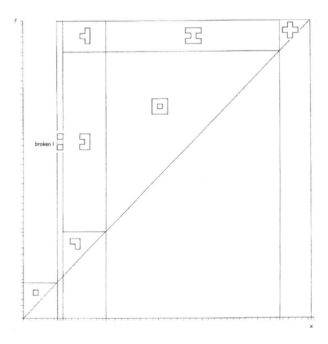

FIGURE 5 The area of morphospace closest to the origin, where simple rectangular plans, Ls, Us, single courts, Ts, Hs and X-shapes are found. From Steadman *Building Types* p. 175

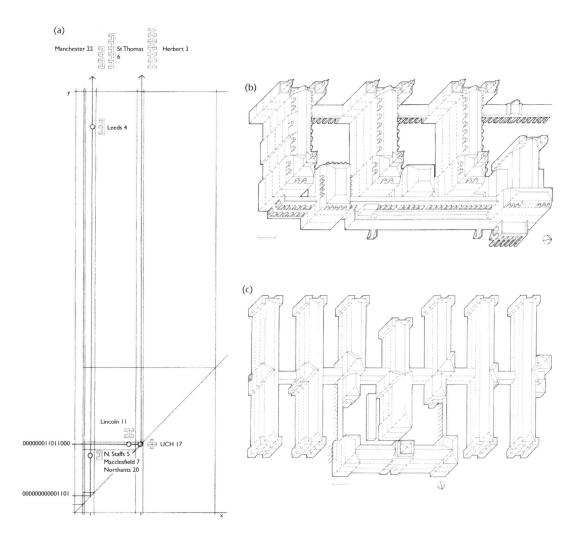

FIGURE 6 (a) The two (heavy) lines in morphospace on which the plans of the ward blocks of nineteenth-century 'pavilion hospitals' are found. The lines correspond to two plan types: with wards on one side of a central circulation spine, as in St Thomas' Hospital of 1865–71 designed by Henry Currey (b); and with wards on both sides of the spine, as in the Herbert Hospital (c) of 1861–65 designed by Douglas Galton. From Steadman *Building Types* pp. 74–75, 80, 179

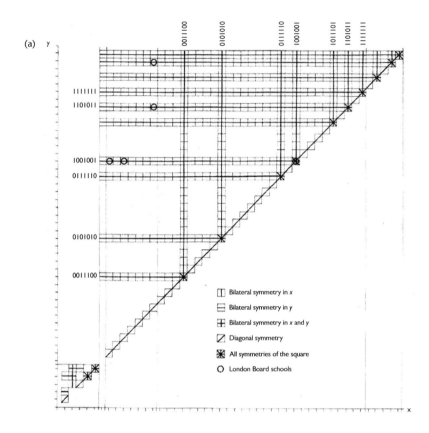

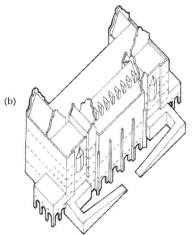

FIGURE 7 (a) Plans with different types of symmetry (bilateral, diagonal) in morphospace. The positions of some late nineteenth-century London Board schools are marked with circles. These 'central hall schools' are represented by inserting halls into the courtyards of the archetypal building. (b) A typical bilaterally symmetric London Board school with central hall designed by E R Robson at Oban Street, Tower Hamlets, 1881. From Steadman *Building Types* pp. 127, 184

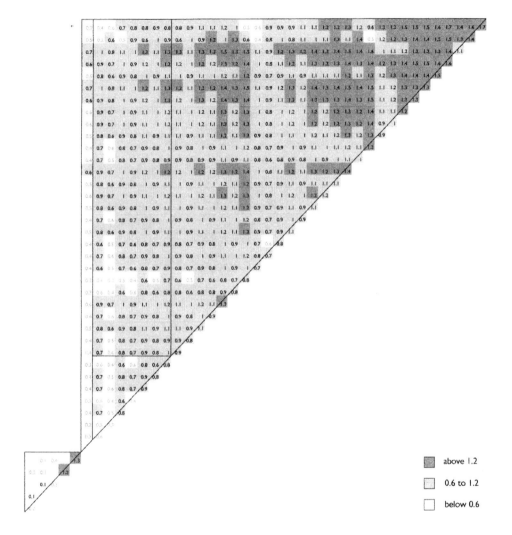

FIGURE 8 Values for floor space index (total floor area divided by site area – a measure of density) calculated for all plans in morphospace, given a set of standard values for the dimensions of day-lit and artificially lit strips and courtyards. Notice how the FSI values rise towards the upper right corners of the zones for different plan shapes, because plans with larger numbers of strips of accommodation occur here. From Steadman *Building Types* p. 395

236 Theoretical approaches to built form

to compute different dimensional properties of the resulting forms, such as the ratio of volume-to-wall area. This is a quantity that we might expect in general to have a bearing on heat loss and on the costs of construction. Another such property is Floor Space Index (the ratio of floor area on all floors to site area), an indicator of the densities achievable with different forms (Figure 8). Measures of circulation distances would also be possible. Notice that these are objective geometrical measures of built form, not predictions of people's activities. They can give an (admittedly crude) indication of the relative performance of different built form options, whatever the particular behaviour of the eventual occupants.

There are many limitations to this architectural morphospace in its present form, and I make no claims for comprehensiveness. The forms of many actual buildings can already be represented. But the scope is confined obviously to a rectangular geometry, and beyond that, there are further restrictions on the classes of rectangular built form that can be represented. Extension to the third dimension would however be straightforward, allowing for forms with different numbers and types of floors. I would emphasise that this is a first attempt at mapping worlds of possible built forms at this level of abstraction, one that could be greatly developed. The purpose is to contribute hopefully to architects' strategic knowledge of these worlds – knowledge that they can then deploy in design. Trade-offs between different aspects of performance can be studied, by contrast with allowing the computer to 'optimise' plans on one or a few criteria, as in the early layout methods and in some more recent systems employing genetic algorithms.

Might practitioners be interested in this kind of activity in 'architectural science'? The work on enumerating room layouts of the 1970s had little impact on practice, partly because at that time the idea that options for design might be limited by intrinsic geometrical factors was an unpalatable one. My own belief is that, since these limits indubitably exist, it is better to understand them and their consequences. Such knowledge is not constraining but liberating.

Notes

1 Ivan E Sutherland, *Sketchpad, A Man-Machine Graphical Communication System*, PhD thesis, Massachusetts Institute of Technology 1963; published by Garland, New York 1980.
2 Tom Willoughby, 'Understanding building plans with computer aids', in D Hawkes ed., *Models and Systems in Architecture and Building*, Construction Press, Lancaster 1975, pp. 146–153.
3 William J Mitchell, Philip Steadman and Robin S Liggett, 'Synthesis and optimisation of small rectangular plans', *Environment and Planning B*, Vol. 3, 1976, pp. 37–70.
4 George Stiny and William J Mitchell, 'Counting Palladian plans', *Environment and Planning B*, Vol. 5, 1978, pp. 189–198.
5 Bill Hillier, *Space is the Machine*, Cambridge University Press, Cambridge 1996, pp. 275–277.
6 Philip Steadman, *Building Types and Built Forms*, Troubador, Leicester 2014: see also www.buildingtypesandbuiltforms.co.uk.

12

ARCHITECTURAL MORPHOSPACE

Mapping worlds of built forms

(with Linda Mitchell)

(Environment and Planning B: Planning and Design Volume 37, 2010, pp. 197–220)

The previous paper outlined a method by which a variety of built forms could be produced by cutting them from an 'archetypal building'. This paper goes into more technical detail. The forms are characterised in terms of day-lit and artificially lit zones, rather than detailed room layouts. How is it possible to count and catalogue all possible plans and forms of this type? This paper explains.

In essence the method consists of dividing the plan of the complete archetypal building into a number of strips in the x and y directions. If a strip is to be retained in a plan it is coded with a 1, and if it is to be omitted from the plan it is coded with a 0. The resulting sequences or 'strings' of 0s and 1s in x and y create binary codes. All codes can be put in ascending order, providing an exhaustive list of plan possibilities. In principle it would be possible to introduce a third string in z to give a three-dimensional description, although that option is not developed here. Rather than set these possible configurations out in a simple linear catalogue, it is arguably more informative to present them in a two-dimensional table or morphospace, as indicated in Paper 11.

Some applications to a geometrical history of building types are sketched in the second part of the paper, with examples from nineteenth-century pavilion hospitals, English elementary schools and early New York skyscrapers. The purpose is to provide a classification of built forms, to understand their interrelationships in a systematic way, and to see how building types have followed characteristic 'morphological trajectories' through this space of forms. It is a tool with which to approach the history of architecture from a geometrical point of view. The paper's argument is extended and elaborated to book length, with many more historical examples and analyses, in Building Types and Built Forms *(2014).*

The idea of a 'morphospace'

The term 'morphospace' has gained currency in biology, to refer to a means for representing the ranges of actual and possible forms for the bodies or organs of plants or animals. Typically such a representation locates forms within some coordinate system in which the axes correspond to dimensional parameters that describe the forms. The quantitative scientific study of biological form goes back to D'Arcy Thompson but it was the University of Chicago palaeontologist David Raup who laid the foundations of modern morphology and who

238 Theoretical approaches to built form

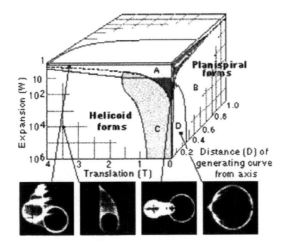

FIGURE 1 A morphospace for gastropod shells, from D M Raup, 'Geometric analysis of shell coiling', *Journal of Paleontology*, Volume 40, 1966, by kind permission of the Society for Sedimentary Geology. Only the regions A, B, C and D are occupied by the shells of actual species, of which examples are illustrated. Other regions describe shells that are 'theoretically possible' but are not found in nature

introduced the computer as a modelling tool.[1] Figure 1 illustrates Raup's three-dimensional morphospace for the shapes of gastropod shells. The shells of actual species are found only in the regions labelled A, B, C and D. Other parts of the space correspond to shells that are in some sense theoretically 'possible' but do not occur in nature. Biologists have developed morphospaces for several other classes of natural forms, as for example the shapes of dicotyledon leaves.[2]

In this paper we define an architectural morphospace for a class of rectangular forms of building. The plans of these built forms are all located within a two-dimensional coordinate system. The system could in principle be extended to a third dimension to describe the buildings' heights. This morphospace differs however from its biological counterparts, in that it serves to map a world of distinct 'dimensionless' configurations for built forms. *Each configuration can then have values assigned to dimensional parameters as required.* The typical biological morphospace, by contrast, maps parametric transformations of just one underlying configuration. It is the fact that the forms of buildings are generally much simpler than those of organisms that allows this two-level approach, treating first configuration and then dimension.

An 'archetypal building'

The paper builds on previous work in which a method was proposed for encoding built forms by reference to what was termed an 'archetypal building'. For full details the reader is referred to previous publications by the authors.[3] (L J Mitchell was formerly L J Waddoups.) We give a resumé here. Figure 2 shows the archetypal building diagrammatically. It is made up of floors of three different types: basement floors; above those, deep-plan floors that extend continuously across the complete building; and above those again, floors punctuated by a

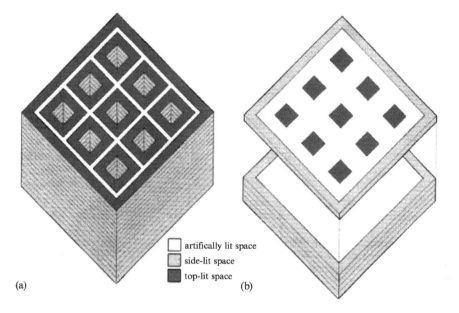

Figure 2(a) The archetypal building. (b) The lower deep-plan floors of the archetypal building, all but the topmost of which can be artificially lit at the centre and side-lit round the edges. Parts of the topmost deep-plan floor can have top lighting from the bases of the courts above

regular pattern of courtyards. The diagram shows an array of three by three courts, although there could be more. The archetypal building should not however be imagined as an arbitrarily selected fragment from some infinite array. Rather it is bounded by window walls on the four facades.

The interior of the archetypal building is divided into three kinds of zone, distinguished by their types of lighting. Space adjacent to the four outer walls, and space surrounding the courts, can be side-lit with windows. Space on the topmost courtyard floor, and below the bases of the courtyards in the topmost deep-plan floor, can be top-lit with roof lights. All remaining space in the interior of the building must by necessity be artificially lit. In Figure 2 these lighting types are shaded in different tones. See how the courtyard floors are in effect divided into a series of 'strips' of space with these various lighting conditions. (Of course in practice the boundary between side-lit and artificially lit space might not be quite so clear-cut, especially if the two strips were not separated by a wall.) Notice the strips of artificially lit space between the pairs of side-lit strips on the courtyard floors. These might correspond to corridors, although that is not their only interpretation in architectural terms.

All dimensions of the archetypal building are to be conceived as being parameterised (Figure 3), including in the vertical direction the numbers of floors of each type and their storey heights, and in the horizontal plane the widths of the strips of accommodation and the widths of the courts. Should any such dimensional parameter be assigned the value zero then the element in question will disappear. Thus in the vertical direction it is possible for example to select just some number of courtyard floors, by assigning suitable storey heights, and to suppress all basement and deep-plan floors by giving storey heights of zero throughout. Similarly in the horizontal plane it is possible to select certain of the strips of accommodation in x and

240 Theoretical approaches to built form

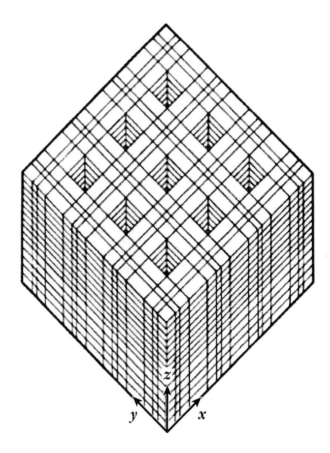

FIGURE 3 The archetypal building set in an x, y, z coordinate system, showing how the plan is divided into courts and 'strips' of accommodation with different lighting conditions

y by assigning positive values to their widths, and to remove all other strips by giving zero value to their widths. In this way a large variety of different configurations can be produced through what amounts to a method of carving or cutting away pieces from the complete archetypal building. The constraints of day lighting and natural ventilation are however always respected.

Many systematic approaches to the representation and enumeration of architectural forms and architectural plans to date have concentrated on the level of individual rooms and their spatial interrelationships.[4] Notice how the present representation moves to a higher and more abstract level, instead treating zones or strips of accommodation, each of which might be subsequently subdivided into a number of rooms. Detail is sacrificed by this tactic of course. But the gain from the point of view of exhaustive enumeration is that the combinatorial task of counting configurations is still tractable at the scale of entire large built forms, where an enumeration of arrangements of separate rooms would be combinatorially out of the question.

Binary encoding of plan forms derived from the archetypal building

In earlier papers we have shown how all possible plan arrangements for built forms derivable from the courtyard floors of the archetypal building can be indexed and catalogued using a method of binary encoding. Figure 4 illustrates this method for simplicity with the case of a single courtyard archetype on one storey. The general approach is then readily extendable to more courts as in Figure 2. (From this point onwards in the paper we ignore any deep-plan floors.) The courtyard is set in plan in an (x, y) coordinate system (Figure 4a). There are seven strips running in the x and the y directions, corresponding in sequence to space of the different types: side-lit; artificially lit; side-lit; the court; side-lit; artificially lit; side-lit. Let us assign to each strip either a 0 if it is to be removed, or a 1 if it is to be selected. We thus obtain two seven-digit binary strings, in x and y. Let us agree to list these by convention in order, first the x string, then the y string, to produce a 14-digit binary code. An alternative way of thinking of this coding is to consider the plan as an array of 49 cells. If *both* the x value and the y value referencing a cell are 1, then the cell is retained. If *either* the x value or the y value is 0, the cell is removed. Figure 4b illustrates how this method of encoding can be used to define a wholly side-lit **L**-shaped form with the code 0001101 0001101.

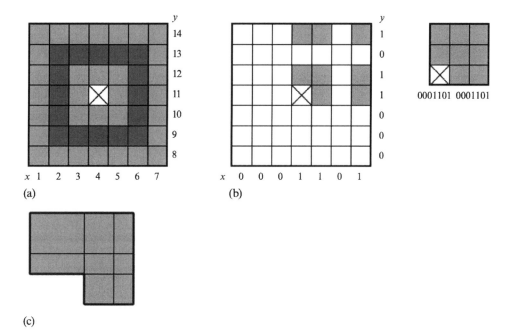

FIGURE 4 (a) A single-court archetypal building in plan view. The central X is the court. The light grey tone signifies day-lit space. The dark grey tone signifies artificially lit space. The presence or absence of strips of accommodation in any plan derived from the archetype is represented by 1s and 0s in the x and y strings. (For each cell in the array, if the product of its x value and its y value is 1, then the cell is present. If the product is 0, then the cell is absent.) (b) The binary coding 0001101 0001101, which corresponds to a wholly side-lit **L**-shaped configuration. (c) This **L** can be given any desired dimensions

242 Theoretical approaches to built form

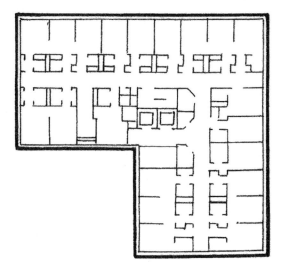

FIGURE 5 Plan of the Blue Bonnet Hotel, Fort Worth, Texas; architects Elmer Withers, Mauran, Russel and Crowell, from S Holl, *The Alphabetical City* 1980 p. 39. The plan has the 14-digit binary code 0001111 0001111

The binary code describes a dimensionless configuration. Each of the strips present in the plan – designated by the 1s – can then be given some specific dimension of width as required. (In practical day lighting terms there will be an effective limit on the possible widths of the side-lit strips.) A dimensioned example of the **L**-shaped form is illustrated in Figure 4c. Figure 5 shows the plan of an actual **L**-shaped building – the Blue Bonnet Hotel in Fort Worth, Texas – that has artificially lit corridors and whose code is therefore 0001111 0001111.[5] It will be clear that a similar method of coding can be applied to the nine-court archetype of Figure 2, for which the length of each binary code is 30 digits. It is possible to imagine different ways in which the encoding method might be extended to the vertical direction by adding a third z string to represent the presence or absence of floors of the different types – although we do not develop this aspect in the present paper.

All of these codes are binary numbers (albeit with zeros in the first few places in some cases) and can be put in ascending order, so as to catalogue all possible plan forms obtainable from the archetype. However not every binary number corresponds to the plan of a distinct and architecturally meaningful built form, by any means. Many groups of binary numbers correspond to plan configurations that are identical under rotation and/or reflection. We have developed methods for identifying and removing such isomorphs, and retaining by convention the instance coded by the *lowest* binary number. Some binary numbers correspond to configurations that make little sense architecturally, as for example where side-lit strips that are notionally lit from courts are present but the courts themselves are not. All these cases have been suppressed from the catalogue. Finally there are a small number of instances where configurations with different codes are effectively equivalent under dimensioning as explained in previous work.[6]

With all these duplicates and meaningless codes removed, the numbers of remaining codes for arrangements derived from archetypal buildings with different numbers of courtyards are as follows:

1 court	(7 × 7 strips, 14-digit codes)	675
4 courts	(11 × 11 strips, 22-digit codes)	36,462
9 courts	(15 × 15 strips, 30-digit codes)	1,708,518

The 675 permissible 14-digit codes for the one-court archetype have all been catalogued and set alongside plan diagrams of the respective configurations.[7] Listing the codes in ascending order results, by and large, in a grouping of plans of similar shape together in the list. From the one-court archetype it is possible to produce plans of five generic shapes: simple rectangular blocks, **L**s, **U**s, □s (complete courts) plus what we have termed 'broken **I**s'. Each generic shape is found in many versions, since each arm or wing of the shape can be made up of different combinations of side-lit and artificially lit strips. The 'broken **I**' shapes are generated by selecting just the single central strip of accommodation incorporating the courtyard itself, as seen in Figure 6. As a result, the actual built form falls into two disconnected parts separated by the (two-sided) court, as shown. Such forms might arguably have been rejected as incoherent; however we have chosen to retain them since they correspond to the plans for example of certain narrow-frontage courtyard houses.

In the catalogue of binary codes the **L**-shapes are all found together, followed by the **U**s, followed by the □s. (The simple block and broken **I** forms are however scattered throughout the list, as we will see.) Obviously the organisation of this catalogue is linear, one-dimensional. There seem to be several advantages to be gained in visualisation by rearranging the same configurations into a two-dimensional morphospace. The key here is the recognition that the various generic plan shapes can be produced by the combination of different 'shape generators' corresponding to the x and y strings that make up the binary codes.

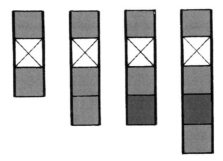

FIGURE 6 Examples of 'broken **I**' forms, in which the plan is broken by the court into two separate parts. The court is marked X in each case. These could correspond to the plans of small courtyard houses

244 Theoretical approaches to built form

'Shape generators' and their relationships to the plans of built forms produced from the archetypal building

The **L** generator for a one-court archetype takes the form 0001> where the three 0s and the single 1 (representing the court) are fixed, but the three positions marked by asterisks can be filled with either 0s or 1s, so long as there is *at least one 1*. The resulting permutations of 0s and 1s correspond to the various possible combinations of side-lit and artificially lit strips in the given arm of the **L**-shaped plan. By combining two **L** generators (for the *x* and *y* strings) and permuting 0s and 1s in all allowed positions in each generator, we produce all possible codes for **L**-shaped forms within the terms of the representation. These range from forms consisting of just one strip in each arm of the **L**, as for instance 0001001 0001100, to the unique form with three strips in both arms 0001111 0001111 as in the building of Figure 5. The example of 0001101 0001101 in Figure 4 provides an intermediate case.

For the one-court archetype there are just three shape generators: the **L** generator 0001★★★, the **U** generator ★★★1★★★ and the [broken] **I** generator 0001000. **L**-shaped forms are produced by combining two **L** generators (**LL**) as already explained. **U**-shaped forms are produced by combining an **L** generator with a **U** generator (**LU**), and □-shaped (full court) forms by combining two **U** generators (**UU**). Broken **I** forms are produced by combining the **I** generator with either of the other two generators (**IL**, **IU**). In addition there are ten distinct solid block forms, generated from five different seven-digit strings 0000001, 0000010, 0000011, 1000001 and 1000011 in the combinations shown below in Figure 9. Walls containing windows necessary for side lighting are shown in the diagrams in broken line. The heavy lines mark walls that could in principle be 'blind' or party walls.

Let us now consider generators for plan shapes in archetypal buildings with four courts or nine courts, to which similar principles apply. With four courts we have shape generators of 11 digits and binary codes of 22 digits. The new generators are:

> **T** 0001★★★1000
> **F** 0001★★★1★★★
> **E** ★★★1★★★1★★★

As before, there must be at least one 1 in each 'open' group of positions marked by three asterisks. With nine courts we have generators of 15 digits and binary codes of 30 digits. The respective generators at this level, labelled **t**, **f** and **e** for their analogies with the **T**, **F** and **E** generators are:

> **t** 0001★★★1★★★1000
> **f** 0001★★★1★★★1000
> **e** ★★★1★★★1★★★1★★★

It is of course possible to produce single-court or four-court plans from the nine-court archetype (as well as two-court, three-court and six-court plans) by suppressing the appropriate number of courts in the relevant positions. In these circumstances it is necessary to add an extra eight 0s to the front of the **I**, **L** and **U** shape generators, and an extra four 0s to the front of the **T**, **F** and **E** generators. Table 1 lists all allowable combinations of the resulting 15-digit generators, together with diagrams of the resulting generic shapes themselves (not all of which now correspond to letters of the alphabet) and the numbers of versions of each

TABLE 1 Shape generators and binary codes for the nine-court archetype

Shape generators	Plan shape	Binary code	Number of instances
–	■	(solid blocks: see Figure 8)	10
IX	▮	000000000001000 (any other generator)	1867
LL	┐	000000000001★★★ 000000000001★★★	28
LU	⊐	000000000001★★★ 00000000★★★⊐★★★	196
UU	□	00000000★★★1★★★ 00000000★★★⊐★★★	406
LT	┤	000000000001★★★00000001★★★1000	35
LF	╡	000000000001★★★ 00000001★★★1★★★	343
LE	╕	000000000001★★★ 0000★★★1★★★1★★★	1274
UT	╟	00000000★★★1★★★ 00000001★★★1000	140
UF	╢	00000000★★★1★★★ 00000001★★★1★★★	1372
UE	╫	00000000★★★1★★★ 0000★★★1★★★1★★★	5096
TT	┼	00000001★★★1000 00000001★★★1000	15
TF	╪	00000001★★★1000 00000001★★★1★★★	245
TE	╪	00000001★★★1000 0000★★★1★★★1★★★	910
FF	╫	00000001★★★1★★★ 00000001★★★1★★★	1225
FE	╫	00000001★★★1★★★ 0000★★★1★★★1★★★	8918
EE	⊞	0000★★★1★★★1★★★ 0000★★★1★★★1★★★	16653
Lt	╡	000000000001★★★ 0001★★★1★★★1000	196
Lf	╡	000000000001★★★ 0001★★★1★★★1★★★	2401
Le	╡	000000000001★★★ ★★★1★★★1★★★1★★★	8575
Ut	╫	00000000★★★1★★★ 0001★★★1★★★1000	784
Uf	╫	00000000★★★1★★★ 0001★★★1★★★1★★★	9604
Ue	╫	00000000★★★1★★★ ★★★1★★★1★★★1★★★	34300
Tt	╪	00000001★★★1000 0001★★★1★★★1000	140
Tf	╪	00000001★★★1000 0001★★★1★★★1★★★	1715
Te	╪	00000001★★★1000 ★★★1★★★1★★★1★★★	6125
Ft	╫	00000001★★★1★★★ 0001★★★1★★★1000	1372
Ff	╫	00000001★★★1★★★ 0001★★★1★★★1★★★	16807
Fe	╫	00000001★★★1★★★ ★★★1★★★1★★★1★★★	60025
Et	╫	0000★★★1★★★1★★★ 0001★★★1★★★1000	5096
Ef	⊞	0000★★★1★★★1★★★ 0001★★★1★★★1★★★	62426
Ee	⊞	0000★★★1★★★1★★★ ★★★1★★★1★★★1★★★	222950
tt	╫	0001★★★1★★★1000 0001★★★1★★★1000	406
tf	╫	0001★★★1★★★1000 0001★★★1★★★1★★★	9604
te	╫	0001★★★1★★★1000 ★★★1★★★1★★★1★★★	34300
ff	╫	0001★★★1★★★1★★★ 0001★★★1★★★1★★★	58996
fe	⊞	0001★★★1★★★1★★★ ★★★1★★★1★★★1★★★	420175
ee	⊞	★★★1★★★1★★★1★★★ ★★★1★★★1★★★1★★★	750925
Total:			1,745,655

246 Theoretical approaches to built form

shape. These numbers are calculated using two elementary counting rules, the sum rule and the product rule.[8]

Plotting plan arrangements in morphospace

The (rather simple) idea for displaying these possible configurations across a two-dimensional plane is to define an (x, y) coordinate system and plot the x string from each binary code on the x-axis and the y string on the y-axis. Each configuration is thus mapped to a unique (x, y) location. Figure 7 shows the result for the nine-court archetype and 15-digit x and y strings. Because of symmetry about the main diagonal only half the area between the (positive) x and y axes is occupied.

The position of each string on the relevant axis corresponds not to its value as a binary number, but to its index number when all strings are listed in ascending order. In this order, it is generally the case that all versions of a given shape generator are found in a continuous unbroken sequence. This happens, in the early part of the listing, with the **L** and **U** generators.

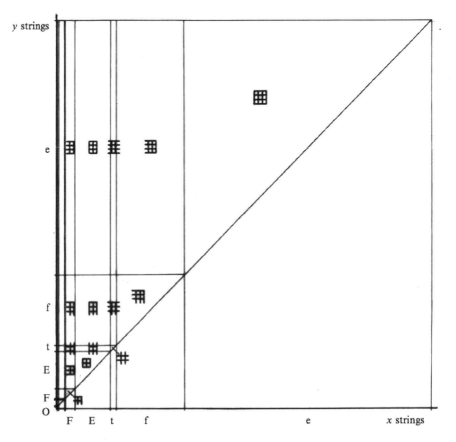

FIGURE 7 Morphospace for the nine-court archetype and 15-digit x and y strings. These strings, and the corresponding shape generators, are listed along the x and y axes, and individual forms are thereby mapped to unique (x, y) locations. Some generic shapes are indicated, to which rectangular and triangular zones in morphospace correspond

Versions of the **T** generator however are found interspersed at regular intervals among the strings corresponding to the **F** generator. Similar problems arise with the **t** and **f** generators. This phenomenon occurs because both **T** and **t** generators (and their analogues for yet longer strings) end with groups of three 0s. There is a comparable situation – although unique to the shape in question – with the solid block forms, three of whose generators occur at the very start of the list and two others much later on.

Two options thus arise for mapping morphospace in these terms: either to preserve the strict sequential listing of all strings and accept the intermingling of some shape generators; or to re-order the strings in places, so that all instances of a given shape occur within a discrete area of morphospace. The second of these routes has been taken here, despite the undeniable

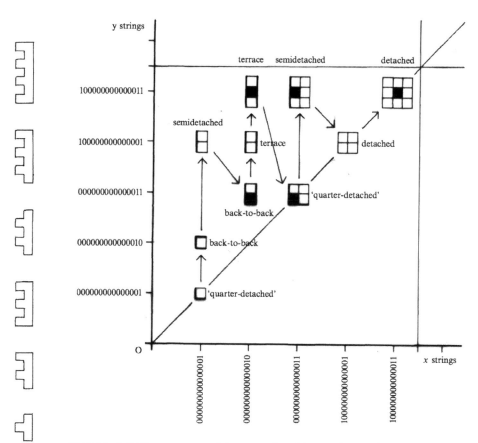

FIGURE 8 (*left*) The sequence of shapes produced by combining the **L** generator with other generators, along a line parallel to the *y*-axis

FIGURE 9 (*above*) The rectangular zone in morphospace closest to the origin in which the ten solid block forms are found. Arrows show the sequence of 30-digit codes in ascending order. For each form, artificially lit zones are in solid black and blind facades in heavy line. The ten forms correspond to the plans of simple house types, as indicated (see text)

248 Theoretical approaches to built form

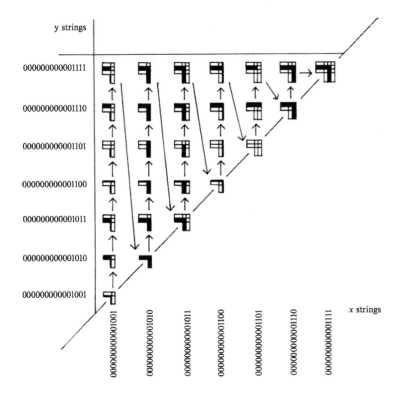

FIGURE 10 The triangular zone in morphospace containing all **L**-shaped forms. For each form, artificially lit zones are in solid black and blind facades in heavy line. Forms with diagonal symmetry lie on the main diagonal.

loss of conceptual elegance. All solid block generators are placed in ascending order at the very start of the list; all **T**s following the **U**s; and all **t**s following the **E**s. Otherwise strings are listed in ascending order throughout.

With this adjustment, each generic shape corresponding to some pair of shape generators has its own rectangular or triangular zone in morphospace (see Figure 7). Moving in either the positive *x* direction or the positive *y* direction across the space, the transition from one zone to the next is marked by the addition of one or two more 'wings' or 'arms' to the plan shapes – with the exception of the shapes created by the **T** and **t** generators, where the same number of wings is reorganised. So, for example, following the shapes created by combining the **L** generator with other generators, moving parallel to the *y*-axis, we find the sequence shown in Figure 8. 'Squarer' plan shapes including the single-court, four-court, and nine-court forms lie close to or on the main diagonal while 'thinner' plan shapes are found near to the *y*-axis.

Let us zoom in to the part of morphospace close to the origin, to examine some of the patterns in which individual configurations are arranged within the zones for each generic shape. Figure 9 shows the ten solid block forms immediately adjacent to the origin, with the ascending sequence of their binary codes marked by arrows. Not every location is occupied

Architectural morphospace   **249**

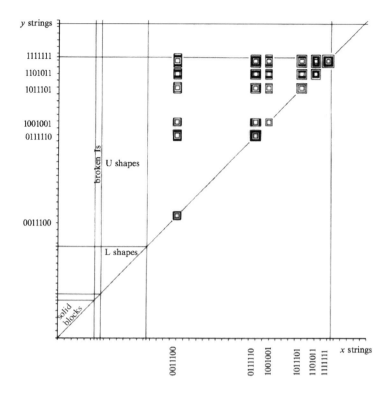

FIGURE 11 The triangular zone in morphospace containing all □-shaped forms. Just those forms with bilateral or fourfold symmetry are illustrated, for which either the *x* or the *y* string, or both, are palindromic. Only the last seven digits of the *x* and *y* strings are given. For each form, artificially lit zones are in solid black and blind facades in heavy line. The forms with fourfold symmetry lie on the main diagonal

by a configuration because of the phenomenon of equivalence under dimensioning mentioned earlier. Artificially lit space is shown in black, and 'blind' facades – through which daylight is not received – are shown by thicker lines. Notice how the configurations are organised according to their overall 'widths' (measured as numbers of strips), increasing in both *x* and *y* as the strings come to include more 1s and fewer 0s. All of them correspond to the plans of small rectangular houses, following the standard typology of 'detached', 'semi-detached' and 'terrace' as indicated on the figure. There are also two versions of the 'back-to-back' type common in some British cities in the nineteenth century; and two versions of what one might call 'quarter-detached' plans, also found on occasion, which can be grouped together in fours.

Figure 10 shows the **L**-shaped configurations, where every location in the triangular zone is now occupied. Again, black denotes artificially lit space, and thicker lines mark blind facades. Notice how all those arrangements that fall precisely on the main diagonal possess diagonal symmetry, since in every case the *x* string and *y* string are identical, by definition.

Other symmetries are to be seen among the □ shapes produced by the combination of two **U** generators (Figure 11). Should one of these generators be palindromic (the initial eight 0s being ignored) then the associated forms will be bilaterally symmetrical in either *x* or *y*.

250 Theoretical approaches to built form

There are six such palindromes among versions of the **U** generator: 0011100, 0111110, 1001001, 1011101, 1101011, and 1111111. Should generators in *both* x and y be palindromic, then the associated form will display fourfold symmetry. These cases (and only these) are illustrated in the figure. It should be said that these are all symmetries of the dimensionless configurations. The implication is that dimensioned versions *could* also be symmetrical, but only if those dimensions were assigned symmetrically.

Applications to a geometrical history of buildings

The first purpose of this representation, this architectural morphospace, is didactic and explanatory. It is intended to show the consequences of the constraints placed on formal possibility by some of the generic functions of buildings, in particular natural lighting and natural ventilation. Clearly the representation has its limitations – even within the restrictions imposed by a general rectangularity – and it is not possible to generate the forms of many real buildings from the archetypal building, even approximately. Only forms that are prismatic in the vertical direction can be produced: forms with setbacks on upper levels are not allowed for (at present at least). In forms with protruding wings these must be of all the same length in x or y, even when dimensioned. The strips of accommodation are always of standard width across the plan, where in real buildings the plan perimeter might be articulated – within limits – with some parts recessed or pulled forward.[9]

The representation *does* nevertheless allow the forms of many actual buildings of common types to be approximated – as our earlier references to houses and hotel buildings have indicated. We see the potential for demonstrating systematic relationships between the forms of many real buildings by plotting them in morphospace. This makes it possible to give more precision than is usual to the definition of building types in formal terms. The historical and evolutionary trajectories of types may be tracked through morphospace. And it is possible to demonstrate why certain built forms should have occurred at specific times and places in history and not others. We continue the paper with three brief examples intended just to suggest the potential for such explorations in morphospace.

Pavilion hospitals

From the mid-1850s a distinctive new type of hospital made its appearance in Britain, which became known as the 'pavilion hospital'.[10] The design was linked in England to the name of Florence Nightingale who vigorously promoted it, although in fact it had its origins in France in the late eighteenth century, and a series of studies and schemes by medical and architectural experts at the Académie des Sciences in Paris.[11] Over sixty pavilion hospitals were built in Britain up to the First World War, and many others throughout the world.

Before the microbiological discoveries of Pasteur it was believed that disease was carried by polluted or stagnant air ('miasmas'). The pavilion hospital was arranged therefore to be as well ventilated and windy as possible. Each ward block was narrow in plan and was day-lit and cross-ventilated with large windows along both sides. The wards branched off a linear circulation spine, and were separated by wide courtyards. These courts were not closed on the fourth side so that breezes might circulate freely. Internally the plan had, as a consequence, a tree-like circulation structure arranged such that dirty linen, dressings or bedpans never needed to be carried through other wards, and patients from different wards with different

Architectural morphospace 251

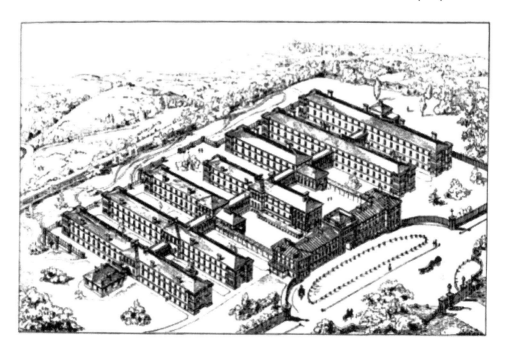

FIGURE 12 The Herbert Military Hospital, Woolwich, London, 1861–65, designer Capt. Douglas Galton, assisted by R O Mennie. Pavilion wards branch off both sides of the central circulation spine

FIGURE 13 St Thomas's Hospital, London, 1865–71, architect Henry Currey. Pavilion wards branch off one side of the circulation spine (at the rear in this view; the arcades at the front do not carry the main circulation)

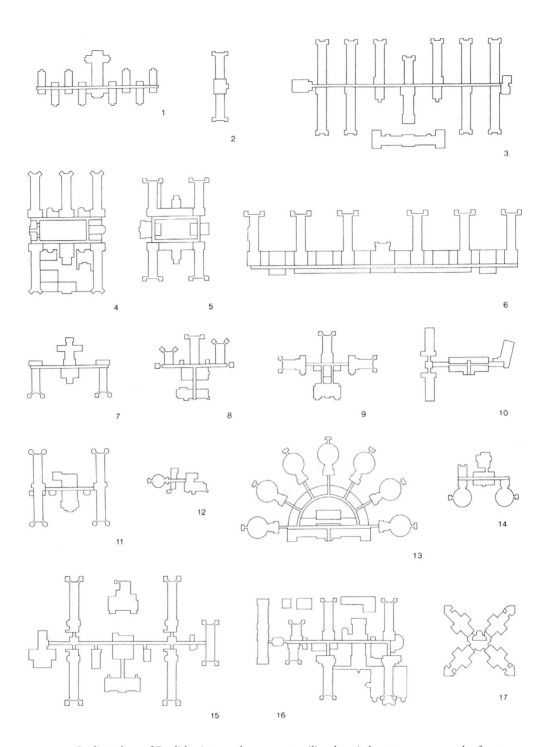

FIGURE 14 Outline plans of English nineteenth-century pavilion hospitals to a common scale: from J Taylor, *The Architect and the Pavilion Hospital* 1997, with kind permission of Jeremy Taylor. The Herbert Hospital is at 3, St Thomas's at 6, and University College Hospital, London at 17. Many of these hospitals, besides ward blocks, also have outpatient departments, administration blocks and other units. These are ignored in the present analysis

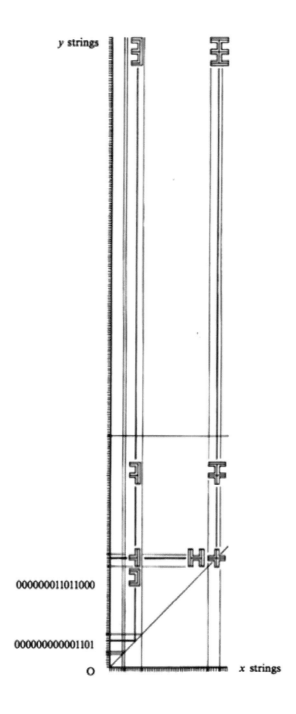

FIGURE 15 The lines in morphospace on which the grouped ward blocks of nineteenth-century pavilion hospitals are found. Those with central circulation spines like the Herbert Hospital lie on the line corresponding to the **T** string 000000011011000. Those with offset circulation spines like St Thomas's lie on the line corresponding to the **L** string 000000000001101

254 Theoretical approaches to built form

diseases could be kept separate. The bathrooms and WCs were at the very tips of this tree structure, at the far ends of the ward blocks. Figure 12 shows the Herbert Military Hospital at Woolwich of 1861–65, which served as a model for many later buildings. Here the wards branched off both sides of the circulation spine. In other cases the wards all lay to one side of the spine, as in St Thomas's Hospital, London of 1865–71 (Figure 13). Depending on the size of hospital required, more or fewer wards might be provided. In minor provincial hospitals there could be just one or two blocks. (Often in addition there were separate administrative buildings, outpatient departments and so on, which we ignore here.) Outline plans of a range of pavilion hospitals, drawn by Jeremy Taylor, are illustrated in Figure 14.[12]

In terms of the shapes represented in morphospace, it will be seen that all possible plans for the connected ward blocks of pavilion hospitals can be approximated by the sequence of forms corresponding either to the **L** generator (for plans with wards on one side of the spine) or the **T** generator (for plans with wards on both sides) in combination with other generators in each case. The cruciform produced by two **T** generators is exemplified by University College Hospital where four ward blocks radiate from a central circulation core in order to save space on a restricted square site in London. Since the wards consisted always of two strips of side-lit space, one for each side of the ward, with no central artificially lit space, these hospital plans in fact all lie on single lines in morphospace corresponding to the unique binary strings 000000000001101 (**L**) and 000000011011000 (**T**) (Figure 15).

In this example, therefore, a building type defined in formal terms – the pavilion hospital – is shown to consist of a theoretical *set* of forms, any of which may be said to exemplify the type. Some members of this set were actually built in the nineteenth century. Others were not, but might have been; and if they had been, would have qualified equally as belonging to the pavilion type. There are formal affinities with the French and American 'telegraph pole' type of prison, examples of which would be classified in a similar way.

English elementary schools, 1870–1940

Our second example follows the architectural evolution of English elementary schools from the late nineteenth century to the 1940s. Between its foundation in 1870 and its closure in 1904 the School Board for London built some 475 new schools across the capital under the direction of its successive chief architects E R Robson and T J Bailey.[13] In the early years experiments were made with a variety of plans, but by the mid-1880s the Board converged on a standard three-storey arrangement that became known as the 'central hall' type. Figure 16 shows the Ben Jonson School, which dates from 1872 but which served as a prototype for many buildings of the 1880s and '90s. The hall rose through either two or three of the storeys and was surrounded, usually on three sides, by classrooms. Much teaching was done in these Board schools by relatively inexperienced 'pupil teachers' in their teens, who were themselves part-time students in the same schools. Part of the logic of the plan was that the headmaster could patrol the central hall, look into the classrooms via their glazed doors, and intervene if a pupil teacher was losing control. Another virtue was that the hall served as a general circulation space and money could be saved by eliminating corridors.

The central hall design soon came in for criticism however, because of its considerable depth in plan and the fact that it was, as a consequence, difficult to ventilate. Also the classrooms were day-lit from only one side, and were not always ideally orientated. There was growing alarm at the poor state of health of Britain's school children at the turn of the century, and

Architectural morphospace **255**

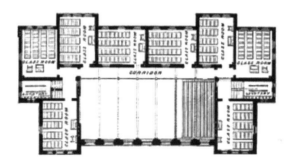

FIGURE 16 Jonson Street School, Stepney, London (later the Ben Jonson School), 1872, architect T Roger Smith. This was the prototype of the 'central hall' Board Schools of the 1880s

increasing emphasis was placed by medical experts on the benefits of sunshine for healthy development and adequate lighting to protect children's eyesight. The result was a new kind of plan for elementary schools, pioneered among others by county architects in Derbyshire and Staffordshire, in which the classrooms were peeled away from the hall and set out along branching and in many cases single-loaded corridors, so that they could be cross-ventilated and day-lit from two opposite sides.[14] Figure 17 shows some examples. In some such plans all classrooms were oriented south for maximum sunlight. Similar developments took place elsewhere in Europe and the United States. The fact that in England the employment of pupil teachers had been largely abandoned by 1900 and teaching had become fully professionalised meant that supervision from the centre was no longer so important.

This process of evolution of school buildings can be plotted in morphospace (Figure 18). In order to model the central hall we extend the representation to allow the possibility of a court being filled with a single-storey hall, either top-lit, or else side-lit from one exposed wall. In the figure these halls are marked by diagonally crossed lines. In these circumstances clearly there can be no strips of accommodation that are side-lit from the court – since there is no court. The figure shows a sample of schools from different dates through the period.

256 Theoretical approaches to built form

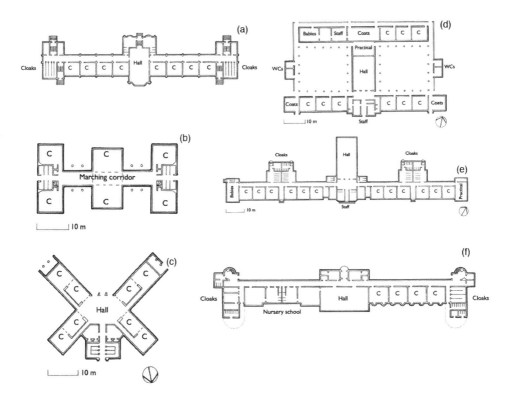

FIGURE 17 Examples of English elementary and junior school plans from the first three decades of the twentieth century, in which the classrooms were set out along single-loaded corridors in order to provide improved ventilation, cross-lighting, and in some cases preferential orientation to the south. (a) Durnsford Elementary School, Wimbledon, London 1910; architect W H Webb. (b) Highfields Elementary School, Long Eaton, Derbyshire, 1911; architect George Widdows. (c) The Glebe Elementary School, Normanton, Derbyshire, 1911; architect George Widdows. (d) Junior School, Wyken, Coventry, 1930s; architect A H Gardner. (e) Infant and Junior School, Scarborough, 1930s; architects Overfield and Alderson. (f) Infant and Junior School, Willesden, London, 1938; architects F Wilkinson and G F Rowe

Central hall schools cluster among **U**-shaped forms – the court of the **U** being filled with the hall – corresponding to the palindromic **U** generator 1001001 where the initial and final 1s are the single-aspect classrooms.

The plans of post-1900 schools take a variety of shapes, since the corridors along which the classrooms are now dispersed can be arranged in different ways. There are examples here of **T, E, +,** and **H** shapes. See how the change over time corresponds broadly to a move in morphospace in the direction of the y-axis, as the plan shapes are opened up and extended. The hall is now situated typically at the centre of the plan where the wings join. The common factor is that these are in every case single-loaded corridors consisting of just two side-lit strips, one for the classrooms and the other for the (side-lit) corridor itself. The result is plans that are significantly shallower than those of the central hall schools.

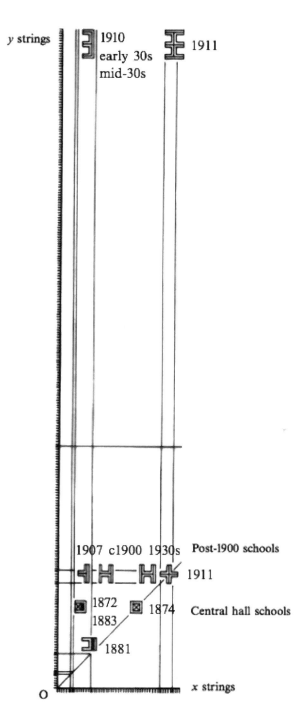

FIGURE 18 The evolution of English elementary schools, 1870–1930, plotted in morphospace. Halls in central hall schools are marked X. The central hall schools cluster among the **U** and **+** forms, while the early twentieth-century schools take **T**, **E**, **+** and **H** shapes. The change in time corresponds generally to a move in morphospace in the direction of the *y*-axis

258 Theoretical approaches to built form

These differences in plan depth can be compared in quantitative terms. We have modelled the archetypal building in an Excel spreadsheet in which it is possible to enter the binary code for a built form, together with values for all the dimensional parameters listed earlier – storey height, widths of side-lit and artificially lit strips, widths of courts and so on. The model computes totals for floor area (F) whether day-lit or artificially lit; roof area; external wall area (W) and volume (V). Also calculated are the area of the building footprint and the total area of courts. From these, some simple ratios are produced, such as wall area to floor area (W/F), and volume-to-wall area (V/W).

For this sample of schools, the differences in plan depth are reflected more or less directly in the ratio of volume-to-wall area (V/W). (For a simple straight block in which the end walls are ignored, $V = (dW)/2$, where d is plan depth.) For three central hall schools the mean value for V/W is 6.01, and for eight post-1900 schools 4.05. (For comparison the mean value for 14 pavilion hospitals is 3.55. These are even shallower overall than the post-1900 schools, in part because of their thin circulation spines.) It is worth noting that, at the same time, a lower value for V/W tends in general to be associated with higher construction costs, since the same volume of building is enclosed by a larger area of (expensive) external wall. In these early twentieth-century schools, and the pavilion hospitals, the additional costs were presumably thought to be worth paying. But later in the century English schools were made more compact again to cut construction costs – both by reducing the area of exterior walls, and eliminating some of the floor area devoted to corridors.

The spreadsheet model also calculates the total areas of external wall facing exactly or approximately north, south, east and west. In the nature of the situation, given that the buildings have rectangular geometry, the areas for north and south are equal, as are those for east and west. Unfortunately in the printed sources from which the present plans are drawn, the actual orientation is not always shown, in which case a north point has been assigned arbitrarily. What *is* always possible however is to compare the larger with the smaller of these wall areas. This ratio then gives an indication of the maximum area of wall that *could* be made to face south (or in any other direction) should the building be appropriately oriented. For the central hall schools this ratio takes values between 1.6 and 1.9, and for the earlier twentieth-century schools, between 1 and 1.75. For the 1930s schools that were deliberately designed with all classrooms facing south by contrast, the ratio rises to between 3 and 4.5. These are buildings with long thin plans aligned east-west (see Figure 17 (e) and (f)).

Early New York office skyscrapers

The new American high-rise office buildings of the end of the nineteenth century were built as speculative investments whose overriding goal was to provide the maximum possible area of rentable floor space. This objective was constrained in three ways. The height of a building was limited by construction technology and – from early in the twentieth century – by legislation to control overshadowing and excessive densities. The depth of the plan was limited by the fact that, at this date, before fluorescent lighting and air conditioning, the offices relied predominantly on natural light and natural ventilation. The overall dimensions of the building in plan were limited by the size and shape of the given site. The historian Carol Willis neatly captures the nature of the designer's task in the title of her essay on Chicago skyscrapers, 'Light, Height and Site'.[15]

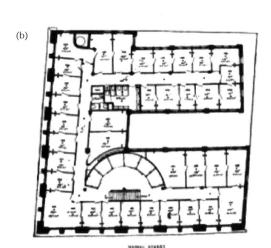

FIGURE 19 Upper storey plans of three late nineteenth-century New York office skyscrapers. (a) Central Bank Building, 1896–97: architects J T Williams and W H Birkmire. (b) American Tract Society Building, 1894–95; architect R H Robertson. (c) Manhattan Life Insurance Company Building, 1893–94; architects Kimball and Thompson

Figure 19 illustrates the upper storey plans of three New York office buildings of the 1890s: the Central Bank Building (a) and the American Tract Society Building (b), both on corner sites, and the Manhattan Life Building (c) whose site runs across the centre of a block, with frontages on parallel streets, Broadway and New Street. All three were simple prisms in form – with the exception of the very topmost storeys – and were not set back in the 'ziggurat' style effectively mandated later by the 1916 New York Zoning Ordinance. In the contemporary architectural literature it was said that space more than 20 to 25 ft (6 to 7.5 m) from a window wall would be too poorly lit to be acceptable to tenants.[16] In these New York buildings, the side-lit strips are in fact mostly just 4 or 5 m deep, which presumably reflects typical sizes for individual offices rather than the extreme limit for day lighting. The corridors are typically 1.8 m wide. As for the light wells, it is difficult to quantify a precise limit on their acceptable minimum width. In the three buildings of Figure 19 the courts are around 8 to 10 m wide, which given that the heights vary between 15 and 20 storeys mean that the effective cut-off angle is around 80°. These wells were often lined with white tiles or glazed

260 Theoretical approaches to built form

bricks to increase the reflectivity of the walls, but even so, the inward-looking offices on the lower floors must have been quite gloomy.

Under these constraints, what built form options were open to designers? We can use morphospace to investigate. Let us take the case of the Manhattan Life Building, whose architects were Kimball and Thompson. The site measured 37 m on the long sides, and 20.4 m on the short sides facing on to the two streets. Let us assume that the building footprint fills or nearly fills the site in order to maximise floor area. In terms of the binary codes, if we assume that the short edges of the site are aligned with the x-axis, then the x string of any feasible built form must begin and end with 0s, since both of the long sides of the building will lie on shared site boundaries and must be blind; similarly the y string will begin and end with 1s for the day-lit facades on the two streets.

Let us assume for the sake of demonstration some standard dimensions for the various elements of possible plans: 5 m for the widths of the side-lit strips of offices, 1.8 m for the artificially lit corridor strips, and 10 m for the widths of courts. These default dimensions can then be applied to all forms in morphospace. A complete single court on these assumptions would have overall dimensions of 33.6 × 33.6 m. It is clear that only plan configurations derived from a single court will fit on the site of the Manhattan Life Building, and that we therefore do not need to consider plans derived from two or more courts. Allowable 14-digit binary codes must therefore take the form:

0**1**0 1**1**1

The court, represented by the 1 at the centre of each string, must clearly be present, otherwise the building could only be a solid block and the interior could not be day-lit. Figure 20 shows the relevant area of morphospace, with the positions of all built forms demarcated by squares. Squares corresponding to forms whose codes do not meet the requirement above are marked thus: ⊞. By assigning the standard dimensions to each form we obtain the overall size of the plan in x and y. Cases where this size exceeds that of the site in either x or y must be discounted. Such instances are marked by a diagonal line thus: ◳. Forms for which the x string is 0001000 are broken Is, and are therefore split into two disconnected parts. They are marked in the figure by a diagonal line thus: ◨. All these too are rejected as unfeasible.

We are left with a number of forms denoted by empty squares. Many of these could be acceptable as open plan offices. All can be adequately day-lit, and all fit within the site boundaries. However New York buildings of this period were always divided into cellular offices (see Figure 19). Since in plans of this type the artificially lit strip corresponds to the corridor, and every individual room must be accessible from a corridor, it follows that wherever there is a day-lit office strip it must have an artificially lit corridor running alongside. For the x string this limits the options to 0001110 and 0111110. For the y string the options are 1101011, 1101111 and 1111111. (To turn all of these into 15-digit strings we need of course to add eight 0s at the start in each case.)

Only three combinations now remain, shown as squares in heavy outline in Figure 20. For these (as for every form) it is possible to calculate the total area of day-lit office space on a single floor. It is this quantity, we may assume, that the developers and architects worked to maximise. Of the three forms identified, that with the largest area of day-lit floor space (368 m², marked by the solid black square) has the 14-digit code 0001110 1111111. This is the code of the Manhattan Life Building. A schematic plan with the standard dimensions applied is shown at the top of the figure, for comparison with the real plan in Figure 19. (The schematic plan is rotated through 180° relative to the real plan.) It turns out that Kimball and Thompson were indeed successful in meeting their overall goal. By automating searches along these lines it should be possible to carry out more general types of analysis, to look systematically at the variety of plans allowable on sites of different shapes, sizes and arrangements of day-lit and blind facades. One could for example compare the generic

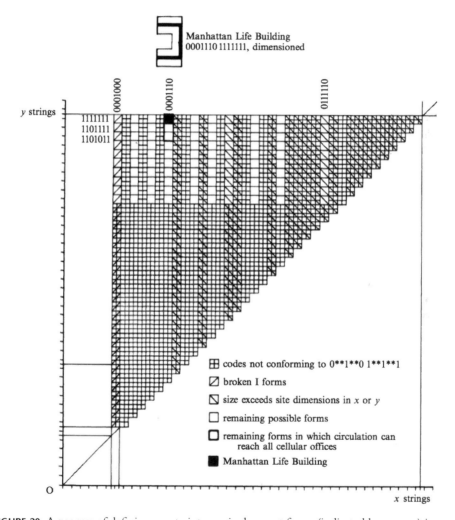

FIGURE 20 A process of defining constraints on single-court forms (indicated by squares) in morphospace, corresponding to the dimensions of the site, and the necessary configuration of blind and day-lit facades of the Manhattan Life Building. A further constraint is imposed on binary codes to ensure that all cellular offices are accessible from (artificially lit) corridors. The three forms meeting all these constraints are indicated with heavy outline. Of these the form with the largest area of day-lit floor space (marked in solid black) has the 14-digit code 0001110 1111111. This is the code of the Manhattan Life Building, whose dimensioned plan is drawn at the top. See text for more detail

262 Theoretical approaches to built form

constraints imposed on the built forms of tall office buildings at this period by the typical dimensions of Manhattan blocks, with those in Chicago or other cities.

Discussion

The principal purpose of the work described here, as mentioned, is to provide a means for mapping the forms of many actual buildings so as to understand their morphological relationships, and to plot the evolutionary trajectories of building types over time. It is a tool, that is to say, for a quantitative, geometrical approach to the history of architecture.

The New York office buildings provided an example for which it can be plausibly argued that a single simple 'fitness function' applied: that of maximising day-lit rentable floor area. The cases of the Victorian schools and hospitals were more complex. Here the goals of achieving oversight of junior teachers in schools and reducing walking distances in hospitals, which tended towards more compact plans, were traded off against the perceived imperatives of ventilation and sunlight, which encouraged the spreading and elongation of plans. Over the periods in question, educational and medical developments, evolving architectural beliefs, and resulting changes in norms and standards, meant that the relative emphases given to these competing goals changed, and the types underwent processes of formal 'evolution' in consequence. These processes can be explored and mapped in morphospace.

[*In the original paper there was a concluding proposal for possible applications of these ideas in computer aids to design, using genetic algorithms. I have since changed my mind about these ideas and have omitted them. Any applications to current practice would be in laying out the 'ranges of choice' open to designers.*]

Notes

1 W D'Arcy Thompson, *On Growth and Form*, Cambridge University Press, Cambridge 1917; D M Raup, 'Computer as aid in describing form in gastropod shells' *Science* Volume 138, 1962 pp. 150–152; D M Raup, 'Geometric analysis of shell coiling: General problems' *Journal of Paleontology* Volume 40, 1966 pp. 1178–1190.
2 M A Lyon and S L Wing, 'A quantitative morphospace for dicot leaves' *Conference of the Botanical Society of America*, Austin, Texas, 16 August 2005.
3 J P Steadman, 'Sketch for an archetypal building' *Environment and Planning B: Planning and Design*, 25th Anniversary Issue, 1998 pp. 92–105; J P Steadman, 'Every built form has a number', 3rd International Space Syntax Symposium, Georgia Institute of Technology, Atlanta, Georgia, USA, June 2001; J P Steadman and L J Waddoups, 'A catalogue of built forms, using a binary representation', *Proceedings*, 5th International Conference on Design and Decision Support Systems in Architecture, Nijkerk, The Netherlands, August 2000, pp. 353–373; L J Waddoups, *A Binary Representation for Built Forms*, PhD thesis, Open University, Milton Keynes, 2001.
4 J P Steadman, *Architectural Morphology*, Pion, London 1983.
5 S Holl, *The Alphabetical City*, Pamphlet Architecture No. 5, Pamphlet Architecture Ltd and William Stout Architectural Books, San Francisco 1980.
6 Waddoups, *A Binary Representation* pp. 60–61.
7 Ibid.
8 A Tucker, *Applied Combinatorics*, Wiley, New York, 2nd edn 1980; details are given in Waddoups, *A Binary Representation* pp. 119–123.
9 Further limitations are discussed in Waddoups, *A Binary Representation* pp. 53–54 and pp. 158–172.
10 J Taylor, *The Architect and the Pavilion Hospital: Dialogue and Design Creativity in England 1850–1914*, Leicester University Press, London and New York, 1997.
11 M Foucault, B B Kriegel, A Thalamy, F Beguin and B Fortier, *Les Machines à Guérir. Aux Origines de l'Hôpital Moderne*, Architecture + Archives/Pierre Mardaga, Brussels and Liège, 1979.
12 Taylor, *The Architect and the Pavilion Hospital* p. 215.

Architectural morphospace **263**

13 E R Robson, *School Architecture*, John Murray, London 1874; republished in 'The Victorian Library' series, Leicester University Press and Humanities Press, New York 1972; D E B Weiner, *Architecture and Social Reform in Late-Victorian London*, Manchester University Press, Manchester and New York 1994.

14 H Myles Wright and R Gardner-Medwin, *The Design of Nursery and Elementary Schools*, Architectural Press, London 1938; M Seaborne and R Lowe, *The English School: Its Architecture and Organization, Vol. II 1879–1970*, Routledge and Kegan Paul, London 1977.

15 C Willis, 'Light, height and site: The skyscraper in Chicago' in J Kukowsky ed, *Chicago Architecture and Design, 1923–1993: Reconfiguration of an American Metropolis*, Art Institute of Chicago and Prestel, Munich 1993 pp. 119–139.

16 C Willis, *Form Follows Finance: Skyscrapers and Skylines in New York and Chicago*, Princeton Architectural Press, New York 1995 pp. 24–30.

INDEX

Note: 'n' indicates chapter notes; italics indicate figures.

adaptive radiation 125
adjacency constraints 196–197, 203–204,
   209–211
air conditioning
  and building geometry 132, 138, 142, 148n16
  department stores 98–99
  and energy use 149, 157, 159–160, 162
  offices 34–38, 138, 258
allometry
  and plan depth 131–138
  as term 131
  in Virtual London model 142–146
Altes Museum, Berlin *10*
American Tract Society Building, New York
  258–259
apartment buildings 134, 136–138, 141
Apple computer company, Cupertino, California
  21
arcades, shopping 61, 87, 89, 93–94
'archetypal buildings' 133
  binary encoding of 241–246
  enumeration of 229–231
  and 'morphospace' 238–240
  and 'shape generators' 244–246
Architects' Journal 191
'architectural doughnuts', as term 21–22
  see also circular plan buildings
Architectural Record, The (journal) 104–105, 107,
  126
arrangements of shapes on grids 11–13
artificial lighting
  'archetypal buildings' 229, 231–232, 239–244,
  246–249

department stores 99
  offices 138, 160–162, 260–261
  pavilion hospitals 254
  schools 256
assembly rooms 92–93
atrium form 81–83, 89–96, 98
Auburn Prison, New York State 58
auditoria 6, *8*
Australia Square skyscraper, Sydney 34–36
Autorimessa (multi-storey garage), Venice 104,
  116–117

Bailey, T J 254
Baker, G 109, 112, 123, 126, 149–150, 161
Barker, Robert 25
Barry, Charles 59
Batty, Michael 131–147
bazaars 86, 92–93
Bemis, Albert Farwell 4, 6, 16, 19n2
Benjamin, Walter 94
Ben Jonson School, Stepney 254–255
Bentham, Jeremy
  Panopticon prisons 25–26, 36–38, 43–64,
  64n1, 77–79
  in Russia 67–69
Bentham, Mary Sophia 69, 71–76, 78, 79n16,
  80n17
Bentham, Samuel 25, 49–50
  Panopticon of 67–79
  in Russia 67–69
  School of Arts, St Petersburg 69–74
Berghauser Pont, Meta 170–172, 177–183
Bertrand Goldberg Associates 31–32

266 Index

Binny, John 61–62
Bloch, Cecil J 20n5
Blue Bonnet Hotel, Texas 242
Boileau, Louis-Charles 81–82, *91, 95*, 96
Bon, Ranko 131–136, 142–146, 177
Bonadè, Vittorio 21
Bon Marché, Au, department store, Paris 81–89, *91*, 95–96
bories (huts), Vaucluse region, France *18, 19*, 23
Boucicault, Aristide 87
Bowser Parking System 108–109
Bozovic, Miran 47
bricks 16
Bristol terrace houses 198–200
Brown, Frank 134, 137, 146, 189–224
Bruyère, André 6, *8*
building blocks 139, 147
building services 96–98
Bunce, Samuel 72–74
Burnham, Daniel 182–183

CAD *see* computer-aided design (CAD)
Cafritz office block, Washington 33–34, 126
Camden Town roundhouse, London 23–25, 37–38
Capitol Records tower, Los Angeles 34–36, 39n17
car parks *see* garages, multi-storey
cars 33–34, 98–100, 103–104
Central Bank Building, New York 258–259
Centre for Land Use and Built Form Studies, Cambridge University 22–23
'chase' (rectangular frame for type) 16–17
Chrest, P 123–124
Christie, Ian 75
circular plan buildings 36
  'architectural doughnuts', as term 21–22
  high-rise car parks 29–33
  hospital wards 26–29, 37–38
  'jam doughnuts', as form 21–25
  'morphospace' of 37–38
  offices 33–38
  railway roundhouses 23–25, 37–38
  transitions to rectangular 17–19
  two types of 21–24
  see also Panopticons
'City of Towers' (Hood) 167–170, 185n3
classically planned buildings 9–10
cloth, woven 16–17
'combinatorial explosion' 191, 229
commercial buildings *see* offices; non-domestic buildings
components in buildings, packing of 16–17
computer-aided design (CAD) 226–236
  'architectural morphospace' 231–236
  enumeration of 'archetypal buildings' 229–231

exhaustive enumeration 227–229
  see also DIS software
configurations 15
constraints
  adjacency 196–197, 203–204, 209–211
  dimensional 197–199, 211
  see also house plans
convexity 11–12
Costain houses *222*
cottages, working-class 206–214
  background and characteristics 206–208
  plans 191–192, 208–212
country houses 9, 134
'court' form 169–170, 172–183
courtyards 139, 204
  in circular plan buildings 21–24
  and energy use 150–151, 159
  multi-storey garages 104, 126
Crawford, William 59, 64
Cruikshank, George, 'Newgate Prison Discipline' cartoon *45*
Crystal Palace, Hyde Park 95
Currey, Henry 233, 251
'cut-off angles' 172–174, 176–178, 181, 185n3

Darwin, Charles 124–125
day lighting
  and building geometry 133–138, 142, 148n9
  department stores 87, 92, 96–98
  and generative design 229, 231–232, 235
  and 'morphospace' 241, 250, 254, 256, 260–262
  offices 34–38, 169, 176, 181
density 167–184
  'City of Towers', Raymond Hood 167–170
  'court'/'street'/'pavilion' forms 169–170, 172–183
  and semi-detached houses 214
  'Spacemate' diagram 170–172, 177–183
  Walled City of Kowloon, Hong Kong 184
Department for Energy and Climate Change (DECC) 152
department store buildings 81–100
  construction technology 94–98
  influences on 83–89, 98–100
  lighting 89–94
  suburban 98–100
depth *see* geometry (plan depth, volume, wall areas)
Descartes, René 5
design, computer-aided *see* computer-aided design (CAD)
design grammar 222–223
detached houses 133–135
  see also cottages, working-class; semi-detached houses

D'Humy ramps 104, 118–123, 126
dimensional constraints 197–199, 211
dimensions, packing 13–16
DIS software 189–192, 221–224
  semi-detached houses 218–220
  terrace houses 196–205
  working-class cottages 208, 212–213
domestic buildings *see* house plans
'downtown' Los Angeles 98–99
Dumont, Etienne 77
Duncan, R S 60
Dutton, G 143

Eastern State Penitentiary, Philadelphia 25, 59,
  63–64
Eiffel, Gustave 81–82, 100n2
Ekistics (journal) 132
elevator garages 105–112
Elmes, James 64
energy use 149–165
  electricity and gas 152–158, 162–164
  morphological factors 163–165
  and plan depth 151–157, 159–162
  and surface area 149–150, 157–159
enumeration
  of 'archetypal buildings' 229–236
  exhaustive 192, 227–229, 240
Escher, M C 16
Euclid 5, 142–143
Evans, Robin 66n41, 74, 76
Evans, Stephen 149–165
evolutionary radiation 124–126
exhaustive enumeration 192, 227–229, 240
exterior curvilinear geometry 6, *8*

facades 6, *8*
Farneti, Fauzia 19
Fenwick's department store, Newcastle 86
Ferris wheel principle, parking 110
Filene, Edward 85
Flannery, Kent 17–18
flats *see* apartment buildings
Flemming, Ulrich 189, 192
floor space index (FSI) 168–177, 181, 183–184,
  235–236
Foster and Partners (architects) 36
Foucault, Michel 44, 65n30
Fresnel pattern 22–23
Funaro, B 109, 112, 123, 126
furniture 16

Galeries Lafayette department store, Paris 85, 98
galleries 9–10, 19
Galton, Douglas 251
garages, multi-storey 103–126
  circular 29–33, 37–38

elevator 105–112, 125
emergence of 103–104
'evolution' of 104–105, 124–126
ramp 112–124
types 113–124, 126
Garden City movement 207
Gehry, Frank 9–10
geometry (plan depth, volume, wall areas) 131,
  146–147, 224n9
  and allometry 131–138, 142–146
  and energy use 149–157, 159–165
  and 'morphospace' 254, 256, 258
  and Virtual London model 131–132, 139–146,
  153–157
'Gherkin'/St Mary Axe skyscraper, London 36
glasshouses (horticultural) 94–95
glass roofs 89–96
glazed roofs 95
Goff, Bruce 9, 11, 15–16
Gordon Riots of 1780 54
Gould, Stephen Jay 132
gravity 4–5
greenhouses 94–95
'ground space index' (GSI) 170–171
Gudea of Ur statue *5*
Guggenheim Museum, Bilbao 9–10

hallways 195–197, 200–204, 208–211, 218–219
Hamilton, Ian 149–165
Hampstead Garden Suburb 207
Hanson, J 118
Harry Seidler and Associates (architects) 34–35
Haupt, Per 170–172, 177–183
Haviland, John 59–61, 64
Hawkes, D 207–208
helical ramps 4, 21, 30–31, 33
  multi-storey garages 104, 116–119, 123–126
Herbert Military Hospital, Woolwich *233*,
  250–251, *253*
hexagons, packings of 9–13, 15
high-rise buildings
  circular car parks 29–33, 37–38
  density 181–183
  early New York offices 258–262
  Walled City of Kowloon, Hong Kong 184
Hillier, Bill 118, 229
Hill's Garage, Los Angeles 107
Hong, S-M 164
Hood, Raymond, 'City of Towers' 167–170,
  185n3
Hopkins, Alfred 55
horizontal plane 5, 9
hospitals 21
  circular wards 26–29, 37–38
  pavilion 26–27, 231–233, 250–254
hotels 21, 136, 138, 141

House of Industry (workhouses) 74
house plans 191–193, 221–224
  allometry in 133–138
  semi-detached houses 134, 141, 214–221
  terrace houses 134–135, 141, 193–206
  and Virtual London model 131–132, 139–146
  working-class cottages 206–214
Housing (journal) 213
Housing and Town Planning Act of 1919 206,
  208
Howard, Ebenezer 207
Howard, John, *The State of the Prisons* 45–46
huts, round 18–19
Huxley, Julian 142

Isle of Pines prison, Cuba 43
isovist (field of view), prisons 54, 57–58, 63

Jacques, F 126
Jakle, J A 107, 125
Japanese shelters, northern Neolithic 6–7
Jebb, Joshua 59–60, 64
Jelinek-Karl, R 118
Johnson, Timothy 226
Johnston, Norman 64, 76
Jones House 15–16
'justified graphs' 118–119

Kahn, Louis 118
Kelsall, A F 203
Kent garages 106–107
Kimball and Thompson (architects) 259–261
Klose, Dietrich 31, 106–110, 113, 126
Koepelgevangenis (cupola prison), Arnhem, the
  Netherlands 43–44, 64n2
Koolhaas, Rem 64n2
Krichev, Russia
  Bentham brothers in 67–68, 75–76
  proposed Panopticon at 78–79
Krüger, M J T 4, 16

Lackington, James 92
Lambot, Ian *184*
Leplanche Alexandre 81–82
Letchworth garden city 207
'lettable' floor area, circular plan buildings 36–38
Liggett, Robin 191, 227–228
lighting *see* artificial lighting; day lighting
Lloyd George, David 206
Logone-Birni village, Cameroun 18
Longley, P A 142–143
Longstreth, Richard 99

MacCormac, Richard 169
Mandan earth lodge 6, 7
Manhattan Life Building, New York 258–261

*Manual on the Preparation of State-aided Housing
  Schemes* (Local Government Board)
  208–214, 216
March, Lionel 22–23, 38, 167–184
Marina City carpark, Chicago 31–33, 37–38,
  39n15
Marrey, Bernard 92–93, 98
Marshall, John 26–28
Marshall Field's department store, Chicago
  85–87
Martin, Leslie 22–23, 167–184
Mayhew, Henry 61–62
Mendelsohn, Eric 96–98
Mennie, R O 251
Metzelaar, J F 43
'minimal gratings' 20n5
Miozzi, Eugenio 104, 117
Mitchell, Linda 237–262
Mitchell, William (Bill) 191, 227–229
Monadnock Building, Chicago 182–183
Mongolian yurts 6–7
'morphospace' 237–262
  for 'archetypal buildings' 238–240
  binary encoding of 241–246
  of circular plan buildings 37–38
  and computer-aided design (CAD) 231–236
  and early New York skyscrapers 258–261
  and English elementary schools 254–258
  and pavilion hospitals 250–254
  plan arrangements 246–249
Morrison, Kathryn 97
Müller, Georg 29–31, 104, 107–109, 116
multi-storey garages *see* garages, multi-storey
museums 9–10, 19
Muthesius, Stefan 198

Naidorf, Lou 34
Narrenturm hospital, Vienna 21–22
naval architecture 6, *9*, 68–69, 75–76
Neolithic shelter, northern Japanese 6–7
Netherlands, residential density 170–172,
  177–183
New Earswick garden city 207, 213
Newgate Gaol, sacking of *45*, 54
New York high-rise offices, early 258–262
'Nightingale wards' 26–28
nomadic communities 18
non-domestic buildings 138–146
  energy use 149–157
  see also office buildings
Nordbeck, S 143
North, Roger 134, 137

octagons 15–16
office buildings
  geometry 138, 159–162

Index **269**

lighting and ventilation 34–38
New York high-rise 258–262
'park at your desk' 33–34, 126
and Spacemate 181–183
Oxford Street department stores, London 84–85

packings 9
   rectangular 13–16
   of squares, triangles and hexagons 9–13
Palladian villas 229
Panopticons
   prisons 24, 25–26, 36–38, 43–64, 64n1, 64n3,
      65n30
   proposed, Krichev, Russia 78–79
panoramas 25
Pantheon Bazaar, Oxford Street 92–93
paper, shape of sheets 16
parallelograms 11
Parker, Barry 207–208, 213
'passive zones' 35, 147, 162
Patout, Pierre 98
'pavilion' form 169–170, 172–183
pavilion hospitals 26–27, 231–233, 250–254
Paxton, Joseph 95
Pentonville prison, London 25–26, 43–46,
   59–63, 76–77
permanent settlements, early 17–19
Philomorphs (seminar) 132
Pico Boulevard department store, Los Angeles
   83
Pigeon Hole Parking 108–110
Pitt, William 68
poché 9–10
Potemkin, Grigory 67–69
prefabrication 4, 119
Price, Joe, house for 9, *11*
Priestley, Philip 61
primitive houses 6–7
printed type 16–17
Printemps, Le, department store, Paris 85, 89, *90*,
   96, 98
prisons
   Panopticon 24, 25–26, 36–38, 43–64, 64n1,
      64n3, 65n30
   radial 25, 59–64, 76–79
psychology of spatial perception 5
public housing 206–208, 211
   Local Government Board manual 208–214,
      216
Pure Oil garage, Chicago 106

radial prisons 25, 59–64, 76–79
railway roundhouses 23–26, 37–38
Ramp Building Corporation, New York 118
ramps, in multi-storey garages 112–119
   see also D'Humy ramps; helical ramps

Ratti, Carlo 149–150, 159, 161–162, 176
Raup, David 237–238
Raverat, Gwen 85
rectangular dissections 189–192, 227–228
rectangularity in buildings 3–19
   components, packing of 16–17
   departures from, in plans 6–9
   and 'high architecture' 19
   hypotheses on 4–6
   and packings of non-rectangular shapes 9–16,
      20n5
   transitions from circularity 17–19
Reilly, C H 98
religious buildings 6–7, 75
residential buildings *see* house plans
Reveley, Willey 49–56
Ricker, E R 123–124, 126
Robertson, Howard 98
Robson, E R 234, 254
Rode, P 158
Roebuck, Sears 98
Rookery Building, Chicago 182
roundhouses, railway 23–26, 37–38
Rudofsky, Bernard 18
Rupert Street car park, Bristol 118
Russian Orthodox Church 75

St Mary Axe skyscraper/'Gherkin', London 36
St Thomas' Hospital, London *233*, 250, *253*
Salat, S 147, 150, 159, 162
Sausset-les-Pins apartment building, France 6, *8*
Saxon Snell, Henry 27–28, 37–38
Schinkel, K F 10
Schlesinger and Mayer building, Chicago 96–97
Schneider-Esleben, Paul 116
School of Arts, St Petersburg 69–74, 79n16,
   80n17
   and radial prisons 76–77
   supervision in 74
   writings on 75–76
schools, English elementary 231, *234*, 254–258
Sculle, K A 107, 125
Sears Roebuck Company 83, 99
Sédille, Paul 89, *90*
Selfridge's department store, London 84–85
semi-detached houses 134, 141, 214–222
   background and characteristics 214–218
   plans 191–192, 218–221
Semple, Janet 44, 75
Sennett, Richard 86, 101n23
Séroux d'Agincourt, J-B 6–7
'shape generators' 244–246
shape grammars 227–229
shear transformation 14
Sheerness naval arsenal, England 75–76
ships 6, *9*, 69–70

270 Index

showrooms 86–87, 89, 92
similarity transformation 14
Sing Sing prison, New York State 58
'Sketchpad' system 226–227
skyscrapers *see* high-rise buildings
Smirke, Sydney 92–93
Smith, T Roger 255
Snaith, William T 99–100
Spacemate 170–184
　'court'/'street'/'pavilion' forms 169–170,
　　172–183
　staircases 199–203, 208–209
Stateville Penitentiary, Illinois 25–26, 36, 43–44,
　55
Steadman, Philip 133–134, 137, 146
Steemers, K 149–150, 160
Stiny, George 229
Stokes Redden, John 83
'street' form 169–170, 172–183
Sullivan, Louis 96–97
Sundt House project 9, *11*
Sutherland, Ivan 226
Swenarton, M 206
Swindon office buildings 138, 140–141, 160

Tallensi huts 6
Taylor, Jeremy 27, 252
'Temple of the Muses, The' bookshop, London
　92
terrace houses 134–135, 141, 193–206
　background and characteristics 193–196
　plans 191–192, 196–206
tessellations, semi-regular/Archimedean 15
theatres 6, *8*, 19
Thompson, W D'Arcy 237
timber 16
topological relations 208, 218
Torgovye Ryadi arcades, Moscow 94
torus/'ring doughnut' buildings 21–22
Tour Maîtresse prison, Geneva 77
Trace, M 176
triangles, packings of 9–15
trulli (dwelling), Apulia 19, 23
Tudor Walters Report (Unwin) 207–208, 210–212

Universal South Building, Washington 33–34
Unwin, Raymond 207–208, 210–213

Vahlefeld, R 126
Vaucher-Crémieux, Samuel 77
ventilation
　and building geometry 131–133, 138, 147
　department stores 81, 95–96, 98
　and energy use 152–153, 160, 162, 164
　and 'morphospace' 240, 250, 254, 256, 258,
　　262
　Panopticons 46, 50
　and urban density 177, 183
ventilation, office 34–38
vernacular houses 6–7, 17–19, 23
villages, primitive 17–19
villas 9
Virtual London model 131–132, 139–146,
　150–160
volume *see* geometry (plan depth, volume, wall
　areas)

wall areas *see* geometry (plan depth, volume,
　wall areas)
Walled City of Kowloon, Hong Kong 184
warehouses 86–87, 89, 142, 150, 152,
　163–165
Warner, Leroy L 33, 126
Warren, Paul 55
Welton Becket and Associates (architects) 34
Werrett, Simon 68, 75
Western culture, geometry in 5
Whiteley, William 85, 87–88
Willis, Carol 258
Woldenberg, Michael 132, 143
workhouses 74
World War One 206
woven cloth 16–17
Wright, Frank Lloyd 9, 11
Wyatt, James 92–93

Zidpark garage, London 107–108, 110–112
Zimmermann, William Carbys 25
Zola, Émile 88